CRITICAL QUEER STUDIES

Gender in Law, Culture, and Society

Series Editor
Martha Albertson Fineman, Emory University School of Law, USA

Gender in Law, Culture, and Society will address key issues and theoretical debates related to gender, culture, and the law. Its titles will advance understanding of the ways in which a society's cultural and legal approaches to gender intersect, clash, and are reconciled or remain in tension. The series will further examine connections between gender and economic and political systems, as well as various other cultural and societal influences on gender construction and presentation, including social and legal consequences that men and women uniquely or differently encounter. Intended for a scholarly readership as well as for courses, its titles will be a mix of single-authored volumes and collections of original essays that will be both pragmatic and theoretical. It will draw from the perspectives of critical and feminist legal theory, as well as other schools of jurisprudence. Interdisciplinary, and international in scope, the series will offer a range of voices speaking to significant questions arising from the study of law in relation to gender, including the very nature of law itself.

Critical Queer Studies

Law, Film, and Fiction
in Contemporary American Culture

CASEY CHARLES
University of Montana, USA

ASHGATE

Published by
Ashgate Publishing Limited
Wey Court East
Union Road
Farnham
Surrey, GU9 7PT
England

Ashgate Publishing Company
Suite 420
101 Cherry Street
Burlington
VT 05401-4405
USA

www.ashgate.com

British Library Cataloguing in Publication Data
Charles, Casey, 1951-
  Critical queer studies : law, film, and fiction in
  contemporary American culture. -- (Gender in law, culture,
  and society)
  1. Sexual minorities--Crimes against--United States--
  Case studies. 2. Sexual minorities--Legal status, laws,
  etc.--United States. 3. Culture and law. 4. Legal films--
  United States--History and criticism. 5. Homosexuality and
  motion pictures--United States. 6. Gays in motion
  pictures--Case studies. 7. Trials in motion pictures--
  Case studies. 8. Milk, Harvey--Assassination. 9. White,
  Dan, 1946-1985--Trials, litigation, etc. 10. Van Sant,
  Gus. Milk.
  I. Title II. Series
  340.1'15'0973-dc23

Library of Congress Cataloging-in-Publication Data
Charles, Casey, 1951-
  Critical queer studies : law, film, and fiction in contemporary American culture / by Casey Charles.
    p. cm.
  Includes bibliographical references and index.
  ISBN 978-1-4094-4406-0 (hardback) -- ISBN 978-1-4094-4407-7 (ebook) 1. Homophobia--Law
  and legislation--United States. 2. Gays--Legal status, laws, etc.--United States. 3. Gay rights--United
  States. 4.
  Homosexuality--Law and legislation--United States. 5. Hate crimes--United States. 6. Transgender
  youth--Violence against--United States. I. Title.
  KF4754.5.C43 2012
  346.7301'3--dc23

                                                                                          2012001684

ISBN 978-1-4094-4406-0 (hbk)
ISBN 978-1-4094-4407-7 (ebk)

Printed and bound in Great Britain by the
MPG Books Group, UK.

Contents

List of Figures

Table of Cases

Introduction

In the introduction to a recent issue of *South Atlantic Quarterly* on "Writing since Queer Theory," the editors lament a lack of contributions from scholars working in film and legal studies.[1] This book seeks to fill that gap by examining recent American films and documentaries that dramatize the intersection of law and queer life. *Critical Queer Studies* focuses on the way contemporary film and fiction integrate and influence crucial issues of queer law, including jury selection, unwanted sexual advance, negligence, hate crimes, and gay marriage. Works like *Milk, Brokeback Mountain, Boys Don't Cry, The Laramie Project,* and *Howl* have become barometers of the changing face of queer law in our country; their production and reception participate, I will argue, in a world of discourse that necessarily interacts with legal pronouncements through processes of articulation, citation, and commemoration. Film renditions of the stories of Harvey Milk, Brandon Teena, Matthew Shepard, and Ennis del Mar re-enact, to borrow Victor Turner's formulation, dramas of social conflict that participate, critique, and even foment legal doctrine, illuminating the reciprocity between legal and cultural representation and demonstrating how the law maintains its hold over the queer subject through a series of ideological fictions, and conversely, how these works of film, drama, and fiction draw upon the realities of queer legal status to dramatize their narratives.[2]

Critical Queer Studies finds its bearings at the intersection of two discrete paths of critical inquiry—queer studies and law and literature. Within these parameters, I engage questions of film adaptation and archival citation, drawing for example in the Harvey Milk chapters on a compilation of documentary (Epstein's *The Times of Harvey Milk*), docudrama (Emily Mann's *Execution of Justice*) and mainstream film (Van Sant's *Milk*) as well as trial transcripts, case law, and other media. A cultural studies approach facilitates a more thorough examination of the heterosexist strategies of queer erasure, exclusion, and scapegoating that inhabit criminal and civil legal process both inside and outside the parameters of

---

1   "We note, most obviously, the scarcity of contributions from people working in film and cultural studies . . . as well as the near total absence of essays from people working principally in law." Janet Halley and Andrew Parker, "Introduction to a Special Issue: After Sex: On Writing since Queer Theory," *The South Atlantic Quarterly* 106:3 (summer 2007): 422.

2   My study relies heavily upon Victor Turner's exploration of the relations between social conflict, legal trial, and drama in *From Ritual to Theatre: The Human Seriousness of Play* (New York: Performing Arts Journal Publications, 1982).

literary and cinematic production. More specifically, this broadened methodology supports my major contention that the tragic paradigm—as detailed Aristotle's *Poetics* and reconceived in the work of Augusto Boal—informs legal as well as dramatic representation in ways that reveal the influence of literature upon legal process.[3] Yet even though the ideology of the tragic queer informs the narratives in this study, these stories do not necessarily embrace that dominant discourse. Expressions of sexual freedom as represented in these works also expose, in Judith Butler's words, "the performative practices by which heterosexualized genders form themselves through the renunciation of the *possibility* of homosexuality." Thus, these films, docudramas, and stories engage a critical queer critique even as the prevailing mythos of catastrophe informs their narrative trajectories, revealing how the law of tragedy continues to determine the queer subject in aesthetic, social, and legal arenas.[4]

Exaggerated Reports of the Demise of the Law and Literature Movement

Recent studies of law in Renaissance and nineteenth-century literature remind us that connections between the worlds of letters and law have roots as deep as Aristotle's alignment of tragedy with justice, the Inns of Court with Elizabethan drama, and nineteenth-century American men of letters with an oratorical tradition that combined legal and literary training.[5] The more contemporary law and literature movement, which began with the work of scholars like James Boyd White and others, has grown out of an interdisciplinary approach that seeks in part

---

3 Augusto Boal, *Theatre of the Oppressed* (New York: Theatre Communications Group, 1985).

4 Judith Butler, *Bodies That Matter: On the Discursive Limits of Sex* (New York: Routledge, 1993), 235.

5 I will discuss Aristotle's *Poetics* and its relation to justice *infra*, relying on Augusto Boal and his critics. Kieran Dolan's *A Critical Introduction to Law and Literature* (Cambridge: Cambridge University Press, 2009) discusses the Inns of Court; Guyora Binder and Richard Weisberg in *Literary Criticisms of the Law* (Princeton: Princeton University Press, 2000) review the connections between letters and law in nineteenth-century America at 14–16. (See also Robert A. Ferguson, *Law and Letters in American Culture* [Cambridge, MA: Harvard University Press, 1984].) Other recent analyses of law and literature outside queer studies include Ravit Reichman, *The Affective Life of Law: Legal Modernism and the Literary Imagination* (Stanford: Stanford Law Books, 2009), Susan Heinzelman, *Riding the Black Ram: Law, Literature, and Gender* (Stanford: Stanford Law Books, 2010) (unruly women on trial), and Joseph P. Tomain, *Creon's Ghost: Law, Justice, and the Humanities* (Oxford: Oxford University Press, 2009). Richard Posner's *Law and Literature* (Cambridge, MA: Harvard University Press, 2009)—with its controversial insistence that literary discourse can help lawyers grow as individuals but has no bearing on the realism of the legal profession itself—is now in its third edition.

to bring the lessons of critical theory to a more pragmatic legal profession.[6] In Julie Stone Peters's recent review of the history of this movement, she concludes that the largely unrealized promise of this interdisciplinary field—namely that literature could somehow "humanize" the study of law—has ironically had the salutary impact of leaving scholars less preoccupied with questions of boundaries and more able to focus on the possibilities of a "disciplinary multiplicity" that finds a "comfortable habitation" where studies in "law, culture, and the humanities" can proceed without the demands that literature and its critical landscape produce greater material effect or that the law become more empathetic.[7] In keeping with Peters's assessment, *Critical Queer Studies* adopts this cultural studies approach toward the interplay of these disciplines, endeavoring, in Sara Murphy's words, less "to reify law and literature as opposing entities" than to "examine the ways both engage in the production of social norms, sustaining them at times and subverting them at others."[8]

Peters's account of the impenetrability of much of the legal profession to the lessons of hermeneutics, deconstruction, and narrative theory, however, must undergo some re-evaluation in light of one constitutional law professor's embrace of legal empathy theory in his choices for the Supreme Court—a theory that resonates with the way Martha Nussbaum in *Poetic Justice* understands the potential humanizing effect of the literary imagination on the law.[9] Importantly, Nussbaum, in her Introduction, turns to *Maurice*, an early queer novel that has no particular legal focus, to make her case for the ethical imperative of the literary imagination—for the way in which literature allows all readers, including lawyers and judges, to understand how "people different from oneself grapple with disadvantage" (Nussbaum xvi). In discussing Forster's posthumously published novel, Nussbaum claims:

> The strategy in *Maurice* is to select as hero a man of strong and exclusive homosexual tendencies who is in no other way "unnatural." In fact, he is a boring, snobbish, middle-class English stockbroker of mediocre talent and imagination. The reader is not thrilled by him, but his kindness and his general good nature evoke sympathy. The emotional structure of the novel relies on the ease with which the reader will see Maurice as average, and then see, year by year, how the treatment society accords to his desires ... renders him terribly nonaverage and also deeply unequal ... This inequality is enforced by social

---

6   James Boyd White, *The Legal Imagination* (New York: Little, Brown, 1973).

7   Julie Stone Peters, "Law, Literature, and the Vanishing Real: On the Future of an Interdisciplinary Illusion," *PMLA* 120:2 (March 2005): 442–453, at 451.

8   Sara Murphy, "The Law, the Norm, and the Novel," in *Studies in Law, Politics, and Society: A Special Issue: Law and Literature Reconsidered*, ed. Austin Sarat (Bingley, UK: JAI, 2008), 53–77, at 74.

9   Peters 444; Martha Nussbaum, *Poetic Justice: The Literary Imagination and Public Life* (Boston: Beacon, 1995).

prejudices that justify themselves with language of nature that derives from religious tradition. (97)

Maurice, the queer anti-hero, gains his stature from withstanding the internal and external obstacles of heterosexist social norms. He serves as a case study of "a different person" in need of the same empathy that Justice Sotomayor and President Obama recognize as a legitimate part of legal adjudication. Maurice's exemplarity points to the way heteronormativity establishes him as the empathetic legal and social subject par excellence, one whose disadvantages are arbitrarily upheld by the unverifiable assumptions of legal bias and one whose predicament has given rise to compelling fictional narratives, like Forster's novel, which dramatize the need for understanding.[10]

Nussbaum is not naïve; she realizes that her empathy theory, even among her students, will face "years of institutional abhorrence and discrimination" (xvii), yet she nonetheless champions empathy as an ethical imperative. Her theory has its critics. Maria Aristodemou, for example, reminds us that, as Terry Eagleton noted, not everyone who reads *King Lear* necessarily becomes a good person; there is, in other words, no "ethics of reading in itself" which will somehow transform the legal profession.[11] For Aristodemou, both law and literature are deeply rhetorical enterprises, both create narratives that seek to "legislate" meaning, advancing in the case of *Maurice*, the deeply political message that legal and social opprobrium governs the queer subject. On the other end of the critical spectrum, moreover, followers of Judge Posner also believe that legal process should ultimately have no truck with the vagaries of aesthetics. Critics like Paul Heald, for example, agree that Nussbaum's empathy has the potential to change human beings who read fiction, but insists the existence of such empathy does not in any way diminish the status of the law as an "independent and objective arbiter of disputes."[12] Others see this claim to legal objectivity as deeply ideological, the law's resistance to the lessons of semiotics merely evidence of how far the legal profession will go to "conceal its artificial origins."[13]

The debate over the role and influence of empathy within the fields of law and literature revisits in small the larger tension, which *Critical Queer Studies* explores, between the more professional legal field and a more scholastic discipline of the humanities, between the "real world" of the law and the "academic" world of

---

10   Forster refused to publish the novel during his lifetime, and a terminal note to *Maurice*, written in 1913 and later updated, notes that even in 1971 homosexuals in Britain continue to be prosecuted for consensual sexual acts (Nussbaum 97).

11   Maria Aristodemou, *Law and Literature: Journeys from Her to Eternity* (Oxford: Oxford University Press, 2000), 5. For Aristodemou law is always already literature, and literature always already law (4).

12   Paul J. Heald, "The Death of Law and Literature: An Optimistic Eulogy," *The Comparatist* 33 (May 2009): 20–26, 26.

13   Aristodemou 1.

literature—between, on a broader plane, the worlds of nonfiction and fiction. Those who see both areas of study participating in what Jane Baron calls the "collective meaning-making" of texts—who find that the humanities provides "a faithful mirror of justice" which challenges us to search for "higher law"—understand literature and law as intertwined in a process of adjudicating and assessing the intricate relationships of norms, laws, and concepts of justice.[14] Even if I recognize, as a trial attorney turned literature professor, that a closing argument before a jury may have far greater material consequence than a lecture in queer literature class, I can still acknowledge a use of similar rhetorical practices in conveying my message. And as I move further into the academic profession, teaching in a field as politically, legally, and socially fraught as queer studies in a western state like Montana, I continue to realize how the spheres of influence in legal and academic practice become more and more intertwined. For legal cultural critics like Binder and Weisberg, the ongoing critiques of the legal profession as somehow never able to attain an idealized objectivity or as too formal to entertain subjectivity miss the mark by casting the humanities as a "redemptive Spirit" that can somehow breathe life into the "rigid, cynical, and calculating," letter of the law.[15] Literature, like law, participates in "the arena of social conflict" and its readers, like lawyers, come to its texts with their own set of adversarial positions.[16] A documentary like *The Times of Harvey Milk* does not profess neutrality in its arrangement of archival material any more than an opening statement presents a version of the facts that is not selective and geared toward telling a story from a client's point of view. Even a work as potentially "neutral" as Annie Proulx's famous short story, "Brokeback Mountain," began, by the writer's own assessment, as an attempt to depict "rural homophobia."[17]

What the study of law *avec* literature can promote is a re-thinking of the law's decision-making authority as a "necessarily figurative and constructive representation of society's will."[18] As Gadamer and others have maintained, the law inevitably makes a rhetorical appeal to aesthetic judgment through its use of narrative in the same way a docudrama like *The Laramie Project*, with its wide dissemination in schools across the country, makes its own appeal for the codification of sexual orientation clauses in non-discrimination policies, including hate-crime legislation.

---

14   Jane B. Baron, "Law's Guilt about Literature," *Studies in Law, Politics, and Society* 36 (2005): 17–30, at 20. See also Tomain, xviii (on humanities as "mirror of justice").

15   Binder and Weisberg 18.

16   Guyora Binder, "Aesthetic Judgment and Legal Justification," *Studies in Law, Politics, and Society: A Special Issue: Law and Literature Reconsidered* 43 (2008): 79–113, at 80.

17   Annie Proulx, "Getting Movied," *Brokeback Mountain: Story to Screenplay* (New York: Scribner, 2005), 30.

18   Binder 80

Whether one argues that law *and* literature share a rhetorical and textual common ground, or law *in* literature can edify the legal profession itself or at least the individual practitioner—whether one follows a critical legal studies position that recognizes the ideological fictions that inhere in the legal profession or finds oneself in the academic position of teaching in a field like queer studies that has legal and social bias as one of its central concerns—there can be little doubt that the current legal debate about the status of the queer subject in society informs contemporary LGBTIQ narratives in ways that both highlight fictional constructs in the law and reveal the legal consequences of aesthetic production.[19] Jill Mann's *Execution of Justice*, for example, a docudrama about the trial of Dan White for the murder of Harvey Milk, trenchantly exposes the arbitrary bias in trial practice through a dramatization of a jury selection during which every gay juror in the pool was dismissed by the judge for cause, the court assuming gay jurors to be incapable of neutrality while neighbors of Dan White were impaneled without question as reasonable men and women. Similarly, a defamation case that arose in connection with Fox Searchlight's *fictional* but "based-on-a-true-story" biopic of the Brandon Teena case (*Boys Don't Cry*) illustrates the potential legal consequences of an artistic product as widely disseminated as this major motion picture. These interpenetrations evidence a dialectic between fields that have traditionally depended on discrete epistemes for maintenance of their authority; they teach us not only how literature acts as a "constitutive dimension of law," but also how law, within the contexts of much contemporary queer representation, has in turn underwritten the dramatic trajectory of artistic production.[20]

Admittedly, the rhetorical and aesthetic components of legal process are more readily apparent than the legality of artistic representation. In Richard Schneck's recent essay, "The Laws of Fiction," he argues for a focus on "literature *as* law" through his discussion of the use of evidence in Cooper's *Pioneers*, where the novel supplies its own representation of evidentiary truth as a replacement for the flawed legal process described during Natty Bumppo's trial.[21] Schneck's argument relies in part on Derrida's 1992 essay, "The Mystical Foundation of Authority," which uses Montaigne's observation that the source of legal authority resides in a

---

19   For a sampling of early Critical Legal Studies works, see Jerry Leonard, ed. *Legal Studies as Cultural Studies: A Reader in (Post)Modern Critical Theory* (Albany: SUNY Press, 1995); Peter Goodrich, *Legal Discourse: Studies in Linguistics, Rhetoric and Legal Analysis* (New York: St. Martin's, 1987); Mari J. Matsuda, *Where is Your Body? And Other Essays on Race, Gender and the Law* (Boston: Beacon, 1996); Patricia Williams, *Alchemy of Race and Rights: Diary of a Law Professor* (Cambridge, MA: Harvard University Press, 1992); Ruthann Robson, *Gay Men, Lesbians, and the Law* (New York: Chelsea House, 1997); Carl Gutíerrez-Jones, *Critical Race Narratives: A Study of Race, Rhetoric, and Injury* (New York: New York University Press, 2001).

20   Binder 19. See also Michel Foucault, *The Archaeology of Knowledge and the Discourse on Language*, trans. A.M. Sheridan Smith (New York: Pantheon, 1972).

21   Richard Schneck, "The Laws of Fiction: Legal Rhetoric and Literary Evidence," *European Journal of English Studies* 11:1 (April 2007): 47–63, 49.

kind of fictional fiat of power. Schneck makes the case that law derives its authority from a performative act—a narrative declaration of a history of originary custom or practice—which in itself is neither "just nor unjust" and which in fact contains no "previous law with its founding anterior moment" that guarantees a claim to validity.[22] If the law establishes its monopoly on truth and justice by resorting to fictional genealogies of ancient norms, which are nothing more than arbitrary acts of force, then literary representations of the law often reflect an awareness of this rhetorical nature of legal power, an awareness that in turn empowers literary representation to supply its own version of legal authority within the parameters of story-telling. In Hillis Miller's reading of Kleist's "Michael Kohlhaas," for example, he argues that this fictional narrative portrays the arbitrary nature of legal authority in so far as it purposely "fails to account" or justify the events it relates by keeping secret the prophesy of the gypsy's prediction which Michael receives before his death.[23]

Hillis Miller's essay, part of a collection that includes Derrida's original article, also focuses on the way literary production, like the enactment of law, derives its power through an appeal to precedent and citation (1508). To be socially effective, "a work of literature must be canonized, surrounded by a complex set of editions, reviews, commentaries," Hillis Miller notes, in the same way a statute both appeals to precedent in its enactment and relies on enforcement and sanction after it is enacted. "The appeal to precedent in law means, most often, the appeal to an agreed-upon narrative of particular cases, often agreed upon only after lengthy and expensive litigation" (1493). In the ensuing analysis of versions of the stories of Milk, Shepard, and Brandon Teena—and even Proulx's presentation of the "gay" cowboy—a complex set of editions and commentaries act, I will argue, as a form of citational authority, a mode of repetitive and performative enactment of roles played by the paradigmatic queer subject, roles that borrow in large part from the provisions of a generic code of tragedy, as discussed below. In this way, wide dissemination of the cinematic rendition of the award-winning *Milk*, for example, reinforces one version of the queer subject, acting as a form of cultural authority.

---

22   Jacques Derrida, "Force of Law: The 'Mystical Foundation of Authority,'" in *Deconstruction and the Possibility of Justice*, ed. David G. Carlson, Drucilla Cornell, and Michel Rosenfeld (New York: Routledge, 1992), 13; quoted in Schneck 50. Judith Butler applies an analogous argument through her contention that the law of gender performatively enacts its own legitimacy through claims of origin and naturalness in *Gender Trouble: Feminism and the Subversion of Identity* (New York: Routledge, 1990). Queer practices undermine claims that gender, the cultural assumptions tied to sex, are indelibly linked to sexed anatomy in the same way that literary representation of law can reveal the mystical authority of the law. See Judith Butler, "Deconstruction and the Possibility of Justice: Comments on Bernasconi, Cornell, Miller, Weber," 11 *Cardozo Law Review* 1715 (1990).

23   J. Hillis Miller, "Laying down the Law in Literature: The Example of Kleist," 11 *Cardozo Law Review* 1491–1514, 1514 (1990).

Though my study analyzes representations as varied as case law, newspaper editorials, and short stories, its central focus on film originates in large part from the power of that medium's popularity, its ability to circulate and disseminate in ways that rival the law's methods of promulgation and citation. The cinematic image—whether it be of Ennis's blood-stained shirt in Jack's closet or the buck fence where Matthew Shepard was tied and left to die—garners a lasting symbolic, almost legislative authority as a depiction of continuing social opprobrium. If filmmakers have become to some degree "the unacknowledged legislators of the world," to tweak Shelley's famous adage, documentarians and biopic auteurs like Kaufman, Epstein, Peirce, Van Sant, Muska, and Jill Mann are arguably the drafters of such legislation, in large part because the content of their works often *includes* material from the legal archive.[24] As part of its narration, *The Times of Harvey Milk* incorporates the famous tape recording of Dan White's confession, used as evidence in the trial, just as the police interrogation of Brandon Teena figures prominently in Muska and Olafsdottir's award-winning documentary, *The Brandon Teena Story*. In many of the works treated in this study, the law *becomes* literature; its content crosses over into the world of aesthetic production, thus rendering legal precedent as a source and basis for cultural representation. This crossover, moreover, underscores the way recent struggles of the queer subject for legal and social recognition have produced what Tony Kushner has called a "drama of the real," scripts as compelling as any improbable fiction. The "true stories" that biopics like *Boys Don't Cry* and *Milk* are based upon more often than not involve legal and political episodes of social history that become part of the film's dramatic process, thus blurring not only disciplinary boundaries but also the reputedly distinct realms of nonfiction and fiction.

While the more specialized field of film and law has recently received crucial critical attention, an emphasis on queer studies in law and film has garnered less.[25] In a collection entitled *Law's Moving Image*, Leslie J. Moran brings queer studies, film, and law together in an essay on film versions of Oscar Wilde's three trials. This essay investigates the role of "realism" in two 1960s movies about Wilde: one starring Robert Morley (based on the stage play of 1938) and the other Ken Hughes's *The Trials of Oscar Wilde* starring Peter Finch. Relying in part on Christian Metz's observation that the screen must unfold a spectacle of

---

24   P.B. Shelley, "A Defense of Poesy," in *Shelley's Critical Prose* (Reno: University of Nevada Press, 1967), 3:36.

25   See Austin Sarat, Laurence Douglas, and Martha Merrill Umphrey, eds. *Law on the Screen* (Stanford: Stanford University Press, 2005); Orit Kamir, *Framed: Women in Law and Film* (Durham, NC: Duke University Press, 2006); Steve Greenfield, Guy Osborn, and Peter Robson, *Film and Law: The Cinema of Justice* (Portland: Hart, 2010), at 249, on gay film; David A. Black, *Law in Film: Resonance and Representation* (Champaign Urbana: Illinois University Press, 1999) on genre; Anthony Chase, *Movies on Trial: The Legal System of the Silver Screen* (New York: New Press, 2002); Ross D. Levi, *The Celluloid Courtroom: A History of Legal Cinema* (Westport: Praeger, 2005).

"make believe" which at the same time maintains an effective deception of "an air of truth," Moran shows how the Finch film, which takes more liberty with the facts, received greater critical praise because it fulfilled the generic expectations of emotional realism that adhere to the genre of cinema, even though the film medium from its inception has claimed—more than language—the capacity for a more exact realism, namely, the ability "to close the gap between the thing represented and the representation" through the camera.[26]

While Moran's essay does not at any length discuss the queer aspects of the Wilde films other than briefly note the refusal of American production companies to accept the controversial screenplay, his essay explores how the generic expectations of film have their own "laws of verisimilitude" which govern reception. These laws ironically are governed by a "cultural norms" of a "social world" which determine a film's value in relation to a particular "cultural" verisimilitude (91). Finch's version of the Wilde story, he notes, captures the truth of the event not by journalistic accuracy but by becoming an "'honest tragedy'" that gains its authenticity or "air of truth" by turning Wilde into a "martyr" and following a set of generic expectations that attach to cinema and fiction (92). Moran arguably examines the constructed nature of "realism" in these Wilde films in order to illustrate the way an illusory "air of truth" that attaches to the cinematic queer finds its "authenticity" through representing the award-seeking performance of Oscar Wilde as flawed and suffering tragic subject, punished for his refusal to comply with the heteronormative dictates of the law.[27]

The Wilde story, with its archive of films, trial transcripts, historical accounts, and dramas, serves as one prototype for the case studies that *Critical Queer Studies* undertakes in relation to the more contemporary legal and cultural status of the LGBTIQ American. Other historical queer film and law precedent includes representations of the life of Edward II in the play by Marlowe and Derek Jarman's film version of the deposition and assassination of the medieval king who fell in love with Gaveston. Melville's *Billy Budd*, also based on an historical account, filmed and dramatized in many modes, arguably represents a nineteenth-century American precedent for exploring the way the "queer" as legal subject provides material for tragic legal narrative. I will explore Hellman's *Children's Hour* later in this introduction as a central prototype for the chapters in this book. Each of these early cases points to the way works of Robin West and Peter Brooks on the connections between literary genres and jurisprudence inform queer social,

---

26   Christian Metz, *The Imaginary Signifier: Psychoanalysis and the Cinema*, Trans. Celia Britton et al. (Bloomington: Indiana University Press, 1986), 72, in Leslie J. Moran, "On Realism and the Law Film: the Case of Oscar Wilde," *The Law's Moving Image*, ed. Leslie J. Moran, Emma Sandon, Elena Lozidou, and Ian Christie (London: Glass House, 2004), 77–93 at 91.

27   For more recent parts of the Wilde archive, see *Wilde*, dir. Brian Gilbert (Sony Pictures 1998); Moisés Kaufman, *Gross Indecency: The Three Trials of Oscar Wilde* (New York: Vintage, 1998); Stephen Rudnicki, *Wilde* (Los Angeles: Dove, 1998).

cultural, and legal subjectivity, defining the sexual outlaw as destined for tragic catastrophe in film and fiction.[28]

The Myth of the Queer Hero: Aristotle's Tragic Paradigm

The queer subject as represented in literature and film has a long history of close affiliation with the catastrophes of the tragic genre, whether through suicide (Martha in *The Children's Hour*), disease (Richard in *The Hours*), punishment (Edward II in Marlowe's play), or murder (Sebastian in *Suddenly Last Summer*). The subjects of this study—Matthew Shepard, Harvey Milk, Brandon Teena, Ennis del Mar, and Jack Twist—are no exception, so it behooves us to think at the outset about how and why the queer scapegoat continues to capture the popular imagination as recently as Ford's remake of Isherwood's classic novel, *A Single Man*, in 2009 – to explore how and why the only-good-queer-is-a-dead-queer narrative still sells tickets in spite of the recent legal and political inroads made by cases like *Lawrence v. Texas* (overturning sodomy statutes) and *Perry v. Schwarzenegger* (holding California's ban on same-sex marriage unconstitutional).

In addition to its adjectival capacity as a descriptor of calamitous events, the word "tragedy" has a long citational history as a category, a taxonomic designation within the world of literary representation—in short, a genre. Derrida describes the concept of genre as a principle of precedent that derives its authority from establishing limitations around the form and content of a text.[29] His analogy between law and generic expectation in his essay "The Law of Genre" points to the way the description of works as tragic—whether documentaries, films, short stories, or dramas—participates in a classification that not only designates certain components of form and content but also necessarily "contaminates" the text (59). For Derrida, the law of the law of genre is a "principle of contamination through citation" (59), a mark that is also a remark about the parameters of the designation itself (64). Hence, if we are to consider queer narratives as "tragic," we must explore how these works both fit and do not fit into the markings of this genre, not purely for aesthetic reasons but also because the tragic designation continues to "contaminate" the queer subject beyond the world of literary representation. The story of the tragic queer both invokes the vexed question of literary categorization and also carries with it an epithetic authority that continues to render queer

---

28   Peter Brooks and Paul Gerwitz, eds. *Law's Stories: Narrative and Rhetoric in the Law* (New Haven: Yale University Press, 1996); Robin West, *Narrative, Authority, and the Law* (Ann Arbor: University of Michigan Press, 1994). I argue in my conclusion that Epstein and Friedman's recent film about the obscenity trial surrounding the publication of Ginsberg's *Howl* breaks with the "tragic" tradition by dramatizing a legal victory for queer rights.

29   Jacques Derrida, "The Law of Genre," trans. Avital Ronell, *Critical Inquiry* 7:1 (autumn 1980): 55–81, 56.

subjectivity—in both the aesthetic and social imagination—as necessarily destined for catastrophe.

In Stephen Halliwell's introduction to his translation of Aristotle's *Poetics*, he revisits some of the misconceptions about the philosopher's description of the tragic genre. Though Aristotle understands that most tragedies take their material from heroic saga or myth, the philosopher of *The Poetics* puts greater emphasis on the "failure of human action" than the mistake or *hamartia* of a single character.[30] Tragic mimesis, which is more than pure imitation of nature, presents "people in action" who can be either good or bad (73); it has as its primary focus a representation of "ethically serious subjects" (36)—the dramatic enactment of action which is "complete, and of a certain magnitude" and which, by virtue of its presentation of reversals (*peripeteia*) and recognitions (*anagnorisis*), arouses pity and fear in the audience, effecting the catharsis of such emotions. In spite of the historical re-interpretation of tragedy in *The Poetics* as a genre that focuses on a flawed hero who misses the mark and faces calamitous consequences, for Halliwell, Aristotle's text finds the heart of tragedy in action or plot structure rather than character or thought (87). Though tragedy has as its subject the dramatic enactment of "agents engaged in the pursuit of the ethical goals of life" (89), its emotional power originates in the components of plot structure (or organization of events), in a set of actions that produce pity and fear (sympathy and identification) in the spectators who originally were the main characters in early dramatic enactments.[31]

Halliwell's commentary reminds us that the now fetishized Aristotelian paradigm has through history undergone a revision, shifting tragedy from a story of a series of events to the narration of character development, a shift that has ramifications for our understanding of the application of notions of tragedy to queer narratives. Because the stories of Harvey Milk, Brandon Teena, and Matthew Shepard are as much the stuff of history as fiction, they initially face the generic obstacle of falling outside the parameters of tragic mimesis, in part because fiction concerns itself, according to Aristotle, not with historical reporting of events but with "things as they might possibly occur"—tragic mimesis dealing with probability rather than what actually transpired.[32] Though history deals more specifically with individual occurrences and tragic mimesis with universal necessities, nothing, Aristotle reminds us, prevents events that have actually occurred from "belonging to the class of the probable or possible" (18). History, and the documentaries, docudramas, and biopics it produces, therefore, can gain the power of tragic mimesis if their content follows the pattern of reversal, mistake,

---

30   Stephen Halliwell, *The Poetics of Aristotle: Translation and Commentary* (Chapel Hill: University of North Carolina Press, 1987), 15.

31   Boal 33.

32   O.B. Hardison, Jr., *Aristotle's Poetics: A Translation and Commentary for Students of Literature*, trans. Leon Golden (Gainsville: University of Florida Press, 1981), 18 (Aristotle) 156–7 (Hardison's commentary).

catastrophe, recognition, and catharsis Aristotle enumerates. The quintessential queer narrative gains its tragic status, therefore, not necessarily because of the essentialized heroic actions of a single character—not because a queer hero somehow fits into the "better than us" formula Aristotle cites though does not insist upon—but because these LGBT histories dramatize "pitiful and fearful incidents."[33] These incidents involve "people in action" whose ethical status run the gamut from Brandon Teena to Harvey Milk, from John Lotter to Dan White. Aristotle's theory, Halliwell states, "does not require either tragedy or comedy to be restricted to certain kinds of social character or material" (76).

This reconsideration of the focus of Aristotle's tragic mimesis from character to plot warns against an inclination to construct the queer hero as tragic protagonist—to turn, as it were, Harvey Milk into Hamlet or even Dan White into a Creon. Because the legal and social status of the queer subject in many parts of the world, including the American West, is still in the process of moving from outlaw and social pariah to singled-out minority (*Romer v. Evans*), the reading of these queer characters as generic heroes must inevitably come up against a lack of public empathy or capacity for identification (even if the character is played by a heterosexual icon like Sean Penn), making it difficult to garner the empathy needed to induce the cleansing pity and fear which tragic representation must invoke in the audience. Yet within the terms of Halliwell's correction of Aristotle's emphasis, these necessary affective results arguably still emerge in such stories not by virtue of character, but through representation of the pursuit of what Aristotle calls "virtue," the struggle to exercise "free behavior without coercion"[34]—in these cases struggles by queer subjects to socialize and legitimate their sexuality. Calamity ensues as a result of sexual expression, dramatizing a community's extra-legal impulse to violently repress that expression.

Although Augusto Boal's *Theatre of the Oppressed*, written in 1973, has undergone some trenchant critique for its over-simplification and vilification of Aristotle's theories, its influential reading of tragedy in *The Poetics* as a form of cultural repression continues to garner attention, in part because of the analogy he draws between Aristotle's theories of drama and justice.[35] In Boal's reading of

---

33   For "better than us," see Halliwell 15; for "fearful incidents," see Hardison 21.

34   Boal 17.

35   Paul Dwyer, "*Theoria Negativa:* Making Sense of Boal's Reading of Aristotle," *Modern Drama* 48:4 (winter 2005): 635–658. Dwyer challenges Boal's notion that *The Poetics* is a deeply conservative text based on Greek legal hierarchies. For Dwyer, though Aristotle was by no means a radical, his conception of justice was not always aligned with the workings of law (641) as Boal suggests. Dwyer goes on to question whether theatrical history, at least until Brecht, has acted as a repressive tool of the state, and critiques Boal's static Marxist sense of base/superstructure (652) that fails to take into account the subversive possibilities of traditional drama as well as the way Boal's emancipatory and participatory theater of the oppressed (TO) is subject to a commodity fetishism that could render its liberatory goals as purely symbolic. See Kathleen Gallagher's work on Boalian theater, in which she discusses a young black Seventh Day Adventist's unwillingness to play the

Aristotle's theory of tragedy (which functions in its own right as a kind of impure citation of the kind Derrida ascribes to all genres), politics is the sovereign art form, and theater, as the cultural agent of the political, has as its mimetic goal the representation of "the actions of man's rational soul … which consists in virtuous behavior, remote from the extremes, whose supreme good is justice and whose maximum expression is the Constitution" (23–24). For Boal, Aristotelian tragedy performs a repressive function by representing action "*directed against the laws*" (32), action that creates pity and fear in the audience as it witnesses a cathartic purging of an "extraneous element" in society and eventually restores the social fabric to its status quo ante. Though Boal reads Aristotelian tragedy as purely a theater of containment without a possibility of subversion—a reading maintained in the service of advancing his own alternative theater of the oppressed [TO] (a people's theater in which the "spect actor" participates in the unfolding of the drama)—nevertheless his notion of Aristotle's "coercive tragedy" lays important groundwork for exploring the reciprocity between drama and justice on the one hand, and more generally between what Victor Turner calls social drama and trial— between, more theoretically, the workings of fiction and those of legal history or fact (Boal 40).

In Boal's claim that Aristotelian tragedy acts as a "powerful system of intimidation" (46), he emphasizes the way dramatic catastrophe and its witnessing by an identificatory public purge "all antisocial elements" and reinstates a universe of moderate and accepted values (47). Whether this return to equilibrium can or cannot include the queer subject, whose controversial actions can still produce panic in many segments of society, becomes one of the organizing ethical questions of my treatment of the dramatic unfolding of mistake, reversal, and catastrophe of these works. As both potential antagonist and protagonist, tragic agents like Jack Twist or Brandon Teena pursue their sexual freedom within social arenas that often define their normative equilibrium through a strict exclusion of non-heterosexual behavior. In Boal's reading of the classic Hollywood Western, moreover, he suggests that audience empathy resides more often than not with the villain— "the bad guy" who wreaks havoc on the community and enacts the aggressive tendencies of a spectatorship which identifies with, though is intimidated by, the

---

part of a "homosexual" during a TO session, as indicative of the social resistance to the power of aesthetics (Radhika Rao, "Editor's Review of *The Aesthetic of the Oppressed* by Augusto Boal, translated by Adrian Jackson and *The Theatre of Urban Youth and Schooling in Dangerous Times* by Kathleen Gallagher," *Harvard Education Review* (fall 2008), http://www.hepg.org/her/abstract/660. Others besides Boal have examined the connection between the analysis of drama Aristotle's *Poetics* and legal process. In *Poetic and Legal Fiction in the Aristotelian Tradition* (Princeton: Princeton University Press, 1986), Kathy Eden reminds us that Aristotle and Sidney after him align the rhetoric of legal oratory with the technique of fiction rather than the reportage of history. Her book demonstrates how the notion of *anagnorisis* or recognition is closely aligned in Aristotle with methods of legal proof.

energy of one who takes the law into his own hands—an antagonist the audience admires for his or her power (47). Though *Brokeback* and *Boys Don't Cry* are not classic Westerns, this film genre clearly informs their narratives in the same way the Barbary Coast tradition of San Francisco underwrites the Harvey Milk story and the "live and let die" mentality of the West looms behind Matthew Shepard's buck-fence murder. The convergence of a "gunfighter-nation" ethos with the story of the dubious queer hero gives Boal's observation about cinematic permutations of the tragic paradigm singular relevance to the way these narratives may act as a cultural means of "purging all the spectator's aggressive tendencies" and eliminating queer antisocial elements from the western landscape.[36]

The notion that an audience's pity and fear—its empathy for and identification with a character's misfortune, action, and punishment—might reside not with Brandon Teena but with her attacker John Lotter, not with Matthew Shepard but with his murderer Aaron McKinney may, however counter-intuitively, provide an important key for understanding the continued appeal of queer tragedy within mainstream cultural representation. For Boal, an audience takes vicarious pleasure in the violence of the antagonist, in an aggressivity that enacts its own form of vigilante justice against queer ruptures, even though the spectators, in witnessing the punishment of those antagonists, are also intimidated. After the tragic denouement, however, the townspeople return to their "square dances" and church picnics, pleased to be rid of the pervert but realizing the law of moderation prevents them from condoning the aggression of even one as otherwise admirable as Dan White—policeman, fireman, veteran. Boal's proposition that the appeal of Westerns resides in empathy for the antagonist underscores tragic mimesis as a representation not just of above-average characters that happen to love the same sex or be transgendered but also of an organized action that dramatizes the ethical conflict between sexual expression and the forces of heteronormativity. To this degree, Proulx's statement that the focus of her story is "destructive rural homophobia" retains its resonance, in spite of those who have challenged her generalization.[37]

If, as Binder and Weisberg have suggested, tragedy is an "epiphany of law, of that which is and must be"—if tragedy thus portrays a subject who transgresses and must succumb to the natural order—then the queer hero, like Antigone, emerges as a figure whose ethical exercise of freedom necessarily confronts an order that is itself flawed.[38] As recent studies like *Homophobias: Lust and Loathing*

---

36   See Richard Slotkin, *Gunfighter Nation: Myth of the Frontier in Twentieth-Century America* (Norman: University of Oklahoma Press, 1998).

37   See David Peterson's "'Everything built on that:' Queering Western Space in Proulx's 'Brokeback Mountain,'" in *Queering Paradigms*, ed. Scherer Burkhard (Oxford: Peter Lang, 2009), 281–298, for the argument that the Rocky Mountains function as a "heterotopia" (an inverted rendition of a homophobic space as queer center) (286).

38   Binder and Weisberg 211, citing Northrop Frye's *Anatomy of Criticism.* "Tragedy dramatizes a sacrificial ritual and so resonates with the Fall of man and the Passion of

across Time and Space and Fetner's *How the Religious Right Shaped Gay and Lesbian Activism* have demonstrated, queer subjectivity sustains its tragic status through a process of subjectivization, a process that involves a continued internal and external opprobrium that queer culture has challenged and must continue to face—especially in the law of the West.[39] These tragic works thus dramatize the ethics of queer socialization—from legal, political, geographical, and domestic dimensions—representing the unfolding of what Aristotle calls "ethically serious subjects."[40]

While queer controversy has no doubt emerged in the production of successful Hollywood films like *Philadelphia, Brokeback,* and *Milk* as a fetishized commodity that entertains through selling manufactured conflict, perpetuating from Boal's perspective the dominance of the straight state, a crucial critical question remains about the effect of these works on society as a whole, including the laws of the land.[41] My study seeks to explore how the paradigm of the tragic queer—to whom is necessarily ascribed *hamartia, peripeteia,* and *anagnorisis*—has infiltrated the social imagination and thus functions ideologically within deliberations of both the halls of justice and the theaters of culture. Through a process of individualization that belies a fuller understanding of the scope of the tragic genre and thereby erases the complicity of heterosexism, the tragic queer moves through the legal system always already condemned by an epithet that is also a misnomer. Behind most tragic queers, I will argue, is a tragic homophobe, a tragic social force of blind normalization.

Critical Queer Studies

My book takes its title from the final chapter of Judith Butler's *Bodies That Matter,* situating its argument within a "self-critical dimension" of queer studies that

---

Christ." The analogy between Christ and queer hero has its own social resonance, as evidenced by the controversial attempt to stop production of Terrence McNally's *Corpus Christi,* a queer passion play, at the Manhattan Theatre Club in 1998.

39   David Murray's edited collection *Homophobias: Lust and Loathing across Time and Space* (Durham, NC: Duke University Press, 2009) treats national and global mechanisms of queer prejudice; Tina Fetner's *How the Religious Right Shaped Lesbian and Gay Activism* (Minneapolis: University of Minnesota Press, 2008) provides a historical account of gay activism in the United States since the 1970s. More recently, Joey L. Mogul, Andrea J. Ritchie, and Kay Whitlock have published *Queer (In)Justice: The Criminalization of LGBT People in the United States (Queer Acts/Queer Ideas)* (Boston: Beacon Press, 2011). See Judith Bulter's *Psychic Life of Power: Theories of Subjection* (Stanford: Stanford University Press, 1997) for subjection as a complex process of agency and interpellation.

40   Halliwell 36.

41   See Margot Canady's *The Straight State: Sexuality and Citizenship in Twentieth Century America* (Princeton: Princeton University Press, 2010).

questions the essentialist assumptions of identity politics and examines the queer subject within the framework of a central paradox, one that is maintained in large part by the law and the norms it underwrites (227). For Butler, the queer subject "who would resist such norms is itself enabled, if not produced, by such norms," and while agency is not "foreclosed" because of this "constitutive constraint," it does make such agency, as Foucault argued, a "reiterative" or citational practice that is "immanent" rather than "external" to power itself (15). For Butler, the *matter* that both constitutes the sexed body and makes a body *matter* acts in large part through performatives—those discursive practices that enact or produce what they name (13). Sex is assumed "in the same way the law is cited" as the bootstrapping repetition of "normalizing injunctions that secure the borders of sex" (14).[42] Against the backdrop of what she calls the materialization of heterosexual hegemony in regulatory norms, Butler in the final section of *Bodies That Matter* posits the contestation of those regulations in the acts of queer subject, whose use of the term "queer" as descriptor seeks performatively to reverse even as it retains the "abjected history of the term" (223). A presentist queer politics that refuses to acknowledge how the genealogy of the abjected homosexual continues to reside within the queer subject necessarily ignores the way "usage" of the term is controlled by forces outside it as much as by those who reclaim it. "If the term 'queer' is to be a site of collective contestation," she writes, "the point of departure for a set of historical reflections and futural imaginings, it will have to remain that which is, in the present, never fully owned, but always and only redeployed, twisted, queered from a prior usage" (228).

In the following chapters on film and fiction, I seek to show how the conflicts between the regulatory norms of heterocentrism and their queer redeployment are dramatized through a set of narratives that borrow from a social and cultural history of tragic abjection as it filters through both legal and aesthetic discourse. Harvey Milk's famous call in the 1970s for lesbians and gays around the country to "come out," for example, takes place within a narrative context of his impending assassination—arguably as a consequence of his own openness—as well as in the context of his own failure to come out of the closet before his own political career. Gus Van Sant's *Milk* tells a story of both liberation and tragic melodrama; it celebrates the sexual revolution of the Castro even as it re-enacts the catastrophes of Puccini's *Tosca*. A critical queer reading of this film and others recognizes the persistence of a tragic injunction in these popular cultural representations of the queer subject, an injunction whose reiteration has the uncanny power to reinstate a stubborn heteronormativity in the courtroom as well as the theater.

Butler's analogy between the performative workings of the queer subject and the citational reiteration of the law leads to the question of which performances

---

42   "If 'sex' is assumed in the same way that law is cited ... then 'the law of sex' is repeatedly fortified and idealized as the law only to the extent that it is reiterated as the law, produced as the law, the anteriori and inapproximable ideal, by the very citations it is said to command" (Butler, *Bodies* 14).

by queer subjects "qualify as an affirmative resignification" and which ones run the risk "of reinstalling the abject at the site of its opposition" (240). In an allusion to the current debate over gay marriage, she asks, "To what extent, then, has the performative 'queer' operated alongside, as a deformation of, the 'I pronounce you …' of the marriage ceremony" (226). If gays and lesbians gain the right to participate in Austin's performative par excellence—the marriage vow and its concomitant thousand rights and obligations—will this assimilation merely re-inscribe a queer couple as heterosexual homos? This question, which Butler's alludes to and one of my ensuing chapters will investigate, speaks to a methodology of *Critical Queer Studies* that borrows from the work of race theorists like Gutiérrez-Jones and critical legal studies scholars like Wendy Brown and Marion Young. Queer studies scholars, I argue, need to recognize the antinomies that inhabit the current trajectories of queer activism and theory—contradictions that exist between the struggle for equality (in marriage, employment rights, and participation in the military) and the demands for liberty in the recognition of difference, i.e. the aesthetic and social call for a unique "queer" culture.[43]

The dilemma created by the divide between assimilationists and separatists, admirably explored by critical race theorists like bell hooks, is exemplified by Michael Warner's polemic against Evan Wolfson and the proponents of gay marriage, in which Warner argues that queer culture has become the victim of "mad vow disease," to use Kate Clinton's comic characterization.[44] Warner's argument, which I discuss in my final chapter, draws on the observations of critical legal studies scholars like Wendy Brown, who insists, "rights must not be confused with equality nor legal recognition with emancipation."[45] Brown's caveat underwrites an ongoing dissension in the queer ranks between academics and activists, constructivists and essentialists, anarchists and utopians, and—from a geographical angle—metronormative city queers and those whom Scott Herring calls "anti-urbanists."[46] The self-critical dimension of queer studies has already taken shape through explorations of homonormativity and homonationalism in works that decry the materialism of queer, especially gay male culture, as well as postcolonial and global studies that have revealed the imperialism of American

---

43   See Marion Young, *Justice and the Politics of Difference* (Princeton: Princeton University Press, 1990) for a discussion of the contradictions inherent in the struggle for equality and identity recognition.

44   Michael Warner, "Beyond Gay Marriage," in *Left Legalism/Left Critique*, ed. Wendy Brown and Janet Halley (Durham, NC: Duke University Press, 2002), 259–289. See also Lisa Duggan, "Holy Matrimony!" *Nation* (March 15, 2004).

45   Wendy Brown, *States of Injury* (Princeton: Princeton University Press, 1995).

46   Scott Herring, *Another Country: Queer Anti-Urbanism* (New York: New York University Press, 2010); Judith Halberstam, *In A Queer Time and Place: Transgender Bodies, Subcultural Lives* (New York: New York University Press, 2005); José Esteban Muñoz, *Cruising Utopia: The Then and There of Queer Futurity* (New York: New York University Press, 2009); Lee Edelman, *No Future: Queer Theory and the Death Drive* (Durham, NC: Duke University Press, 2004).

"out and proud" paradigms.[47] "For whom is outness a historically available and affordable option?" Butler asks in her critique of presentist conceptions of queer identity politics that overlook the way gender, geography, race, ethnicity, and class configure LGBTIQ issues in situationally discrete ways (227).

Aware of the corrections multiculturalism and globality must make to a rights-based and emancipatory trajectory in queer legal studies, the chapters in this volume seek to turn attention toward the way recent American cultural narratives implement a return of the repressed—an uncanny reminder that the queer sobriquet carries with it a history of violent prejudice, one which legal, social, and aesthetic norms continue to enforce. Using the "gunfighter nation" ethos of the West as their *locus amoenus*, these biopics, docudramas, and mainstream films are not purely renditions of shopworn stories of homophobia; they are versions of a heterosexism that is fearless, even a-phobic, in its promulgation of a social system that "denies, denigrates, and stigmatizes nonheterosexual forms of behavior, identity, relationships, or community."[48] This stigmatization, like Eribon's concept of the insult, finds its aesthetic corollary in the way queer cinema borrows from the genre of tragedy to insure the success of its narratives.[49] *The Celluloid Closet* and more recent works on queer cinema, have detailed the paradigms that attach to the history of gays and lesbians on the screen from the pre-Hays Code freedom of male dancing filmed by the Lumiere Brothers to *Philadelphia*'s betrayal of the victimized queer AIDS lawyer, Tom Hanks.[50] From the Jack Lemon jokester in *Some Like it Hot* to serial killer Al Pacino in *Serpico* (later to become Ray Cohn in *Angels in America*), from lesbian vampire to suicidal boarding school transgressor, the history of queers in cinema, to the degree it has evaded censorship, tells a story that more often than not reiterates the calamitous fate of the queer subject. While doom and gloom is not the only queer variety in the larger scope of mainstream film production (*Far From Heaven*, *Angels in America*, for example), queer stories of the West tend to find their gravitas in what Herring calls the simultaneous fetishization and disavowal of the possibility of a "rural queer identification" (173).[51]

The disavowal of the alive-and-well face of homo-hate throughout our great land takes other shapes than the wholesale displacement of such opprobrium on

---

47   Jasbir Puar, *Terrorist Assemblages: Homonationalism in Queer Times* (Durham, NC: Duke University Press, 2007); Lisa Duggan, *The Twilight of Equality: Neoliberalism, Cultural Politics and the Attack on Democracy* (Boston: Beacon, 2004); Martin F. Manalansan IV and Arnaldo Cruz-Malavé, *Queer Globalizations: Citizenship and the Afterlife of Colonialism* (New York: New York University Press, 2002).

48   Herek in D. Wickberg, "Homophobia: On the Cultural History of an Idea," *Critical Inquiry* (autumn 2000): 42–57, 47.

49   Didier Eribon, *Insult and the Making of the Gay Self*, trans. Michael Lucey (Durham, NC: Duke University Press, 2004).

50   Vito Russo, *The Celluloid Closet* (New York: Harper & Row, 1987).

51   Donna Deitch's *Desert Hearts* (Samuel Goldwyn, 1985), based on Jane Rule's novel, is an important lesbian exception.

to the mythos of the rugged conformity of the Wild West. We know that most hate crimes take place near gay bars in cities; we also know that the incidence of anti-queer violence in high schools around the country has not declined with the passage of hate-crime legislation. The god-hates-fags movement is a nationwide enterprise underwritten by a Christian coalition that includes Mormons and Catholics as well as born-again Baptists; its supporters include corporations like Target and Best Buy; news services like Fox, presidential candidates like Michele Bachmann, whose love-the-sinner rhetoric masks an endorsement of conversion therapy. The hostile environment for queers who are involved in the legal profession as litigators or litigants has also received recent attention, uncovering what Pamela Bridgewater and Brenda Smith call an "incredible reluctance to probe for bias based on an individual's either real or perceived sexual orientation."[52] While *Critical Queer Studies* must focus on the "manner in which heterosexuality, has, silently but alienly, maintained itself as a hidden yet powerfully privileged norm," it also takes as its difficult charge an examination of the way docudramas like *The Laramie Project* become sounding boards for prejudice as much as a theatrical call for change. *Critical Queer Studies* must explore how Brandon Teena's and Lana Tisdel's professed "homophobia" evidence a marked unease within the sexual minority consortium known acronymically as the LGBTIQ coalition. It must face the way the paralyzed and closeted Ennis del Mar instead of the more open Jack Twist becomes the star of the show in Ang Lee's subtle and understated film. It must acknowledge, therefore, how these redeployments dramatize the dire consequences of expressions of sexual freedom even as they disseminate the existence and force of sexual expression. Their performances carry forward and reinscribe, in fact "cite" the violence of normativity even as they represent challenges to it.

The probably undecidable question of the ultimate social effect—whether catalyzing or appeasing, subversive or containing—of the dissemination of a docudrama as popular as *The Laramie Project* mirrors in some ways the polarized and mutually exclusive stances that inhabit much of the current conversation about the future of queer subjectivity. *Critical Queer Studies* examines the dialectical interplay of these oppositions through an examination of the material, even legal,

---

52 Pamela D. Bridgewater and Brenda V. Smith, "Introduction to Symposia: Homophobia in the Halls of Justice: Sexual Orientation Bias and its Implications within the Legal System," 11 *American University Journal of Gender, Social Policy, and the Law* 1–128, at 2 (2002). This symposium details the devaluation of claims for loss of income in injury suits brought by partners as well as the lack of credibility ascribed to LGBTIQ witnesses. Judges, litigants, lawyers, jurors, and court personnel regularly disparage queers. In one famous Texas case, the defendant Richard Bednarski, accused of murdering two gay men, received a more lenient sentence because the judge said gays are equivalent to prostitutes (13). The homophobic label, which implies a conscious and overt bias, the authors state, "obscures the existence of heterosexism—or institutionalized domination of GLBT individuals" (16).

consequences of aesthetic production within the larger context of what Sarat calls the "imaginative life of the law and the way law lives in our imagination."[53] My discussion of *Brokeback Mountain* focuses, for example, on how the reality of an unprosecuted hate crime acts as a "phantasm" that defines Ennis del Mar's subjectivity (13). This focus on the proliferation of legal authority into consciousness, geography, and social practice represents, in my view, a valuable corrective to recent studies of queer subjectivity that concentrate, in the case of Lee Edelman for example, on the power of the queer as anti-family representative of the persistence of the death drive, or in the case of Esteban Muñoz, on the utopian possibilities of the queer aesthetic subject. Both of these important studies search for a place of viable resistance for the redeployment of the queer subject, but both could benefit from a greater acknowledgment of what Butler calls the "coded context" through which queers take their stance, from a greater awareness of the way the queer subject is interpellated by forces outside the self, forces that at the same time inhabit the unconscious, framing possibilities of resistance (13).

The chapters in this book explore those coded contexts—not as a way of limiting the scope of queer activism—rather as a means of foregrounding the obstacles that queer America would like to ignore, displace, or deny, in a manner described by Shoshanna Felman in *The Juridical Unconscious*.[54] The goal of such an examination, moreover, is not to deny the utopian impulses of Muñoz, but to embrace, as Drucilla Cornell has argued, the power of the imaginary to overcome the obstacles to queer life, in whatever form that imaginary might take.[55] In that spirit, the struggle for legal rights as well as the emancipatory goals of identity politics have a place, one that recognizes the competing and contradictory claims of queer practice but also understands them not from an either/or perspective but one that affirms the multiple avenues through which queer subjects seek human recognition.

This necessary affirmation grows out of my thinking about how categorization, in Gregory Alexander's words, "poses special risks for members of disadvantaged groups," including the way in which the assertion of identity difference can "operate *on behalf of* domination" through processes of isolation, compartmentalization, and even minority "studies" [italics mine].[56] Queer subject positions are "created not given," Alexander reminds us, and the chapters that follow investigate the architecture of these legal and aesthetic creations—constructions that arise from inside and outside the queer community. These chapters seek to expose and

---

53 Austin Sarat and Jonathan Simon, ed. *Cultural Analysis, Cultural Studies, and the Law: Moving Beyond Legal Realism* (Durham, NC: Duke University Press, 2003) 13.

54 Shoshana Felman, *The Juridical Unconscious: Trials and Traumas in the Twentieth Century* (Cambridge, MA: Harvard University Press, 2002).

55 Drucilla Cornell, *Transformations: Recollective Imagination and Sexual Difference* (New York: Routledge, 1993).

56 Gregory S. Alexander, "Talking About Difference: Meanings and Metaphors of Individuality," 11 *Cardozo Law Review* 1355–1375, at 1373, 1374 (1990).

dismantle illegitimate "sources of domination" that continue to haunt the queer subject in the houses of justice, theater, and academia (1374–1375).

Hellman's Prototype

One of the most amazing moments in the film version of *The Celluloid Closet* comes during the interview with Shirley MacLaine when the famous actress states unequivocally that she and Audrey Hepburn never discussed the topic of lesbianism during the making of Lillian Hellman's *Children's Hour* in the early 1960s. MacLaine is flabbergasted to admit the power of such denial, yet the social and psychological hold of the queer taboo in the 1950s and early 1960s finds corroboration in an equally astonishing absence of homosexuality as a topic of Gordon Allport's compendious *Nature of Prejudice*, published to critical acclaim in 1954.[57] The wholesale erasure of this topic in cinematic and most mainstream academic circles not only underlines the courage of literary authors like Vidal, Baldwin, and the pseudonymous Claire Morgan (Patricia Highsmith), but also emphasizes the ground-breaking nature of Hellman's play about the power of slander. The crime that dare not speak its name—as it was called by another famous queer figure who got mixed up with the law and forgot that truth is a defense to libel—has over the years garnered its power through a dual process of legal censorship and social erasure—a paradoxical combination of criminal naming and civil silencing.

Lillian Hellman's 1934 drama serves as a remarkable model for the more contemporary queer law and literature texts my book investigates. Her play, banned in Boston, was performed at a time when the depiction of homosexuality on the stage was illegal. Its source, a true case of defamation in an Edinburgh boarding school in 1810, was archived by Lillian Faderman in her *Scotch Verdict: Miss Pirie and Miss Woods v. Dame Cumming Gordon*.[58] William Wyler filmed Hellman's play twice: once in a bowdlerized 1936 version called *These Three*, in which the lesbian plot is turned into one of heterosexual adultery in order to appease the enforcers of the notorious Hays Code; the other in the 1963 *Children's Hour* with MacLaine and Hepburn, in which Martha Dobie hangs herself at the film's end. Wyler remade *These Three* as the force of the Hays Code was waning in 1960, presumably as a way to atone for his earlier heterosexualized adaptation.[59]

---

57 Allport's compendious study published in 1954 (500 pages) contains only one mention of homosexuality in a footnote, an omission that attests to erasure as one of the principle strategies of prejudice (Gordon W. Allport, *The Nature of Prejudice* [New York: Anchor, 1958]).

58 Lillian Faderman, *Scotch Verdict: Miss Pirie and Miss Woods v. Dame Cumming Gordon* (New York: Columbia University Press, 1994).

59 *These Three*, dir. William Wyler (Samuel Goldwyn Co. 1936); *The Children's Hour*, dir. William Wyler (United Artists 1961).

This story of two Connecticut boarding school teachers, who are accused by a "jealous" student of having sexual relations, changes its Scottish source by rendering Martha's lawsuit for defamation unsuccessful. Miss Pirie and Miss Wood prevailed in their case against their accuser in 1810 and also won on appeal, successfully proving in court that they did not have sexual relations. On the other hand, Martha and Karen, whose school is ruined long before the trial takes place, lose their suit, even though new evidence at the end of the drama causes the judge to vacate his decision. Once Mrs. Tilford realizes that her niece was lying, she recants her accusation, but the economic and personal damage is done and the tragic, outed homosexual is already well on her way to self-destruction. As the curious case of *Lana Tisdel v. Fox Pictures*, arising from Peirce's *Boys Don't Cry*, will evidence, a false accusation of homosexuality continues to be actionable, reminding us of the continued stigmatization of the queer. Hellman's adaptation rewrites the Pirie case—apparently with the help of Dashell Hammet—in order to dramatize the consequences of such a stigmatization and thereby highlight the tragic conflict between the expression of sexual freedom (real and perceived) and the authority of what Boal calls the coercive force of Aristotelian justice.

The composite of archives and adaptations of Hellman's drama—replete with a 1952 revival of the play as a veiled attack on the hearings of the House Committee on Un-American Activities (HUAC)—sets the stage for the current success of a set of queer films, docudramas, and biopics that have captured a more contemporary American imagination at the turn of the twenty-first century. As David Churchill noted in his study of another famous queer case that had its literary and filmic offshoots (Leopold and Loeb), the linking of "homosexuality with murder and pathology" has served as a vehicle for a "historical ideological process" that produces cultural capital through configuring queers as murderous or suicidal.[60] Hellman's re-writing of the outcome of the Pirie legal drama participates in the creation of that cultural capital in ways that adumbrate the successes of *Boys Don't Cry* and *Brokeback Mountain*. The play's particular understanding of the "imaginary power of the law," moreover, points to *The Children's Hour*'s strange affinity to the struggles of Ennis in *Brokeback*, especially in the fireside scenes when Martha wonders if she really is "like that," daring not to name the crime, masochistically realizing that on the level of consciousness if not behavior, her defamation action, like Oscar Wilde's, is a kind of fraud, a kind of willful closeting she undertakes to appease the powers of normalization at work inside her. Her lawsuit, like the hate crime Ennis witnesses as a boy, gazes at her like a symbolic determination of the self. The truth, which acts as a defense to defamation in the public arena of the law, revolves within the tribulations of Martha's tortured consciousness as both indictment and realization, signaling the power of interpellation, but also forcing Martha to admit her passion for Karen.

---

60   Churchill, David S. "The Queer Histories of a Crime: Representations and Narratives of Leopold and Loeb. Journal of the History of Sexuality. 18:2 (2009): 287–324, at 323 and 296.

Hellman's queer play, therefore, with its documentary and legal history, its tragic outcome, and its history of citational adaptation foreshadows future trials of the queer subject in Nebraska, Wyoming, and California as represented in the films, fictions, and transcripts I will explore. *The Children's Hour* lays a foundation for a set of queer legal dramas at the turn of the twenty-first century that expose the way law, literature, and film have worked together to perpetuate social norms even as they narrate attempts to resist and overturn them.

Contemporary Queer Cases

Chapter 1 explores how the famous 1979 defense of Dan White for the murder of Harvey Milk grounds its success in a combination of gay erasure and vilification in the courtroom, as dramatized by Emily Mann's docudrama, *The Execution of Justice*. This chapter reads Mann's portrayal of the trial's jury selection as indicative of the absent presence of the queer in this famous trial, dramatizing a heterocentrism that allows the tragic focus to shift from victim (Harvey Milk) to defendant, Dan White. The chapter then turns to *The Times of Harvey Milk* to show how Epstein's award-winning documentary reverses the trial's portrayal of Dan White as tragic protagonist, turning Harvey Milk into an idealized and heroic scapegoat.

Chapter 2 revisits the Matthew Shepard murder by examining a recent episode of ABC's *20/20* that sought to recast the case as a drug crime rather than a hate crime. The network's devaluation of anti-gay bias in the case not only ignores the plea of homosexual panic defense used in the trial, but also illuminates the ideological foundations of the doctrine of unwanted sexual advance, which continues to perpetuate social myths about gay men, myths that are both exposed but also perpetuated in *The Laramie Project*. The play's indebtedness to the narrative trajectory of Aristotelian tragedy aligns it with a cathartic and contained form of cultural panic that is analogous to and may reinforce the legal doctrine, even as *The Project* exposes the social conflict that underlies the Shepard murder.

Reading legal, literary, and filmic documents surrounding the famous Brandon Teena case, Chapter 3, subtitled "Branding Brandon," examines two central scenes—Sherriff Laux's interrogation of Brandon Teena as portrayed in Muska's documentary and the final love scene in *Boys Don't Cry*—in order to establish the violence of gender policing in both criminal and civil procedure—a violence driven home by a Nebraska court's decision that the transgendered Brandon was comparatively negligent for continuing to remain in Richardson County after the discovery of his "true" sex. Although the decision in this wrongful death case was reversed on appeal, it points to the persistence of a tragic narrative of gender and sex transgression, a purported flaw that retains its sanctioned legitimacy as stigma, I argue, in defamation lawsuits like that of Lana Tisdel who sued the producer of *Boys Don't Cry*—for falsely portraying her as a lesbian in the final sex scene of Peirce's award-winning film.

Chapter 4 turns to legislation in order to establish a link between the unprosecuted hate crimes that bookend Proulx's love story "Brokeback Mountain" and the narrative paradigm of proposed hate-crime legislation in western state legislatures. The recurrent process of bill proposal, public hearings, and rejection of legislative action has established a tragic trajectory of state-sanctioned animus which also inhabits Ennis's traumatized unconscious, dooming his love affair with Jack to a series of "high altitude fucks" in the pastoral idyll of the Rocky Mountains. Turning to the events surrounding the *Brokeback* phenomenon— including censorship, film criticism, awards ceremonies, and the tangential but synchronous passage of federal hate-crime legislation—this chapter examines how the *Brokeback* phenomenon has exploded generic expectations of what Proulx calls the "land of the pure, noble cowboy," thereby unsettling Sedgwick's homosocial continuum, even as it continues the tragic tradition. *Brokeback* re-writes *Romeo and Juliet* in a way that defamiliarizes love tragedy but also foregrounds the forces of anti-gay hate that impede same-sex love.

In Chapter 4, I explore Gus Van Sant's *Milk* (2008) in conjunction with the current debate over gay marriage between scholars like Michael Warner and the Human Rights Campaign's Evan Wolfson. Through an account of the geographical and chronological convergences that take place in the plaza outside San Francisco's City Hall, I juxtapose the 2008 broadcast of the hearings of the case against Proposition 8 (*Strauss v. Horton*) and the 2008 film footage in Van Sant's biopic of Harvey Milk's famous speech in the City Hall Plaza at the Gay Pride Parade 30 years earlier. Relying on Butler's notions of inscription and citation, this chapter reviews the performances of Ken Starr, Sean Penn, and the language of Judge Walker's decision in *Perry v. Schwarzenegger* as a way of showing how both culture and law effect stable positions by "citing" unstable precedent and ideological narratives. Milk's liberationist rhetoric and the history of his troubled "marriages" allow us to critique both assimilationist and anarchist tendencies in queer thinking, while a reading of Judge Walker's recent decision holding Proposition 8 unconstitutional reveals the myths that underlie the ideology of marriage.

More envoi than summary, my conclusion returns to the work of political theorists like Marcuse and Laclau in order to lay the groundwork for a political aesthetics—one that envisions the production of new queer works that both call for a critique of pure tolerance and narrate stories that complicate the queer tragic paradigm. Boal's notions of aesthetic legislation also envision a transition from the poetics of oppression to a new aesthetic, one that, in the context of this continuing twenty-first century struggle, will harness the power of queer "writes" to promote queer "rights" and introduce a poetics of "the unrepressed." This new aesthetic finds voice and image in Rob Epstein's recent film about the 1957 obscenity trial for the publication of Ginsberg's *Howl*, a story of queer law that documents a historical victory for a poem that celebrates the gay body.

Chapter 1

A Jury of One's Queers: Revisiting the Dan White Trial[1]

The field of critical queer studies examines the discursive formations through which sexual minorities have continued to suffer, in the words of the late Justice Brennan, such a "pernicious and sustained hostility"—such an "immediate and severe opprobrium"—that their only counterparts in the United States are racial groups (*Rowland v. Mad River Local School District*, 470 U.S. 1009, 1014, 105 S.Ct. 1373 [1985] [opinion of Brennan, J., dissenting from a denial of certiorari]). As legal scholar Mari Matsuda has declared, the "criminal justice system is a primary location of racist, sexist, homophobic, and class based oppression in this county."[2] This chapter explores the methodology behind these trenchant assessments by revisiting perhaps the most notorious anti-gay crime in United States history, the assassination of Harvey Milk by ex-policeman and San Francisco supervisor Dan White, who served after his manslaughter conviction a little over five years for the killings of Milk and Mayor George Moscone. Two dramatic re-enactments of this famous trial—one an award winning film, *The Times of Harvey Milk*, and the other a stage play entitled *The Execution of Justice*—provide the data and framework for my exploration of the way the criminal justice system perpetuates queer bias by sanctioning strategies of exclusion and erasure in almost all phases of trial—from jury selection to closing arguments, from expert testimony to pleas of diminished capacity.

The literature on the Dan White trial also dramatizes the larger social impact of this famous criminal proceeding, documenting the shock waves and riots the trial produced in a town that had become in the matter of a decade the hub of a national gay rights movement, a mecca where by 1979 one out of seven residents were gay or lesbian.[3] Taking place on the cusp of an incipient backlash

---

1   This chapter originally appeared as "A Jury of One's Queers: Revisiting the Dan White Trial," *Queer Mobilizations: LGBT Activists Confront the Law* (New York University Press, 2009) 257–280. It is reproduced here with the permission of New York University Press. Some revisions have been made.

2   Mari J. Matsuda, "Crime and Affirmative Action," 1 *Georgetown Journal of Gender, Race and Justice* 309, at 319 (1998).

3   Frances FitzGerald, *Cities on a Hill: A Journey through Contemporary American Cultures* (New York: Simon & Schuster, 1981), 27; Elizabeth A. Armstrong, *Forging Gay Identities: Organizing Sexuality in San Francisco, 1950–1994* (Chicago: University of Chicago Press, 2002), 18.

that would soon usher Ronald Reagan into national office, the trial of Dan White continues to resonate as what Armstrong and Crage call a "commemorable event" in large part because it symbolizes a turning point in the history of a gay rights movement that would soon turn its attention from liberation to survival in the face of political conservatism and the AIDS epidemic.[4] While the White Night Riots in San Francisco's City Hall, which followed the verdict, attest on one level to a dramatic disjunction between legal process and social advancement, the trial also continues to resonate in queer collective memory as a reminder of the deep-rooted homophobia within the criminal justice system—a prejudice evidenced by the long road to the defeat of sodomy laws, the continued use of the homosexual panic defense in some courts, and ongoing debates over adding sexual orientation to hate-crimes legislation in many states.

The story of the rise and fall of the slain Harvey Milk achieved its commemorative status through a discursive explosion that started with the famous footage of now Senator Dianne Feinstein announcing the murders on the morning of November 28, 1978, just days after 900 people from the People's Church had drunk lethal Kool Aid in Guyana: "As president of the Board of Supervisors," her shaky voice spoke into the microphones, "it is my duty to make this announcement: Mayor George Moscone and Supervisor Harvey Milk have been shot and killed. The suspect is Supervisor Dan White" (Mann 151–152).[5] This television footage—a close-up of Feinstein's aghast countenance before a host of microphones—became the opening sequence of Epstein's famous film, a documentary that reproduces the paradigmatic narrative of the fated queer by beginning with Milk's murder before relating Harvey's biography. Almost immediately after the shots rang out in City Hall that November morning, accounts of the homicides began to reverberate through channels of television coverage, newspapers, a recorded confession, courtroom sketches, trial transcripts, an opera, two major book-length accounts, a collection of poems, and some five years later, two important documentaries that used these sources for their dramatic re-creations—Emily Mann's *Execution of Justice* published in 1983, and the 1984 Academy-Award winning documentary film *The Times of Harvey Milk*.[6]

---

4   Elizabeth A. Armstrong and Suzanna M. Crage, "Movements and Memory: The Making of the Stonewall Myth," *American Sociological Review* 17 (October 2006): 724–751, at 726.

5   Emily Mann, *The Execution of Justice* in *Testimonies: Four Plays* (New York: Theatre Communications Group, 1997), 151–152. References within the body of the chapter come from this version of Mann's docudrama.

6   Mann's play begins with the same television coverage. Other retellings of these murders include Randy Shilts, *The Mayor of Castro Street* (New York: St. Martin's, 1982); Mike Weiss, *Double Play: The City Hall Killings* (Menlo Park: Addison Wesley, 1984); Stewart Wallace and Michael Korie, *Harvey Milk: Opera in Three Acts*, in the Gay and Lesbian Archive, San Francisco Public Library (1994) (opera); *I Promise You This: Collected Poems in Memory of Harvey Milk* in the Gay and Lesbian Archive, San Francisco Public Library (1979); Warren Hinckle, *GaySlayer!* (Virginia City: Silver Dollar

These productions—one a film, the other a docudrama—not only cite trial transcripts, interviews, and newspapers; they also cite one another. Both have become part of a cultural commemoration that has incited the building of schools, centers, the creation of scholarships, and the repeal of laws.[7] These two key documentaries also illustrate how the "difficult art" of the drama of the real, as Tony Kushner describes the documentary, undertakes cultural and historical critique as part of its generic structure.[8] In this chapter, I explore first how jury selection in the Dan White case, as dramatized by Mann's docudrama, evidenced a form of homo-exclusion and erasure that led to a jury purged of queers, an audience already sympathetic to the defendant's tragic role before the trial started. Secondly, I examine the way Epstein's film transforms the trial's tragic narrative from the story of the heroic Dan White, who cracked under pressure, into a narration of the martyrdom of Harvey Milk. Both works use the tools of theater and film to critique even as they dramatize the defendant's audiotaped confession and famous plea of diminished capacity, the so-called Twinkie defense, which alleged that the defendant's temporary mental illness resulted from an ingestion of large amounts of junk food.

Throughout my analysis, I rely on Victor Turner's notion that social conflict finds redress through a set of rituals that include the analogous forums of

---

Books, 1985). A trial transcript is available in Kenneth W. Salter, *The Trial of Dan White* (El Cerrito: A Market and Systems Interface Publications Book, 1991). This chapter examines as its primary data Mann's *Execution of Justice*, which premiered in 1984, and Roert Epstein and Richard Schmeichen's film *The Times of Harvey Milk* (Cinecom International, 1986); I treat Gus Van Sant's biopic *Milk* (2008) in another chapter, though it should be noted that he borrows from the Epstein documentary and includes the now iconic image of the distressed Feinstein before the microphones. For background on Milk's rise and fall, see FitzGerald 25–119; John D'Emilio, *Making Trouble: Essays on Gay History, Politics, and the University* (New York: Routledge, 1992), 57–94; Armstrong, *Forging*; and Susan Stryker and Jim Van Buskirk, *Gay by the Bay: A History of Queer Culture in the San Francisco Bay Area* (San Francisco: Chronicle Books, 1996).

7   For the Harvey Milk legacy, see Shilts 347–348. The diminished capacity defense was repealed by the California legislature after the White verdict.

8   Tony Kushner, "The Art of the Difficult," *Civilization* (August–September 1997): 62–67, quoted in Gary Fisher Dawson, *Documentary Theatre in the United States: An Historical Survey and Analysis of Its Content, Form, and Stagecraft* (Westport: Greenwood, 1999), xii. Mann's docudrama has become one of the "exemplar[s] of the staged oral history," a fast-growing body of American docudramas that compile interviews, court transcripts, and other documents to create on-stage dialogue. Anne Deavere Smith, Tony Kushner, and Moises Kaufman have published in this genre (see Ryan M. Claycomb, "(Ch)oral History: Documentary Theatre, the Communal Subject and Progressive Politics," *Journal of Dramatic Theory and Criticism* 17 (spring 2003): 95–119, at 99). Because these documentaries incorporate archival materials into their scripts, my reading of this play and film often leads to examination of the historical documents that Mann and Epstein have integrated into their creative productions.

courtroom, stage, and screen (12).[9] For Turner the trial acts as a form of social theater, a dramatic re-enactment that replays original acts of violence through performances of confession, judgment, and punishment; it functions as a dramatic enactment that seeks to repair a rupture in the social fabric and return a community to a form of civil order (10). From the more specific perspective of Turner's analogy between social conflict and Aristotelian tragedy, the choral jury of Dan White's peers—removed chronologically and socially from the scene of the crime, sequestered, and cautioned—witnessed a legal re-enactment of the 1978 killings, determining varying claims to truth, deciding the mode of redress they felt warranted, parceling out a remedy meant to return San Francisco to its *status quo ante*, an environment where Aristotelian justice might again prevail, where the laws made by those in power might again be obeyed (Turner 11; Boal 22–24).[10] The commemorable resonance of the Dan White case, I will argue, arises in part because the elements of its narrative fit easily within the "existing genre" expectations of tragedy, replete with a protagonist who suffers from a mistake made in the face of misfortune (Armstrong and Crage 726). In many ways, the archive of the Dan White trial itself represents the first in a long line of dramatic retellings of this segment of gay history, though the defense in the Dan White trial uses the heteronormative criminal justice system to shift the focus from victim to defendant, to make White—not Harvey Milk—this tragedy's protagonist. In what follows, I first provide a historical context for the trial and then explore how subsequent dramatizations by Epstein and Mann re-try the Dan White case even as they critique its discriminatory underpinnings. My final section brings critical queer studies to bear on the ideological strategies of these artistic commemorations, asking hard questions about how we can undertake a critique of this homophobic legal history without replicating the very demonization that these docudramas sometimes portray.

Of course, neither the social ritual of Dan White's trial nor the production of these documentaries took place in a historical vacuum. Both arose within a context of an increasing visible and vocal lesbian and gay presence in San Francisco; both narratives, moreover, still continue to function as forms of what Stuart Hall calls articulation and rearticulation—discursive events that transmit and produce power through a complex set of historical practices.[11] These commemorative documentaries have become part of a collective consciousness that continues

---

9   Victor Turner, *From Ritual to Theatre: The Human Seriousness of Play* (New York: Performing Arts Journal Publications, 1982), 12.

10   Augusto Boal, *Theatre of the Oppressed*, trans. Charles A. and Maria-Odilia Leal McBride (New York: Theatre Communications Group, 1985).

11   Stuart Hall, "On Postmodernism and Articulation: An Interview with Stuart Hall,," by Lawrence Grossberg, in *Critical Dialogues in Cultural Studies*, ed. David Morley and Kuan-Hsing Chen (New York: Routledge, 1996); Kevin DeLuca, "Articulation Theory: A Discursive Grounding for Theoretical Practice," *Philosophy and Rhetoric* 32 (1999): 334–348.

to influence social practice, as evidenced in the opening of schools, archives, and centers in Harvey Milk's name as well as the continued push at local and national levels for legislation to protect the queer community. About the same time Dan White was released on parole from Soledad prison in 1984, after serving a sentence of about five years, Epstein's Oscar-winning film was released, reliving and re-trying these events for thousands of viewers, celebrating Milk's life and martyrdom, casting Dan White as homophobic antagonist. Was it pure coincidence that White was found dead in his car a year later, his lungs filled with carbon monoxide, a suicide note left for his estranged wife? Whether or not he ever watched Epstein's film is not known, but this uncanny intersection of culture and event at the very least had the "queer" effect of abrading the boundaries that some critics often draw between artistic representation and what has traditionally been called history.[12] In the early 1980s, White received a "new trial" in the unofficial courts of culture—in Epstein's film and Mann's docudrama, nonfiction accounts that sentenced this "gayslayer" to death by his own hand.

The Historical Context: A Policeman and his Target

> This tape should be played only in the event of my death by assassination ...
> I fully realize that a person who stands for what I stand for—a gay activist—
> becomes a target for a person who is insecure, terrified, afraid or very disturbed
> themselves ... If a bullet should enter my brain, let that bullet destroy every
> closet door. (Harvey Milk's Political Will, made on November 18, 1977)[13]

Harvey Milk taped his prophetic will after he was elected to the Board of Supervisors, the governing body of San Francisco, in November 1977. The tenacious 48-year-old owner of a camera shop on Castro Street had finally prevailed after three unsuccessful attempts to get elected, his victory attributable in part to a proposition passed the previous year that mandated district rather than citywide elections for supervisors. As a result, the first Afro-American, the first Asian American, the first single mother (Carol Ruth Silver) and the first "avowed homosexual" came to

---

12   "Abrade" is Donald Hall's verb for the way queer studies questions discursive categories, in this particular case, the differentiation between a prevailing notion of ineffectual "art" and the privileged stature of "reality." I follow Hall's universalizing position in this chapter. While queer studies, he states, has as its primary focus "putting pressure on simplistic notions of identity and in disturbing the value systems that underlie designations of normal and abnormal identity, sexual identity in particular" (Donald E. Hall, *Queer Theories* [New York: Palgrave, 2003], 14); it also has as its broader scope the intent "to abrade the classifications, to sit athwart conventional categories or traverse several" (13).

13   Portions of Milk's tape appear in Mann 221–222; a full transcript of one of the tapes of the will is transcribed in Shilts 372–375. Only one copy of the tape contains the famous bullet sentence.

govern the city, along with Daniel James White, the 30-year-old Irish Catholic ex-policeman from Visitation Valley, a working-class neighborhood in the southwest part of town.[14] White, a Democrat, had run a law-and-order campaign, framing his appearance with the theme from *Rocky* and big American flags, proclaiming "I am not going to be forced out of San Francisco by splinter groups of radicals, social deviates and incorrigibles" (Mann 164).[15] As part of his law-and-order platform, White opposed building a home for "troubled" youth in his district, but as one of its first orders of business, the board voted in favor of it, Milk casting the deciding vote in favor after considerable deliberation. White never forgave Harvey for his vote. Though he opposed the Briggs Initiative (a failed 1978 proposition which would have mandated the firing of lesbian and gay teachers in the state), White found himself the lone dissenting vote against Milk's gay rights municipal law and street closings on Polk Street for the gay Halloween parade.

The simultaneous rise to political power of both Harvey Milk and Dan White pointed to a set of social contradictions that lay behind a remarkable decade of gay liberation in San Francisco. When 350,000 marchers participated in the Gay Freedom Day Parade on June 25, 1978, Harvey Milk addressing a rally at City Hall Plaza with the opening "I want to recruit you," the "new society" of the Castro had reached what one historian calls "the high point of its development" (Stryker and Van Buskirk 70; FitzGerald 48). In the course of a decade, a plethora of gay bars, bathhouses, theaters, film festivals, newspapers, and political organizations had accompanied one of the most "miraculous" flourishings of culture in queer history (D'Emilio 187; Armstrong 113, 115). But the unprecedented turnout for the 1978 parade also reflected a reaction to a growing anti-gay political campaign, as evidenced by a California ballot measure that sought to keep lesbians and gay men out of public schools. Spawned by Anita Bryant's successful campaign to defeat Dade County's gay rights law a year earlier, the Briggs Initiative was defeated only after an arduous campaign led by Milk. Its viability pointed to an incipient backlash that would become a significant weapon in the Dan White trial.

What Stryker and Van Buskirk call the "cultural visibility" of the gay liberation movement had also made queers ready targets of an escalating incidence of violence in the San Francisco (73). While police raids on lesbian and gay bars were commonplace in the 1950s and 1960s, that antagonism did not disappear in the 1970s, even with the political clout of the tavern owners. Gay murders, bombings of gay business, and arson continued in the 1970s, and the police were

---

14　Milk first followed his lover Jack McKinley to San Francisco in 1968. He grew up on Long Island, living the life of a closeted Goldwater Republican and Wall Street analyst before migrating to San Francisco (see Shilts 12ff.).

15　White grew up as one of eight children in Visitation Valley, a working-class neighborhood south of downtown. At 10, he was a skinny, crewcut kid whose round face made him a "patsy" in the eyes of other boys in the neighborhood. Dan's father Charlie trained his boy to fight back. White became quarterback at Riordan High and a MVP on the police softball league (Weiss 49).

sometimes the perpetrators (77). Although Dan White was not openly homophobic, his campaign rhetoric employed terms like "malignancies of society" and social "blight" to code his distaste for public displays of affection and nudity in the queer community. White's disaffection with deviates and liberals, coupled with his allegiance to the police force, tapped into a growing frustration with the openness on Castro Street, a frustration backed by a long history of institutional erasure and in many cases impunity for violent attack. The simultaneous political success of both Milk and White reflects a dialectic that still accompanies the struggle for queer civil rights; its detractors often growing more virulent in response to success, some like Dan White well aware of the law's history of unchecked oppression of sexual minorities.

On Friday, November 10, 1978, after 10 months in office as a supervisor, Dan White resigned from the board, citing economic and family concerns. Pressured by his friends, he changed his mind a few days later and asked the progressive mayor for his seat back on Tuesday, November 14. At first, Moscone said he would consider the resignation rescinded, but he later discovered the law required him to re-appoint White formally. Milk lobbied against the re-appointment, and when Moscone met with White, he received no assurances that White would vote for any of Moscone's plans, including the settlement of an affirmative action lawsuit against the police department. On November 25, the mayor offered the job of supervisor to Don Horazney without informing White, who heard the news from a reporter on Sunday, November 26.

The next morning White was driven to City Hall by his aide, carrying his loaded .38 in his suit's coat pocket along with a handful of extra shells in a handkerchief. Dropped off at the entrance, he noticed the new metal detectors in place as a result of the recent Jim Jones massacre. He decided to go around the corner and jump through an open window on the side of the building, running up to the mayor's office and asking the secretary if he could see the mayor. When he eventually gained entrance, White shot George Moscone five times, twice in the base of his skull (two so-called *coup de grâce* shots). He then proceeded to his old office, reloaded his gun, and asked Harvey to talk to him, shooting Milk four times, twice in the head. White fled to St. Mary's Cathedral, called his wife, and turned himself in at Northern Station, where his close friend, Lieutenant Frank Falzon, allowed Dan to narrate his confession.

White was tried in San Francisco in May of 1979, on two counts of first-degree murder. Lawyers impaneled an all-white jury with no gays and lesbians, and the defense built its case on the doctrine of diminished capacity, a form of temporary insanity allegedly brought on by White's depression and junk-food binges. The jury found White lacked the mental capacity to act with malice, convicted White of voluntary manslaughter, and sentenced him to seven years in prison. On May 21, 1979, the White Night Riots left 150 injured and millions of dollars in damage to cars and buildings near City Hall. Later the same night, police raids on Castro Street injured dozens of gay men. While commentators have noted that the riots resulted in little social change, given the incipient rise of the Moral Majority in the

1980s, the collective memory of this trial, I will argue, has not gone unexpressed in film, theater, and nonfiction (D'Emilio 93; FitzGerald 79). Through word and image, these articulations have preserved a common heritage that still marks the bravery of both coming out and queer activism.

Ironically, Dan White received no psychiatric treatment while in prison and was paroled early in January 1984. He was found dead from carbon monoxide poisoning in the garage of his wife's house on October 21, 1985, a patriotic Irish ballad rolling on the cassette player in his car. Before his suicide, White invited his friend Frank Falzon to join him at the Olympics in Los Angeles in 1984. In an interview with author Mike Weiss 20 years after the murders, Falzon divulged the content of his talks with White during the games. "I was on a mission," White had told his friend, "I wanted four of them. Carol Ruth Silver—she was the biggest snake of the bunch. And Willie Brown [black Assemblymen and friend of Moscone], he was masterminding the whole thing." White confided in Falzon that his mission was to save San Francisco. During his 1998 interview with Weiss, the retired detective said he wanted finally to get White's confession off his chest.[16]

A Jury of his Peers

After the Stonewall Riots in New York in 1969, "coming out became a profoundly political act," John D'Emilio writes, one that promised "a huge step forward in shedding the self hatred and internalized oppression imposed by a homophobic society" (85). Ironically, this very same act resulted in disenfranchisement during jury selection in the Dan White trial. As Emily Mann details in her collage docudrama, defense counsel Doug Schmidt systematically asked prospective jurors in the case if they ever "supported controversial causes like homosexual rights," requesting the judge dismiss for cause anyone who answered in the affirmative or suggested that they lived with someone of the same sex (157–158). As Mann dramatizes in Act One of her play, Judge Calcagno's rapid removal of any juror that mentioned even marching in the Gay Pride Parade highlights the court's prejudicial presumption that same-sex attraction was tantamount to bias in the case (157–158). In *Execution* as well Epstein's film, we learn through the mouth of a TV reporter that the final jury contained no gays, no blacks, and no Asians; it consisted finally of one ex-policeman, the wife of an ex-county jailer, and four women old enough to be Dan White's mother (159). Most of the jurors were middle class, Catholic, and inhabitants of neighborhoods near White's district. As the docudrama's fast-moving montage jumps quickly from *voir dire* to the transcript of Joanna Lu's TV news report, it raises critical questions about how *coming out* in one venue of San Francisco in 1979 led to a *ruling out* of the constitutional right to participate in the process of trial by jury.

---

16   Mike Weiss, "Dan White's Last Confession," *San Francisco Magazine* (1998): 32–33.

While prosecutor Tom Norman seemed pleased with the rapid impaneling of a law-and-order jury, seeking as he did the death penalty for the homicide of both Harvey Milk and Mayor Moscone, defense counsel Schmidt also expressed the same satisfaction, for he knew his client would "certainly be judged by a jury of his peers" (Mann 159). One of these attorneys was making a major miscalculation. Both documentaries note the surprising alacrity with which the jury was selected. Judge Calcagno had sequestered over 100 prospective jurors and planned on a lengthy selection process, but the 12 were picked within a few days, and the prosecution raised no objection to its composition, in spite of recent California precedent for Sixth Amendment challenges to juries that failed to draw from a "representative cross-section of the community" without excluding any cognizable groups (*People v. Wheeler* 22 Cal.3rd 258, 583 P.2d 748 [1978]). Eight years later the United States Supreme would follow Wheeler's lead by establishing the so-called *Batson* test, holding that jury composition could be challenged if one side shows a group bias in the selection process and the other is not able to rebut that presumption (*Batson v. Kentucky* 476 U.S. 79, 106 S.Ct. 1712 [1986]). Notably most of these early cases concern the racial make-up of juries and involve challenges by defense counsel, so the absence of any challenge in the White case is in some ways explicable, but that absence also indicates a telling erasure of the queer community from the consciousness of what was considered a "representative cross-section" for purposes of jury make-up.

The Supreme Court extended the availability of *Batson* motions to the gender make-up of juries in 1994, and in 2000, the California Court of Appeals in *People v. Garcia* (77 Cal.App.4th 1269, 92 Cal.Rptr. 339) ruled that gays and lesbians are a cognizable class for purposes of the rule that juries must be drawn from a representative cross-section of the community, stating that any exclusion based on their gay affiliation alone violates the state constitution of California. The court held that even though the United States Supreme Court does not give the heightened scrutiny afforded gender and race to laws that affect lesbians and gays, the California constitution requires courts to confront the "terra incognita" of sexual orientation. "Trial by jury presupposes a jury drawn from a pool broadly representative of the community as well as impartial in a specific case," Judge Bedsworth noted, and a "'representative cross-section of the community' is violated whenever a 'cognizable group' within that community is systematically excluded from the jury venire" (77 Cal.App.4th at 1275).

In *Garcia*, the California Court of Appeals held that gay and lesbians satisfy the criteria that establish a cognizable group for purposes of jury challenges, relying in part on *Wheeler*, the 1978 case that ironically was available to the bar at the time of the White trial. Cognizance, the *Garcia* court reiterated, comes first when a group "shares a common perspective arising from their life experience in the group, i.e. a perspective gained precisely *because* they are members of that group" (77 Cal.App.4th at 1276). Whereas common residency in a neighborhood for less than a year was insufficient to form a common perspective, in the case of gays and lesbians, the court reasoned, "it cannot seriously be argued in the era of 'don't ask; don't tell' that homosexuals do not have a common perspective ... They share a history of persecution comparable to that of blacks and women." The court dismissed the prosecution's argument on appeal that there was no common perspective "shared by Rep. Jim Kolbe (an Arizona Republican), RuPaul, poet William Alexander Percy, Truman Capote, and Ellen DeGeneres." In response to the appeal, Judge Bedsworth claimed we should not confuse perspective with personality. "Commonality of perspective does not result in identity of opinion," the court stated; the whole point of the Batson challenge is to assure that sexual minorities, "exposed to or fearful of persecution and discrimination," be included in the jury pool (77 Cal.App.4th at 1277). The second prong of the jury test was also met. Cognizance is not available if others in the community were able to represent the gay and lesbian perspective. The court could not see how any other group could understand the gay position, citing a National Law Journal Poll (November 2, 1998) that found 17.1 percent of prospective jurors admitting a bias which "would make it impossible for them to be fair and impartial in a case in which one of the parties was homosexual" (as opposed to 4.8 percent admitting the same bias against African-Americans and 5 percent against women) (77 Cal. App.4th 1277).[17]

Relying on the 1978 *Wheeler* case, the *Garcia* decision provides a metaleptic commentary on the failure of the justice system to take cognizance of the inequity of the jury composition in the People versus Dan White. In hindsight this structural erasure seems almost willful given the concurrent flourishing of a gay liberation movement that was commanding national attention. As both documentaries detail, Tom Norman, the veteran prosecutor, may never have even uttered the word

---

17 The *Garcia* court's distinction between commonality of perspective and identity of opinion raises important theoretical questions about the imprecision of ascribing value to minority status, even as Judge Bedsworth's progressive ruling, more than 20 years after the White trial, evidences the law's intransigence in taking judicial notice of what Justice Brennan called queer "opprobrium." Without positing the existence of an essential queer identity, the *Garcia* decision found that J. Edgar Hoover and James Baldwin share a common heritage of persecution sufficient to make them cognizable if not to themselves then at least to a court seeking an impartial cross-section of the community for purposes of jury selection. The real existence of past and present homo-exclusion proved convincing and efficacious for Judge Bedsworth, a fact that cannot be overlooked by those critical legal studies scholars who have recently questioned the efficacy of rights claims (see Francesca. Polletta, "The Structural Context of Novel Rights Claims: Southern Civil Rights Organizing, 1961-1966. *Law and Society*. 34 (2000): 367-398.). For the *Garcia* majority, even the availability of passing in the closet—which widens the philosophical gaps between queers in the world—could not obviate the history of sodomy laws, shock therapy, and, most recently, constitutional amendments. (In the 2004 elections, 11 states adopted constitutional amendments prohibiting same-sex marriage, though New York bucked the trend by legalizing same-sex marriage in 2011). Whether or not the successful constitutional challenge to California's amendment (Proposition 8) will be upheld on appeal to the Supreme Court remains an open question.

"gay" during the entire 1979 trial, remaining silent while defense lawyer Doug Schmidt used his challenges to dismiss every juror connected to "controversial homosexuals." When a young male prospective juror appears and is questioned in Act One of *Execution*, the judge wastes no time in dismissing him for cause. "Do you live with anyone?" defense counsel queries. "A roommate," the juror responds. "What does he or she do?" Schmidt follows up. The juror responds, "*He* works at the Holiday Inn," his emphatic pronoun enough to convince the judge that this gay man is too biased to hear the case. Another heterosexual woman is dismissed for cause when she admits to walking in the Gay and Lesbian Freedom Parade (Mann 158). In the end, Schmidt used his peremptory challenges to dismiss any juror who supported gay rights, and the defense faced no objection from the prosecutor, who seemed stubbornly ignorant of the role bias against queers would play in the case.

Instead prosecutor Tommy Norman sought jurors who believed in the death penalty, oblivious to the social reality that those in favor of capital punishment are often aligned ideologically with social conservatives, many empathetic to law officers who—in a fit of tragic diminished capacity—snap and shoot a homosexual and his gay-friendly mayor. Norman got his law-and-order jury, but it produced an audience for this courtroom drama which was predisposed to a public presumption about the deviance of queers and the innocence of law enforcement.[18] One juror, himself an ex-cop, told the court during *voir dire* that he believed White had murdered Milk and Moscone because of "social pressure"—a metaphor for the tensions mounting in the city over gay migration. Even before any testimony, he articulated the exact argument defense counsel would use to excuse the actions of his client.[19]

Ironically, a *Wheeler* challenge to the jury make-up in the White case also depended on the public voice of the district attorney's office, a voice that was largely complicit in the defense strategy of queer exclusion. Most jury challenges come from minority defendants themselves, but in this case the man on trial was not only aligned with the DA's office as an ex-police officer; he was also part of a growing anti-queer faction in San Francisco. Through a successful backlash strategy, the defense argued for a jury of non-queers, as if anti-homosexuals were actually the cognizable minority for purposes of a constitutional challenge. If Harvey Milk's interest as a victim were to be represented, they would have to have come from a prosecution already infused with a structural bias, one that was loathe to recognize, much less argue, that one of San Francisco's finest might have committed a hate crime. While the prosecutor was also admittedly concerned about the interests of the slain mayor, the vigorous refusal to take cognizance of bias against queer perspectives in the jury manifested itself, paradoxically, as a

---

18   See Liz McMillen, "The Importance of Storytelling: A New Emphasis by Law Scholars," *Chronicle of Higher Education* (July 26, 1996): A10.

19   Shilts 309, 324; Weiss, *Double* 287.

virulent insistence that queer viewpoints were themselves inherently prejudicial in the case.

Defense counsel not only used the jury selection process to equate homosexual causes with controversy; he also convinced the judge that every member of this cognizable class was prima facie biased and therefore dismissible as a trier of fact in a case against the confessed murderer of a gay supervisor. The result was a jury of Dan White's peers—one not only without lesbians and gay men but one also resentful of any controversial queer presence—a jury in fact of anti-queers. The prosecution's decision to *erase* Milk's gayness in the case only facilitated the defense's *exclusion* of lesbian and gays from the jury. Under the ideological guise of impartiality, Judge Calcagno impaneled a jury partial to the heterosexual imperative—producing 12 angry straight whites ready to excuse Milk's killer for an act of violence they could understand if not publicly approve.

Emily Mann's collage documentary, *The Execution of Justice*, foregrounds jury venire early in Act One, featuring a screen behind the actors that reads "Jury Selection." The jury phase of the play follows the controversial counterpoint between Sister Boom Boom (a drag queen from the Order of Perpetual Indulgence) and a San Francisco cop who wears a Free Dan White t-shirt. Boom Boom reads from the Book of Dan, which tells the defendant to fear not, for the jury will give him "three to seven with time off for good behavior" while begging for "love, understanding, and forgiveness" when and if some crazy faggot inevitably kills Dan White after he serves time in prison for a few years (Mann 155). The policeman, on the other hand, is proud to say that Dan White showed "you could fight City Hall," especially a faggot-loving mayor who makes the police handle queers with "lavender gloves" in a city "stinkin' with degenerates" (153–155). The movement from dramatic street lingo to the microcosmic selection of jurors highlights the way the "conscience of the community," as Schmidt called it, has no room in its superego for either Boom Boom or queers closeted in a log cabin. "It appears the prosecution and the defense want the same jury," reporter Joanna Lu opines at the end of Mann's jury selection segment, her statement suggesting not so much collusion as an admixture of erasure and exclusion that left the panoptic space of the trial entirely normalized, absent any abnormal queer presence within the halls of justice (159).

A Man among Men

> Good people, fine people, with fine backgrounds simply don't kill people in cold blood, it just doesn't happen, and obviously some part of them has not been presented thus far. Dan White was a native of San Francisco. He went to school here, went through high school here. He was a noted athlete in high school. He was an army veteran who served in Vietnam, and was honorably discharged from the army. He became a policeman thereafter, and after a brief hiatus developed, again returned to the police force in San Francisco, and later

transferred to the fire department. He was married in December of 1976, and he fathered his son in July, 1978. (Doug Schmidt's Opening Statement read by narrator Harvey Fierstein in *The Times of Harvey Milk*; also in Mann 162)

Defense counsel's now famous opening statement—replete with the implicit heterocentric codes of nativism, sports, militarism, and marriage—begins the trial's dramatization of the Dan White story, a narrative that demonstrates how social rituals reproduce the pervasive trajectory of the Aristotelian tragic paradigm, enacting what Victor Turner calls the "dynamic system of interdependence between social dramas and cultural performances," between—on another level—fiction and fact (107). Both documentaries incorporate Schmidt's opening statement into their script, illustrating the way trial practice has its roots in theater, in a social drama "that accords well with Aristotle's abstraction of dramatic form." Turner reminds us that social drama harbors "something of the investigative, judgmental and even punitive character of law-in-action, and something of the sacred, mythic, numinous, even 'supernatural' character of religious action—sometimes to the point of sacrifice" (108). Documentary, I will argue later in relation to *The Laramie Project*, also illustrates the converse; it exemplifies the ways the archives of social reality, including trial transcripts, often re-enact the fictional structure of tragic narrative, the story of a hero's *hamartia* or mistake in the face of misfortune—a flaw with which juries can identify, pitying the fallen protagonist/defendant and fearing that circumstance might have driven them to the same violent catastrophe. The Dan White jury, through a reactionary intersection between legal process and social movement, consisted of 12 citizens already predisposed to an anti-gay bias which they would "never recognize as the obvious prejudice it is."[20] An apt chorus was in place in the Dan White trial well before Schmidt's opening statement.

Augusto Boal calls the Aristotelian trajectory of social drama a theater of the repressed, a kind homeopathic spectacle that allows an audience (and by analogy a jury) to experience an anti-social impulse vicariously, to enact a "purgation of all antisocial elements" through judgment, and then to return to a universe of defined and accepted values, a *status quo ante* that Aristotle calls the existing parameters of justice. The spectator "enjoys the pleasures and suffers the misfortunes of the character, to the extreme of thinking his thoughts," experiencing the "three changes of a rigorous nature: *peripeteia, anagnorisis,* and *catharsis*; he *suffers a blow* with regard to his fate (the action of the play), *recognizes the error* vicariously committed and *is purified of the antisocial characteristic* which he sees in himself" (40). For Boal, this process of empathy represents "a powerful system of intimidation," not because it deters viewers from acting immoderately but because it allows them to re-enact violence and avoid confronting the social inequities that underlie the narrative (46). By enacting a process of punishment for disobedience to a legal system which itself remains unchanged, tragedy itself for

---

20   Edward Ingebretsen, *At Stake: Monsters and the Rhetoric of Fear in Public Culture* (Chicago: University of Chicago Press, 2001), 163.

Aristotle, under the jurisdiction of those in power, becomes the cultural forum of justice (24).

In a relevant adjustment to Aristotle's *Poetics*, Boal maintains that the classic American Western enlists our empathy not for the almost flawless good guy, but for the "bad guy," who gains his admired power through hubris or ambition. Though this anti-hero often lacks recognition of his fault and feels little regret, the audience is still able to purge its aggressive tendencies by watching this hero's necessary punishment and then returning back to its "square dances," back to a system that functions conservatively "to diminish, placate, satisfy, eliminate all that can break the balance—all, including the revolutionary, transforming impetus" (Boal 47). An analogous revisionary poetics of tragedy applies to the Matthew Shepard murder and *The Laramie Project*, in which the killers McKinley and Henderson become the anti-protagonists in that legal drama. The Dan White trial, I think, pivots on an equally audacious defense strategy: the rewriting of this double assassination as the rise and fall of the All-American boy on the Barbary Coast, the story of a heroic but terribly beautiful young man born to root out the rottenness in the state of San Francisco, who must be punished for a fate that cried out to him, pressuring him to set right the strange queer eruption in the city. With the aid of the exclusion and erasure of the love that dare not speak its name from the parameters of the courtroom, Schmidt's performance before the mute and expressionless White, who never testified in the trial, re-created the eponymous young supervisor as nostalgic and idealized heterosexual icon:

> Dan White came from a vastly different lifestyle than Harvey Milk, who was a homosexual leader and politician. Dan White was an idealistic young man, a working-class young man. He was deeply endowed with and believed very strongly in the traditional American values, family and home, like the district he represented. (*Indicates jury*) Dan White believed people when they said something. He believed that a man's word, essentially, was his bond. He was an honest man, and he was fair, perhaps too fair for politics in San Francisco. (Doug Schmidt's Opening Statement in Mann 163)

Mann's docudrama juxtaposes this transcript with an immediate flashback to an excerpt from one of White's own campaign speeches, in which the young politician details the recent "exodus from San Francisco by many of our family members, friends and neighbors. Alarmed by the enormous increase in crime, poor educational facilities and a deteriorating social structure, they have fled to temporary havens." White calls on the "thousands and thousands of angry frustrated people ... to unleash a fury that can and will eradicate the malignancies which blight our beautiful city" (Mann 164). Both speeches work through metonymy and circumlocution to create links between families, honesty, and patriotism while aligning homosexuals with social deterioration and deceit. His proposed eradication of malignancies thinly veils the homo-hate which both the politician and his advocate would later successfully excuse, even justify, during a criminal trial for breach of the law's parameters—an "unleashing of fury" that a jury of White's peers would find entirely understandable.

Mann's juxtaposition of opening statement and stump speech also evinces an awareness of the acute sense of performance that White, the Jack London adventurer and lover of Irish literature, himself demonstrated through his silent composure during the trial and even, as we shall see, during his compelling confession. The cover of Uris's *Terrible Beauty* in his pocket on the day he committed the murders—a cover Mann's docudrama projects on a screen the confession in Act One (181)—Dan read Irish history in prison in between his specially ordered roast beef sandwiches. He also identified with the IRA's Kevin Barry. White masked his savvy behind a "gee-wiz," play-ball front, a dumb-jock veneer that hid calculation within the nonchalant naïveté of a freshman idealist, even though Frank Falzon, who recruited Dan for the Police Officers Association softball team, testified that his best friend was an "exemplary individual" who was "outstanding in pressure situations" not only at bat but also on duty, revealing to an incredulous jury the degree to which White was never out of control of his performance as tragic victim of gay degeneracy (192–193).

Confession

By almost all accounts, the prosecution lost control of its case when it played for jurors the taped confession Dan White made after he arrived at Northern Station from the cathedral on the day of the murders. Part of that audiotape is spliced into the screenplay of Epstein's *Times of Harvey Milk*, a film that seeks to take back the social drama and narrate its own tragic script—the rise and fall of Gimpy Milch, the Long Island Jew who came to San Francisco and fought his way on to the Board of Supervisors until the disturbed, repressed, and homophobic Dan White resorted to violence to sacrifice Holy Harvey. Unlike Mann's play, which primarily documents the trial in surreal pastiche even as it uses parts of Epstein's screenplay, *The Times* is a traditional film, playing on our emotions as it narrates through the crackling voice of Harvey Fierstein the inevitable catastrophe of the heroic Harvey, whose only flaw was his unwillingness to stay in the closet. Flaunt it he did once he left Wall Street. Footage of the gay politician's famous stump speech ("My name is Harvey Milk, and I'm here to recruit you") appears in the film's account of the supervisor's campaign against Proposition 6, the state-wide anti-gay initiative that was eventually defeated. Milk called himself a dreamer, "wearing the fabled helm of Mambrino" on his head, a reference to the barber's basin Quixote dons in *Man of La Mancha*, a musical which Harvey claimed gave him his hope, even though he admitted to tilting at windmills with his dreams for a socialist city, hoping nonetheless he might slay "a dragon" in the bargain (Milk in Shilts 358). The film's depiction of the rise of the Mayor of Castro Street reaches its apogee in footage of the celebratory street fair, where Milk presides and Sylvester sings "You make Me Feel (Mighty Real)," returning viewers to the pre-AIDS days of free gay love.

The Times of Harvey Milk starts with the newsreel of Dianne Feinstein's announcement of the murders in 1978, moving retrospectively to Milk's life story and reaching its catastrophe through a build-up to White's revenge on the liberals who were ruining his life. After presenting a biography of Milk and a social history of the rise of the Castro, the film presents footage of a disgruntled supervisor White, who slams his microphone during a hearing and descries the naked men on Market Street during the annual pride parade. Epstein's documentary then depicts the murder by splicing television clips of the chaos in the huge domed Civic Center after the shootings. Nowhere does the film play out its demonization of the disturbed assassin more mercilessly than in its replay of part of the antagonist's confession during the trial.[21] The technique speaks to one of the film's *raison d'être*: the portrayal of the defendant's inner anger, his petty hatred for a system that refused to let him have his law-and-order way.

For many in the courtroom, the prosecution's replay of the scratchy audiotape was the cathartic turning point in the trial. It brought more than four jurors and many in the audience to tears of pity, just as Epstein's *Times* would recreate those tears five years later in theaters, this time in sympathy for the heroic victims rather than the assailant. White's confession was a 25-minute monologue with few interruptions by the interrogators—a highly unorthodox ramble that included none of the usual probing by homicide investigators, who in this case were the defendant's friends on the force. It gave the prisoner a stage to perform his breakdown, to compose his emotional narrative of the good man making a mistake in the face of a sea of troubles, self-destructing in opposing them:

> We ... it's just that I've been under an awful lot of pressure lately, financial pressure, because of my job situation, family pressure, because of ah ... not being able to have the time with my family ... It's just that I wanted to serve the people of San Francisco well and I did that. Then when the pressures got too great I decided to leave. After I left, my family and friends offered their support and said, whatever it would take to allow me to go back into office—well they would be willing to make that effort. And then it came out that Supervisor Milk and some others were working against me to get my seat back on the board ...
>
> I could see the game that was being played; they were going to use me as a *scapegoat*, whether I was a good supervisor or not, was not the point. This was a political opportunity and they were going to degrade me and my family ... The mayor told me he was going to call me before he made any decision, he never

---

21   The film includes parts of the audiotaped confession. A complete transcript is available in Weiss's *Double Play*, 262–270. Mann excerpts it under a banner called "The Confession" (181–187).

did that. I was troubled, the pressure, my family again, my, my son's out to a babysitter. (Epstein; Mann 182–183)

In White's confessional mode, reminiscent of Christian pastoral tradition explored by Foucault, the extraction of secret knowledge becomes isomorphic with presentation of truth, a moment of inward disclosure that awakens spirals of pleasure and power in listeners who gain access to the unfolding secret. Though Foucault elaborated the mechanisms of confession largely in relation to sexuality, in this case a kind of *scientia criminalis* gives White's emotional words the prominence of a soliloquy in the dramatic trial, a moment when his inner truth is revealed, when the jurors, fascinated and excited by their access to knowledge, find out about the murderer's true motives.[22] The "excitation and incitement" that captured the courtroom, however, did have its sexual component; the words "family" and "pressure" are repeated over and over again as White's voice cracks, signaling in code the squeeze that gay migration had put on him. Even in 1978, "family" had already achieved its over-generalized status as a semiotic banner for anti-gay crusaders, as White in his stump speeches knew only too well, the geographic and mental pressure he feels attesting to his own heightened sense of social and psychological friction with the growing queer community.

As the defendant's tone moves from whining to sudden composure, White speaks of the "game that was being played" with his future as the mayor vacillated and then decided not to re-appoint him after he quit. "They were going to use me as a *scapegoat*," White tells his friend, Lieutenant Falzon. Even at this moment of intense disclosure, the defendant has the capacity to dip into the annals of social ritual to present himself as exemplar of the tragic scapegoat, the sacrificial lamb on whom the sins of society are heaped, his self-exculpation replacing any remorse for the violence done to the actual victims of his political crimes. Such "overriding feelings of victimization" have continued to this day as a frequent litany of right-wing conservatives, who feel vilified for their "moral" bias against homosexuals.[23] White's 1979 confession partakes in a backlash rhetoric that has become commonplace in arguments against proposed hate crime and employment discrimination to protect sexual minorities.

In a remarkable cinematic re-appropriation, Epstein's film captures White's successful "tragedization" of himself, even as it subverts the defense's version of the truth through its own idealization of the victim Milk. Employing a slow zoom on a black and white close-up of White's face during the tape's soundtrack, the sequence begins with a medium shot of candidate White's campaign poster,

---

22   Michel Foucault, *The History of Sexuality: Volume 1: An Introduction*, trans. Robert Hurley (New York: Vintage, 1980), 47.

23   Arlene Stein, *Shameless: Sexual Dissidence in American Culture* (New York: New York University Press, 2006), 116. We see continued claims of victimization in the more recent rhetoric of one candidate for President of the United States, Michelle Bachmann, and her flamboyant husband Marcus, who participates in a "pray-away-the-gay" ministry.

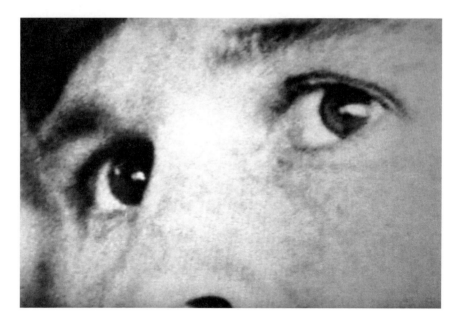

Figure 1.1   Dan White. From *The Times of Harvey Milk* (Criterion Collection)

Source: Courtesy of Robert Epstein

which depicts his tilted profile beside the blurred stars of an unfocused American flag (Figure 1.1) As the tape plays, the crackly sound of the original worn cassette imitates the cracking of the defendant's voice while the prisoner recalls the mounting pressure that led to his reactionary violence. His wife working, his son at a babysitter, White moves his confessional narrative from event (the mayor's failure to call) to his assessment of his own version of "the troubles" via a non sequitur that moves from "troubled" to "the pressure, my family again"—as if he were reminding himself of key phrases. White's high-pitched complaint occurs in the film during a slow zoom into a head shot from the poster, eventually reaching the dark and frightening eyes of the assailant, which is eerily juxtaposed to his emotional confession (Figure 1.2). The camera gives us an insight into an interior altogether more sinister than the sniffling sound effects that accompany White's story, the sounds the jury heard while the defendant sat quietly at trial, his wife in tears. "A certain glint in his eye that, ambiguous a Mona Lisa's smile, could have been determination or something darker; remorselessness, perhaps," one commentator noted about the poster used in the film, its grainy almost abstract zoom suggesting something awry, askance, almost menacing.[24]

---

24   Hinckle in Weiss *Double*, 256–259.

Figure 1.2   Dan White close up. From *The Times of Harvey Milk* (Criterion Collection)

Source: Courtesy of Robert Epstein

By the end of the film's sequence, viewers are gazing at two eyes staring back at them, mirroring their own fascination with this glimpse into the unknown interior of the man on a mission. In the final close-up, the great White hope becomes an abstract pair of eyes—a symbolic composite of black and white specks—the eyes of a man who, after shooting the mayor five times, was "struck by what Harvey had tried to do" and decided to go talk to him. In this extreme close-up, the eyes have become flat black specks on an empty forehead—a heterocentric gaze. Dan's disembodied voice continues as he describes his second murder. He had always been "honest" (straight) with Harvey, who was "devious" (queer): "I started to say how hard I worked for it and what it meant to me and my family an' then my reputation as, a hard worker, good honest person and he just kind of *smirked* at me as if to say, too bad an' then, an' then, I just go all flushed an', an' hot, and I shot him." Like his use of the word scapegoat, White at this moment of supposed loss of control is still able to invoke one of the quintessential gestures that belongs to queer semiotics: the smirk, the simper, that affected manner and smile of the sardonic faggot mocking the tyranny of the All-American boy, who must react like any red-blooded American to such a challenge to his dominance.

Never mind that no prosecution witness was ever called to testify to the butt-patting and smirking that several officers greeted Dan with while they visited him at the police station on the day of the murders, as the documentaries note.

In Dan's bless-me-father confessional, Milk's smirk represented a threat which suddenly forced him to take the law into his own hands. Unlike his reaction to the mayor, White gets "flushed" and "hot" before killing the smirker, using his "transitional object" (as one psychoanalyst called his loaded gun) to wipe the smirk off Harvey's insolent face (Epstein; Mann 208). White's description of his violent reaction to the smirking queer tapped into the rhetoric of the discredited but still extant homosexual panic defense, in which even without sexual advance, the presence of a gay man may provoke a legally excusable overreaction in the straight assailant, whose masculinity is threatened.[25]

By the end of Dan's confession, the jury, as the film's narrator suggests, was putty in defense counsel's hands, the soliloquy having convinced the straight triers of fact that White was an honest, hard-working heterosexual, watching his city go "downhill" so far he "just couldn't take it anymore." His valiant crusade to save his family from an amalgamation of bleeding-heart liberals and smirking queers had brought a "pressure hitting" him so hard he felt his "skull's going to crack"—a tension the jury itself felt as it cathartically lived through the anguish of Dan White's *hamartia* (Epstein; Mann 186). Schmidt would argue in closing that Dan "will be punished. He's going to have to live with this for the rest of his life. His child will live with it and his family will live with it, and God will punish him" (Mann 233). Epstein's film transvalues this scenario by shifting judgment from the trial's mistaken jury to the film-going audience, leaving viewers of this confession scene staring into White's eyes of darkness, eyes that could belong to any frustrated good old boy, any angry American holding a gun without a permit. Harvey's prediction of assassination had come true, and his killer had emerged from the heart of the American dream—the film turning the tragic Danny Boy into a sinister hit man—transforming the protagonist of the trial into antagonist who sacrificed a gay man who had heroically blown open the closet door for a future of queer activism.

Insanity

Even with the evidentiary gift of the prosecution's backfired tape, defense counsel in this famous trial still had to overcome the substantial evidence of premeditation in the White case—the bullets, the window, the reloading, the shots to the skulls' base. The lapse of time between White's decision to visit his victims and the shootings rendered the heat of passion defense unviable, so Doug Schmidt had to find another argument to question the premeditation and deliberation needed for first-degree murder, and/or the malice (intent to do an unlawful act) which was required to prove first- or second-degree murder, regardless of the evidence

---

25   Christina Pei Lin Chen, "Provocation's Privileged Desire: The Provocation Doctrine, 'Homosexual Panic,' and the Non-violent Unwanted Sexual Advance Defense," 10 *Cornell Journal of Law and Public Policy* 195–235 (2000).

of deliberation.[26] To make his case, the young defense lawyer from Michigan turned to his favorite film, Otto Preminger's *Anatomy of Murder*, for his strategy, adopting not only Jimmy Stewart's folksy ah-shucks act in the courtroom but also relying on the argument developed in Judge Voelker's 1957 novel of the same name (published under the pseudonym Robert Travers).[27] In the film, Lieutenant Manion (Ben Gazarra) escapes murder charges by pleading temporary insanity brought on by associative disorder and irresistible impulse. Schmidt, borrowing some frames from his favorite film, relied on California's diminished capacity law, which recognized temporary insanity as a legitimate defense to a charge of malice.

Although neither Mann nor Epstein cite the influence of Preminger's film on the defense strategy, both include segments about the trial's famous psychiatric testimony that was inspired in part by *Anatomy*. Mann's stage direction suggests a multiple series of witness stands which amalgamate all the defense psychologists. Under the heading of "Psychiatric Defense," the docudrama reviews testimony from a handful of hired experts, Schmidt arguing that White suffered from a hidden case of depression, as evidenced by his periodic estrangement from his conjugal visits to his wife. The defendant was also binging on Hostess products, raising his blood sugar levels dangerously high and causing him to lose the superb definition he displayed in a famous shirtless photo of his shamrocked bicep. "Large quantities of what we call junk food," Dr. Blinder testified, "high-sugar-content food with lots of preservatives, can precipitate antisocial and even violent behavior" (Mann 214). For Dan White the "American Dream" had become a "nightmare" as a result of too many Twinkies. When Mary Ann also testified that Dan had admitted to her that he didn't like himself, the jury wept again as she broke down on the stand, explaining her grief for her moody husband. One juror after the verdict said she

---

26   Mann includes the jury instruction in her play. "In the crime of murder of the first degree, the necessary concurrent mental states are: malice aforethought, premeditation and deliberation. In the crime of murder of the second degree, the necessary concurrent mental state is: malice aforethought. In the crime of voluntary manslaughter, the necessary mental state is an intent to kill ... There is no malice aforethought if the evidence shows that due to diminished capacity caused by illness, mental defect, or intoxication, the defendant did not have the capacity to form the mental state constituting malice aforethought, even though the killing was intentional, voluntary, premeditated and unprovoked" (240). Though a vexed term, malice is often understood as *knowledge* of an intention to commit an unlawful act. The jurors decided that White's diminished capacity due to mental illness (depression and diet) vitiated his malice.

27   *Anatomy of a Murder* was an immediate success, spending 61 consecutive weeks on the bestseller list after St. Martin's published it in 1957. Judge Voelker based the novel he called "pure fiction" on the 1952 real-life slaying at the Lumberjack Tavern in Big Bay, north of Marquette (Robert Travers, *Anatomy of a Murder* [New York: St. Martin's, 1957]). After Otto Preminger bought the rights, his film opened in 1959, grossing 5.5 million dollars and garnering seven Academy Award nominations. Preminger hired famed Boston attorney Joseph N. Welch—who had come to fame in the McCarthy hearings—to play the judge in the film (Otto Preminger, *Anatomy of a Murder* [Columbia Pictures 1959]).

reached her decision in part because lengthy imprisonment would have left Mary Ann without her husband (204).

In an article published after the verdict, renowned psychologist Thomas Szasz decried the defense's experts as "psychiatric perverters of our system of justice" who had perpetrated a "judicial crime" by becoming accomplices, lying through their teeth while the court legitimated their testimony and abrogated its duty to determine guilt and innocence.[28] Szasz's attack on bought-and-sold psychiatrists in his field was coupled with a polemic against the "subtle but persistent appeal to the jury's anti-homosexual prejudice." For the fuming Szasz, "with great skill, Schmidt successfully replaced the reality of Dan White, the moral actor on the stage of life, with the abstractions of White's 'diminished capacity' and his 'background'—and then instructed the jury to focus on those fictions and ignore the facts." Instead of using Szasz's direct polemic, Mann imbeds her critique of the psychiatric defense in two characters: the sarcastic Sister Boom Boom, who reads from the Book of Dan (a mock biblical tract), and Jim Denman, the defendant's jailer whom the prosecution decided not to call as a witness. Denman's statements are woven into Mann's post-modern polyphony as a counterpoint to the psychiatric testimony. During the first days after his arrest, Denman reveals that he saw no tears, shame, or remorse in the Dan White he watched in his cell; instead he witnessed an inmate who was regularly visited by members of the force, who patted him on the butt and stood around laughing (Mann 228). When the play's prose breaks into poetic form, as it often does, Denman concludes, "if Dan White was as depressed/ as the defense psychiatrists said he was before he went to City Hall,/ then shooting these people sure seemed to clear up his mind." In *Execution*, Mann exploits the unused testimony of Denman to undermine the credibility of the expert testimony on mental illness, contrasting the abstract expert testimony with the hands-on observation of White's jailer.

Mann's play also employs Sister Boom Boom, San Francisco's famous Sister of Perpetual Indulgence, to provide a more satirical critique of the almost supernatural power of White's experts to magically recast him from premeditated murderer to unbalanced hero. Boom Boom, who read from the parodic Book of Dan at the beginning of the play, returns again to the testament at the end, raising a Twinkie in her hands, and intoning, "Take this and eat, for this is my defense," enacting a mock consecration that turns the sacred body of the defendant into a Hostess product, conflating religion and psychiatry in a way that comments on how the experts in the case were able to narrate a passion of White that turned him into a tragic scapegoat (245).

The science of psychiatry gave defense counsel a link to legal proof that made the narration of his client's "snap" under pressure more than a miraculous transformation. Schmidt's regular repetition of this aural metaphor signaled the un-seaming or "dividing practice" that allowed a jury to accept two diametrically

---

28   Thomas Szasz, "'J'Accuse': Psychiatry and the Diminished American Capacity for Justice," in the Mike Weiss Papers, San Francisco Public Library Archives (1979).

opposed Dan Whites.[29] The antithetical Most Valuable Player and junk food depressive became linked and disconnected by an ideology of breaking or cracking that employed psychiatric truth to separate the tragic hero's *hamartia* from his *peripetaia*, his radical encounter with a destiny of misfortune. In classical tragedy, the very trait that brings about the hero's downfall is ironically instrumental in his rise to power. In Dan White's case, the same paradox was functioning: his hegemonic masculinity, his embodiment of the good, honest, hard-working white male, was intricately tied to the violence he perpetrated.

For the jury to explain this conjunction of American hero and violent homophobe, the discourse of psychology had to provide a theatrical, almost religious "magic" that could make the irrational rational in the court of law, where reason must appear to prevail. Dan's insanity—caused by what Boom Boom points to as the sacred Twinkie—thus provided the reasonable basis for an idealized subjectivity that was also disturbingly illegal. How else could such "a good policeman, good fireman" with so "much promise" also empty nine bullets into the bodies of two of public officials? "Lord God! Nobody can say that the things that happened to him days or weeks preceding wouldn't make a reasonable and ordinary man at least mad, angry in some way," Schmidt argued in closing, invoking what Turner nominates as the "supernatural character" of social ritual, as he asked the jury to feel his client's pain (Mann 230). God, as Mann's Boom Boom suggests, had forced this reasonable man to snap under pressure, just as the jury of his peers would break down in pity of the destruction of their champion, unable to countenance his action, to understand and excuse it, without rendering this moral man temporarily immoral as a means of purging cathartically their own identificatory impulse. The defense, with the help of the prosecution's queer erasure, had produced the very subject the criminal system purported to denounce: a malicious, premeditated assassin whose identification with the ideals of the American way—including the law and order of criminal justice itself—showed the jury the violent and terrible core of their own ideals. The discourse of psychiatry provided the legal means to separate themselves from this homicidal product of their own ideology. In Mann's work, Sister Boom Boom, the drag queen who unabashedly mixes the sacred and profane, reveals the way religious belief combined with bias against sexual minorities was able to underwrite the "science" of the defendant's expert testimony.

The Queer Mirror

The challenge of queer theorization, in my opinion, is to return often to those "sites of becoming," and more importantly, *un*becoming, wherein identity is

---

29   Paul Rabinow, "Introduction," *The Foucault Reader* (New York: Pantheon, 1984), 11.

temporarily constructed, solidified, and then threatened or rendered inadequate in its explanatory power (Donald Hall 109).

The final zoom during Dan White's confession in Epstein's film puts us face-to-face with a fragmentary pair of eyes whose identity is finally as frightening in its mystery as it is in its archival context. Those large black dots on the page and screen belong to every viewer, including, I want to posit finally, the queer gaze. When Dan White committed suicide in his estranged wife's garage in 1985, his death finished a life story that contained striking similarities to features of the archetypal gay narrative, still being enacted in towns everywhere across the country. White was beat up and called a patsy as a kid; he overcompensated in high school by working out incessantly; he was subject apparently to depression; he was regularly estranged from his wife whom he married only a few years before he was incarcerated. He was a man among men, an over-achiever, at sports and works. He was sensitive but regularly ridiculed by his fellow board members for his unwillingness to compromise. He hated himself. He was declared insane. He took his own life. These are the components of a pre-Stonewall novel, but they apply as well to a working-class Irish kid from the unglamorous side of a parochial town we idealize as beautiful San Francisco, a part of this city kids coming on a bus from Altoona, Pennsylvania do not expect to find.

To suggest that this avowed political assassin of the first out elected official in the United States was a repressed gay man, as many including Supervisors Milk and Silver speculated, requires a leap of dubious faith I doubt few of us would want to take, but critical queer theory at the very least requires a recognition of the similarities between Sister Boom Boom and the Free Dan White cop protesting too much about having to walk the streets with "bald-headed, shaved-head men with those tight pants and muscles … putting their hands all over each other's asses" (Mann 154). The classification of White as either a latent queer and/or a homo-hater at some level engages in the very arbitrary construction of identity that has led to the marginalization of lesbian and gay men, establishing within White's presupposed subjectivity an animus that to some extent justifies our own cognizance as a discrete group in need of a place in the jury pool. Cultural retrials of Dan White as closet case, gayslayer, or antagonist in the production of the Harvey Milk legend are not immune from the practices of erasure, exclusion, and narrative catharsis that drove the original jury to a verdict of voluntary manslaughter.

How can we maintain the commemorative resonance of this famous case without replicating the practices of vilification that often mark strategies at work in the trial, Epstein's film, and Mann's play? Even as critical queer legal studies exposes the oppression and hostility of the criminal justice system, it must also search for explanations that move beyond the condemnation of homophobes toward a fuller understanding of the social structures that instantiate that bias. The satisfaction viewers of these artistic retellings find in the demonization of White often impedes the possible creation of what Augusto Boal calls a transformative theater as an alternative to Aristotelian tragedy: the promotion of a legislative stage that moves beyond the portrayal of individual heroes and demons toward dramas that call for change, enactments that are integrated into the social fabric and narrate stories of what Harvey Milk called the "only thing we have to look forward to: hope" (Mann 190). Though Mann's post-modern collage—with its intrinsic critique of jury selection and expert testimony—may do more to focus on the larger concerns of systemic bias than Epstein's film, which follows a traditional generic trajectory, *The Times of Harvey Milk*, through its biographical focus, presents a vision of a pre-AIDS and pre-backlash San Francisco that captures a transformative moment in social and political history.

When Harry Britt, Milk's successor on the Board of Supervisors, announces at the end of Mann's docudrama, "Our revenge is never to forget" (244), he reminds us that these cultural retellings of crucial events in the gay and lesbian archive act as vigilant reminders of the need to constantly forge new articulations which expose queer bias and call for its denunciation. But "what do you do with your need for retribution?" another character asks Britt, who replies, "We will never forget" (245). Mann's staging of the final scene as a stand-off between politicians and rioters outside City Hall anticipates the challenge for queer theorists, like Donald Hall, who envision a form of retribution that neither "solidifies" and therefore replicates violent bias nor avoids taking action against oppression. *The Times of Harvey Milk* captures one form of retribution in its archival compilation of the White Night Riots in City Hall after the verdict, footage of burning police cars and angry queers that can still shock audiences—gay and straight—into recognizing the consequences of social injustice. The film, replayed for new generations of students, acts not only as a part of a collective queer history but also as a social tool, a cultural force that inspires renewed commitment to activism, exemplifying the way artistic commemoration acts as an agent for political change.

By studying these documentaries from a standpoint of critical queer studies, we learn that there is no fixed form of justice, that "not forgetting" must take shape in ways that run the gamut from coming out to protest to making documentaries. Mann's play ends with a tableau reminiscent of both the Stonewall Riots and the encounter that opened her drama: we see Sister Boom Boom in City Hall taunting the police, who raise their shields during the White Night riots—riots that gain compelling resonance in archival footage of *The Times of Harvey Milk*. These dramatic scenes, with their intermixing of confrontation and questioning about forms of retribution, seem to recognize that dramas of social injustice must be played out, as Victor Turner asserts, in the multi-faceted acting of everyday life, whether those scenes take place in the theater, the courtroom, the streets, the classroom, or the bedroom. As the Harvey Milk legacy teaches, we all must struggle inside and outside the halls of justice to insure that trials always impanel a jury of one's queers.

Chapter 2
Panic in *The Project*[1]

Hindsight is *20/20*

On November 26, 2004, ABC television's news magazine *20/20* revisited the Matthew Shepard case, six years after Aaron McKinney and Russell Henderson were sentenced to life in prison without possibility of parole for the murder of the gay University of Wyoming student in 1998.[2] Henderson had plea-bargained to avoid the death penalty, and McKinney was granted life at the request of the victim's family, who conditioned their request on a gag order over McKinney. After ignoring the terms of the sentence and interviewing both prisoners, reporter Elizabeth Vargas disclosed her finding that methamphetamine abuse and robbery were the true motivations for the 1998 beating of Shepard with the butt end of .357 magnum and subsequent abandonment of the victim's body tied to a buck fence on the outskirts of Laramie, Wyoming. The most notorious murder of a gay man in the last decade, Vargas reveals, was never a hate crime at all.[3]

The news magazine begins its story with prosecutor Cal Rerucha, who is also one of the characters in *The Laramie Project*, the oral history drama that has become one of the most frequently produced plays in the country since its opening in 2000 to a Denver audience that included many of those who had been interviewed for the play.[4] On *20/20*, Rerucha recalls how shortly after the beating the media descended on his town "like locusts," one of whom said that Shepard is "going to be the new poster child for gay rights."[5] The prosecutor tells Vargas that Shepard's friends "were calling the media and indicating Matthew Shepard is gay and we don't want the fact that he is gay to go unnoticed." Now, six years

---

1   Casey Charles, "Panic in *The Project*: Critical Queer Studies and the Matthew Shepard Murder," *Law and Literature* 18:2 (summer 2006): 225–252. © 2006 by the Cardozo School of Law. Reprinted by permission of the University of California Press.

2   "New Details Emerge in the Matthew Shepard Murder," *20/20*. ABC. 26 November 2004. The Transcription Company, Burbank, CA, www.transcripts.tv/2020.cfm.

3   Joann Wypijewski, "Hate Crime Laws' Won't Cure Homophobia," *Counterpunch* (November 27/28 2004), www.counterpunch.org/jwil272oo4.html. In her editorial, Wypijewski states that ABC has made "a public claim against the Shepards' effort to turn the story into their sole property."

4   Moisés Kaufman and the Members of Tectonic Theater Project, *The Laramie Project* (New York: Dramatists Play Service, 2001). The Project premiered in February, 2000 at the Denver Center Theater and moved to The Union Square Theatre in New York City in May, 2000. The 2002 HBO-produced film was written and directed by Kaufman.

5   See "New Details" 1.

later, Rerucha informs Vargas, he attributes McKinney's rage and savage pistol-whipping of Shepard not to homophobia or homosexual panic but to drug abuse. "If Aaron McKinney had not become involved with methamphetamines, Matthew Shepard would be alive today," the prosecutor tells ABC.[6]

Many who have commented on Vargas's controversial reconsideration of the case have noticed that the majority of *20/20*'s "emerging details," however, have in fact already emerged. Beth Loffreda's *Losing Matt Shepard*, and articles in *Vanity Fair* and *Harper's* written years earlier, included reports of Shepard's status as HIV positive, a victim of rape in Morocco, and a drug user himself.[7] Even the allegation of McKinney's bisexuality was part of an earlier story.[8] Vargas does report details from two uncorroborated sources: Elaine Baker, a Laramie resident, who says she saw McKinney and Shepard in the back of a limousine with others two weeks before the murder, and Ryan Bopp, one of Aaron's friends and fellow meth users, who claims, "Aaron and I had been awake for about a week or so prior to this whole thing happening" on a "hard-core bender."[9]

---

6   "New Details" 6.

7   *20/20* received criticism from writers Chris Bull, Chris Bull, "When Hate Isn't Hate," *Planet Out* (November 24, 2004), www.planetout.com; Michael Bronski, "A Troubling Vision of Matthew Shepard," *Boston Phoenix* (November 26 – December 2, 2004), www.boston-phoenix.com; and Doug Ireland ("The program's worst omission … was its failure to breath [*sic*] even a hint that violence against those who love differently from the average heterosexual is a daily occurrence in a country drowning in a host of religious superstitions that justify it" [Doug Ireland, "'20/20' and Matthew Shepard," Direland [December 6 2004], www.direland.typepad.com/direland/20oo4/ii/202o-and-matthe.html, 2]). The Shepard case has produced, an explosion of discourse, including five films, a foundation, a book, and numerous articles. See MTV's *Anatomy of a Hate Crime*, dir. Tim Hunter, Lawrence Bender Production for MTV, January 10, 2001. NBC's dramatization with Stockard Channing and Sam Waterston (*The Matthew Shepard Story*, perf. Stockard Channing and Sam Waterston, Alliance Atlantis for NBC, 2002), an A & E documentary (*The Matthew Shepard Story*, dir. Robert Scheiger, Towers Productions for A & E Home Video, 2001) by the same name as NBC's, HBO's production of *The Laramie Project* (dir. Moisés Kaufman, HBO Home Video, 2002), and most recently a film by a resident of Laramie at the time of the killing (*Laramie Inside Out*, dir. Bev Seckinger, New Day Films 2004). Beth Loffreda's *Losing Matt Shepard: Life and Politics in the Aftermath of Anti-Gay Murder* (New York: Columbia University Press, 2000) is the definitive book on the case, and articles by Wypijewski in *Harper's* (Joann Wypijewski, "A Boy's Life: For Matthew Shepard's Killers, What Does It Take to Pass as a Man?" *Harper's* [September 1999]: 61–74) and Thernstrom in Vanity Fair (Melanie Thernstrom, "The Crucifixion of Matthew Shepard," *Vanity Fair* [March 1999]: 209–275) have emerged as important sources. Many others have been writing on the case including Tony Kushner and Camille Paglia, who in her *Salon* column stated that Shepard was cruising for "rough trade" and "lulled into a false sense of security" by the "bombastic excesses of gay activism" (see Richard Goldstein, "The Matthew Shepard Icon," *The Village Voice* [March 13–19 2002]: 52).

8   See Thernstrom 234.

9   See "New Details" 3.

Most tellingly, McKinney and Henderson present their own new versions of the murder from their undisclosed prison location. "I would say it wasn't a hate crime. All I wanted to do was beat him up and rob him," McKinney assures Vargas. The homosexual panic defense McKinney had pleaded at trial, along with the numerous other statements about Shepard making unwanted sexual advances, were just a "tactic," according to the prisoner. His girlfriend, who was convicted of a misdemeanor after agreeing to give evidence, also says now that her statements about McKinney's reaction to Shepard's overtures were fabrications to save Aaron. "I don't think it was a hate crime at all," Kristen Price tells the hour-long version of *20/20*, "I never did."[10] Russell Henderson, assaulted by his mother's boyfriends as a child, emerges as the star witness in this prime-time show. He confides in Vargas that Shepard died "not because me and Aaron had anything against homosexuals," while his friend confides, "It's really hard for me to talk to Russ ... knowing that I'm the one that put him here."[11] The story ends with Henderson's expression of regret: "I am sorry to the nation as a whole because this affected a lot of people and I wish every day I could change or fix it."

Vargas's special has created considerable stir, coming on the heels of the 2004 election in which 11 more states passed constitutional amendments banning same-sex marriage as a Republican administration and Congress were swept into office. ABC online directed those who sent e-mail protests to the network's own blog, where differing opinions about Vargas's special might be aired, discussed, and deflated. Joann Wypijewski, who wrote the *Harper's* article that pitched the murder as socio-economic tragedy, saw the program as evidence that hate-crime legislation "tramples justice" because Shepard has mistakenly become "a holy martyr for enhanced penalties."[12] For Wypijewski, Henderson—the accomplice who did nothing but tie Shepard to the fence and drive the truck—has become the true victim of "the drumbeat over hate," even though Wyoming has never enacted sexual orientation hate-crime penalties in spite of the recent passage of a federal hate-crimes law named after Shepard.

Andrew Sullivan, the conservative logger who served as the single gay-rights advocate interviewed in the story, opines in the segment that Shepard's death "encapsulated all our fears of being victimized."[13] On April 2, 2001, Sullivan's *New Republic* article "Us and Them" compared the killing of Shepard to the pedophiliac rape and murder of 13-year-old Jesse Dirkhising in Arkansas, which, according to conservatives, received little of the media attention Shepard's case garnered. Sullivan argued that hate-crime murders are extremely rare, according to FBI statistics he relied upon, and that "the Shepard case was hyped for political reasons to build support for inclusion of homosexuals in a federal hate crimes

10   "New Details" 5.
11   "New Details" 8.
12   See Wypijewski "Hate Crime."
13   See "New Details" 1.

law."[14] Curiously, *20/20* fails to interview any of the experts on violence against gay men, nor any of those who have already written extensively about the case.[15] Michael Adams of Lambda Legal Defense claimed ABC was trying to "de-gay the murder" and Chris Bull, who spent a year in a fellowship interviewing and writing about a string of 28 anti-gay murders found the network's sensationalism both "mystifying" and "predictable."[16] Relying uncritically on the interviews of men "desperate to make the case that their crime was not motivated by hate after all," ABC, in Bull's view, labored to debunk "the struggle of gay activists for over fifty years to draw attention to the role of lethal animus in attacks on gay men" and "the compelling narrative in the case that has come to exemplify it," Bull noted.[17] His central point is that drug abuse does not vitiate hate; it actually complements it, fulfilling a scenario of multiple motivations in most of the crimes he has studied, all "eerily similar" to Shepard's:

> Young men, fueled by drugs and/or alcohol, believing it a harmless diversion, searched for gay men to harass and rob. Based on anti-gay stereotypes, they believed that gays carried lots of cash, were easy to overpower ... Once apprehended, these men invariably claimed they had been propositioned and were only defending themselves. They believed they were doing society a favor by ridding it of one more queer.[18]

Bull finds it hard to understand how "highly regarded journalists" in television news could return to "the days of denial."

---

14   Andrew Sullivan, "Us and Them," *The New Republic* (April 2, 2001), www.tnr. com/o4o2o01/ trbo4020.html. The call for sexual orientation hate-crime penalties has been largely unsuccessful, Sullivan fails to mention. His statistics are contradicted by a 2004 FBI study that finds sexual orientation hate-crime incidence second only to racial hate crime (see Ireland 2). Sullivan argues that the failure of Dirkhising's murder to stir up the same attention Shepard's death was a "sign of the moral damage that identity politics has already done. It has inured us to simple matters of good and evil. All that matters now, it seems, is us and them." Sullivan's confusion of pedophilia and homosexuality is a common tactic among anti-gay reactionaries.

15   Studies of sexual orientation hate crime include Gary David Comstock's "Dismantling the Homosexual Panic Defense," 81 *Law and Sexuality: Review of Lesbian and Gay Legal Issues* 81–102 (1992), and his *Violence Against Lesbians and Gay Men* (New York: Columbia University Press, 1991); Gregory M. Herek and Kevin T. Berill, eds. *Hate Crimes: Confronting Violence Against Lesbians and Gay Men* (Newbury Park, CA: Sage, 1992); and Chris Bull, "Anatomy of a Gay Murder," *Alicia Patterson Reporter* 20:1 (2001), also in http://aliciapatterson.org/stories/anatomy-gay-murder.

16   See Bull, "When Hate Isn't Hate" 1.

17   Bull, "When Hate Isn't Hate" 1.

18   Bull, "When Hate Isn't Hate" 5.

"It Didn't Happen; It Doesn't Make Any Difference"[19]

If *20/20*'s attempt to set the record straight about Shepard's murder recalls Eve Sedgwick's shibboleth about centuries of erasure of queer readings of literature, the timing of this revisionary news story also mirrors a current political and social climate of increased queer scapegoating. Vargas's attempt to put the Shepard case back in the closet, whatever the motivation, occurs at a historical moment when the Holy War on gays, as Robert Dreyfuss has called it, continues to gain the momentum begun in the 1990s.[20] Even at the time of Shepard's murder in 1998, a consortium of anti-gay forces had begun its controversial "Truth in Love" campaign, an advertising blitz in national newspapers proclaiming "that homosexuals 'can change,' featuring 'ex-gays' who have 'walked out of homosexuality into sexual celibacy or even marriage'."[21] Although the Christian Coalition and Focus on the Family denounced the murder when it occurred in 1998, distancing themselves from the vocal Baptist Fred Phelps (who still visits colleges where *The Project* and his character is staged), Christian leaders received criticism for their support of intolerance during the time of the trial. "Words have consequences," stated Wayne Besen, a spokesman for the Human Rights Campaign, who drew connections between the rhetoric of anti-gay reform groups like Exodus and the brutal killing.[22]

ABC's story is in many ways less an erasure than a devaluation, a version of events that wants to downplay not so much the existence of same-sex relations as the homophobia that surrounds them. It challenges the validity of those who claim homo-hate to be an integral part of our culture and see a deep-seated animus reflected in the continued legal use of the homosexual panic defense. Chris Bull's statement about the "compelling narrative" of queer hate crime and its attempted deletion by ABC points to the importance of thinking about the Shepard murder through the lens of critical queer studies—a phrase that borrows from recent race and feminist scholarship that demonstrates how narratives about ethnicity and gender influence legal processes and how cultural representation reveals justice to be a contested site of meaning.[23]

---

19   Eve Kosofsky Sedgwick, *Epistemology of the Closet* (Berkeley: University of California Press, 1990), 23.

20   Robert Dreyfuss, "The Holy War on Gays," *Rolling Stone* (March 18 1999): 38–41.

21   Dreyfuss 38.

22   Dreyfuss 38.

23   Wai Chee Dimock, *Residues of Justice: Literature, Law, Philosophy* (Berkeley: University of California Press, 1996), 6–10. See Dimock's discussion of the dream of "objective adequation." Critical Legal Studies (CLS) questions the objectivity of legal determination in studies by Young, Leonard, Goodrich, and Sandel, to name a few. See Iris Marion Young, *Justice and the Politics of Difference* (Princeton: Princeton University Press, 1990); Jerry Leonard, ed. *Legal Studies as Cultural Studies: A Reader in (Post) Modern Critical Theory* (Albany: SUNY Press, 1995); Peter Goodrich, *Legal Discourse: Studies in Linguistics, Rhetoric and Legal Analysis* (New York: St. Martin's, 1987); Michael Sandel, *Liberalism and the Limit of Justice* (Cambridge: Cambridge University

   20/20's attempt to re-try the Shepard case in the media presents a telling
intersection of the discourses of law, journalism, and entertainment, a confluence
that also illustrates my larger thesis that law is infused with narrative fictions
and conversely, that fictions (like the dramatic *Laramie Project*) can produce
material—even legal—consequences, including ones that motivate discourses
like television news to challenge the influence of cultural production. For Moisés
Kaufman, the director of the influential *Laramie Project*, his portrayal of this
historical "moment" was specifically designed to begin a national dialogue on
"how we think and talk about homosexuality, sexual politics, education, class,
[and] violence"—his interview-based drama presenting an examination of
gayness on the frontier.[24] *20/20*'s revision of the story recasts Laramie as a town
with a drug—not a hate problem—a new version that works to shift the dialogue
away from queer prejudice, at a time when legislative and religious institutions are
ironically renewing the call for state-supported prejudice in the form of marriage
amendments and rights to exclude. ABC's story, whether by design or not,
participates in a larger movement toward cultural suppression of the homosexual
agenda, as its opponents call it.
   Entwined in this dialogue is the law of homicide, and, more particularly, the
influence that ideologies about gays and lesbians have on the legal doctrine of
justification and excuse in murder trials like that of Shepard. Taking its cue from
Vargas's attempt to debunk the myth of Henderson and McKinney's gay hatred
and render the latter's homosexual panic defense a ruse, this chapter turns first to
the history of the gay panic defense itself as a means of illustrating how ideological
fictions work to support this prejudicial legal doctrine. Drawing from the work of
Critical Legal Studies theorists like Gutierrez-Jones, as well as by some scholars
of the ancillary movement of law and literature, my argument examines how the
"law, like other forms of storytelling, imposes structure on the chaos of experience,
assigns meaning and responsibility."[25] As Liz McMillen has written, "trial lawyers

---

Press, 1982). Works by Rhode as well as Heilbrun and Resnick exemplify studies of the
gendering of justice, while critical race theory in relation to the law appears in Matsuda and
more recently Gutierrez-Jones, whose book discusses hate crimes specifically. See Deborah
Rhode, *Justice and Gender* (Cambridge, MA: Harvard University Press, 1989); Carolyn
Heilbrun and Judith Resnik, "Convergences: Law, Literature and Feminism," 99 *Yale Law
Journal* 1912–1956 (1990); Mari J. Matsuda, *Where is Your Body? And Other Essays on
Race, Gender, and the Law* (Boston: Beacon, 1996); Carl Gutierrez-Jones, *Critical Race
Narratives: A Study of Race, Rhetoric, and Injury* (New York: New York University Press,
2001). A critical queer studies approach has begun in works by Eskridge and Robson, and
more recently Ronner. See William N. Eskridge, *GayLaw: Challenging the Apartheid of
the Closet* (Cambridge, MA: Harvard University Press, 1999); Ruthann Robson, *Gay Men,
Lesbians, and the Law* (New York: Chelsea House, 1997); Amy D. Ronner, *Homophobia
and the Law* (Washington, DC: APA, 2005).
   24   See "New Details."
   25   Blanch McCrary Boyd, "Who Killed Susan Smith?" *Oxford American* (August/
September 1996): 36–42.

... try to tell the story that a jury is most likely to believe."[26] "This is a delicate way of saying," another commentator notes, "that a jurist is most likely to give credence to what he or she already knows ... And what he or she knows *already* is the sum of public presumption on the subject, narratively dispensed and so never recognized as the obvious prejudice it is."[27]

I focus first in this chapter on one of the law's presumed narratives—the homosexual panic defense (HPD)—in its capacity not only as a historical legal doctrine fraught with assumed fictions about gay and straight men but also as a symbolic phenomenon of social condensation—a doctrine that encapsulates the "sudden, overpowering fright, especially when groundless" concerning queer affairs, a fright that continues to grip much of the country.[28] I will argue first that the use and abuse of the legal doctrine of unwanted queer sexual advance, including its attempted employment in the Shepard trial, presents a case study in the influence of ideological narratives—what I am calling "fictions"—on the law. Looking secondly at the text of *The Laramie Project*, I ask whether the play's indebtedness to Aristotelian tragedy aligns it with a cathartic and contained form of cultural panic analogous to the legal doctrine, or whether, in the alternative, the popular *Project* has had a transformative effect on the social fabric, akin to legislation or legal rulings.

Wayne Besen's statement at the time of the Shepard trial that "words have consequences" serves as an uncomplicated summary of the current trends in discourse theory that play a key role in my understanding of the history of the homosexual panic defense. In the *Archaeology of Knowledge* and other works,

---

26   Liz McMillen, "The Importance of Storytelling: A New Emphasis by Law Scholars," *Chronicle of Higher Education*, (July 26, 1996): A10.

27   Edward Ingebretsen, *At Stake: Monsters and the Rhetoric of Fear in Public Culture* (Chicago: University of Chicago Press, 2001), 163. Ingebretsen discusses the Shepard murder in chapter seven. For a further commentary on the influence of narrative on the law, see Richard Delgado, "Storytelling for Oppositionists and Others: A Plea for Narrative," 87 *Michigan Law Review* 2411–2441 (1989), Peter Brooks and Paul Gewirtz, eds. *Law's Stories: Narrative and Rhetoric in the Law* (New Haven: Yale University Press, 1996), and Jacqueline St. Joan and Annette Bennington McElhiney, eds. *Beyond Portia: Women, Law, and Literature in the United States* (Boston: Northeastern University Press, 1997). The extensive law and literature field can be sampled first in Richard Weisberg, *Poethics and Other Strategies of Law and Literature* (New York: Columbia University Press, 1992); James Boyd White, *The Legal Imagination* (Boston: Little, Brown, 1973); and Michael Freeman and Andrew D.E. Lewis, eds. *Law and Literature* (Oxford: Oxford University Press, 1999). See also Julie Stone Peters' review of the field in her article, "Law, Literature, and the Vanishing Real: On the Future of an Interdisciplinary Illusion," *PMLA* 120 (March 2005): 442–453.

28   Pan, the Greek god of forests, wildlife, and shepherds, was represented as having the legs and sometimes the ears and horns of a goat. His appearance often produced a "sudden, extreme, and groundless fear" or panic in those who viewed the harmless god. (See "Pan" and "Panic," *Webster's Collegiate Dictionary*, 5th edn, 1947).

Michel Foucault designates discourse as a broad signifier that represents connections between bodies of knowledge and social control, between discrete institutions that produce regimes of truth within the boundaries of their field—whether medicine, law, journalism, film, or literature, to name a few—and the effects those regimes have on assumed narratives of identity.[29] Although not equivalent to the concept of dominant ideology nor wholly hegemonic in its operation, discourse nonetheless "transmits and produces power" through claims to expertise that enable and constrain the social imagination, even establishing notions of the subject.[30] In the intersection of discourses, Stuart Hall locates his notion of articulation, which he delineates as the "complex set of historical practices by which we struggle to produce identity out of, on top of, complexity, difference and contradiction."[31] Within the discourses of law, drama, and psychiatry—to name some of those at work—the Shepard case, I will argue, produces and challenges gay identity.

"A Gigantic and Senseless Fear"

The history of the homosexual panic defense (HPD), now less viable in many courts but still extant, traces a curious genealogy that moves from pathological latency to justified aggression. It demonstrates how discourses of psychology and law intersect with one another through the articulation of jury trials and, as Peter Brooks argues, the "convictions" that jurors both have and make, in this case about the workings of queer subjects.[32] The public presumptions these discourses have established about gay identity, for instance, allowed the public defender Jason Tangemann to make his argument on October 25, 1999, that Matthew Shepard, while riding in a pickup with the defendant Aaron McKinney, had "reached over and grabbed [McKinney's] genitals and licked his ear"—an unwanted sexual advance that unleashed McKinney's traumatic childhood memories of homosexual abuse by the neighborhood bully and triggered "five minutes of emotional rage and chaos."[33] Tangemann's strategy was to use the homosexual panic defense to negate the premeditation needed for a jury to find first-degree murder. Proving an excusable or justifiable rage at Shepard's provocation would reduce McKinney's

---

29   Aled McHoul and Wendy Grace, *A Foucault Primer: Discourse, Power, and the Subject* (New York: New York University Press, 1993), 34.

30   Michel Foucault, *The History of Sexuality: Volume I: An Introduction*, trans. Robert Hurley (New York: Vintage, 1978), 101.

31   Stuart Hall, "On Postmodernism and Articulation: An Interview with Stuart Hall,," by Lawrence Grossberg, in *Critical Dialogues in Cultural Studies*, ed. David Morley and Kuan-Hsing Chen (New York: Routledge, 1996), 154.

32   See McMillen A10.

33   Christina Pei-Lin Chen, "Provocation's Privileged Desire: The Provocation Doctrine, 'Homosexual Panic,' and the Non-violent Unwanted Sexual Advance Defense," 10 *Cornell Journal of Law and Public Policy* 196 (2000).

offense to second-degree murder or manslaughter.[34] The defense's elaborate narrative of McKinney's torturous closet and Shepard's queer promiscuity, according to *20/20*'s investigation, was a tissue of lies used to convince jurors that Aaron's actions were excusable for the typical or reasonable male. Ironically, the murderers of Shepard are now using the absence of the HPD narrative in seeking the same result—mitigation of their sentences. In both scenarios, homophobia and its erasure have become versions of the "truth" for criminal defense purposes, in the original case blaming Shepard's sexual advance, in the current story claiming that queers fabricated the defendants' homophobia.

HPD has received considerable attention by legal scholars, starting with Bagnall, Gallagher, and Goldstein's 1984 article on bias against gays and lesbians in the court system, in which they argue, "[HPD] raises disturbing questions concerning the extent to which judges and juries are willing to excuse violence toward gays."[35] Law review articles by Mison (1992), Comstock (1992), Chen (2000), and Suffredini (2001) have followed.[36] In spite of criticism from almost every commentator except Dressler, the persistent narrative of provocation and justifiable rage continues to survive.[37] The doctrine, according to commentators, confuses two approaches: self-defense in the face of unwanted sexual advance (violent or nonviolent) and a form of psychological disorder used to medically justify the "violent psychotic reaction in a latently gay defendant."[38] From its inception, therefore, two legal and "public presumptions" about the gay subject co-exist: the expression of same-sex desire is sufficiently anathema to the reasonable juror to warrant violence; and secondly the closet, if disturbed, provokes insanity.[39]

---

34 Tangeman's opening argument admitted that McKinney had "engaged in homosexual acts" with a cousin as a teenager, and at 20 he had become distraught after entering a gay and lesbian church in Florida (see Loffreda 132). Judge Voigt was caught off guard by Tangeman's line of argument and reserved the right to hold it inadmissible during the defense phase of the trial. McKinney plea-bargained before the Judge made a ruling.

35 Robert G. Bagnall, Patrick C. Gallagher, and Joni L. Goldstein, "Burdens on Gay Litigants and Bias in the Court System: Homosexual Panic, Child Custody, and Anonymous Parties," 19 *Harvard Civil Rights-Civil Liberties Law Review* 497–515 (1984).

36 Robert Mison, "Homophobia in Manslaughter: The Homosexual Advance as Insufficient Provocation," 80 *California Law Review* 133–178 (1992); Comstock; Chen; Kara S. Suffredini, "Pride and Prejudice: The Homosexual Panic Defense," 279 *Boston College Third World Law Journal* 279–282 (2001).

37 See Chen 206; Joshua Dressler, "When 'Heterosexual' Men Kill 'Homosexual' Men: Reflections on Provocation Law, Sexual Advances, and the 'Reasonable Man' Standard," 85 *Journal of Criminal Law and Criminology* 726–763 (1995).,

38 See Bagnall in Comstock 82.

39 These scripts find their analogues in *The Celluloid Closet*, the story of gay representation in the history of film, in which the progression from suicide to serial killer is documented in the moves like *The Children's Hour* and *Serpico*. (See Vito Russo, *The Celluloid Closet: Homosexuality in the Movies*, revised ed., [New York: Harper & Row, 1985].)

The homosexual panic disorder (HP) was first formulated in 1920, when clinical psychiatrist Edward J. Kempf studied 19 cases of men who suffered severe psychiatric reactions as a result of their own "perverted cravings" coupled usually with their fear of heterosexuality. For Kempf, the controlling factor in HP was the latent homosexuality of the patient, who, finding himself in a same-gender environment, like a barracks, "feels he is being hypnotized" or fears losing control. Often the panic is precipitated by the departure of a member of the same sex to whom the patient is attached; the reaction to this separation is not outward aggression but self-inflicted punishment, even suicide. Thus the early work into the psychiatric disorder turns the sociological conditions of the closet into a mental disorder, relegating same-sex attachment to a form of insanity. Nowhere in Kempf's research, however, does he link the panic disorder to violent aggression against solicitation from another male.[40]

When clinician Burton Glick returned to the disorder in 1959, he could find little research on the topic and no mention of it in standard psychiatric dictionaries even though the Diagnostic and Statistical Manual of the APA for 1952 officially recognized HP (by 1980, however, it had been declassified in the DSM). Glick found the term "panic" imprecise, designating a range of emotions from discomfort to horrifying fright. Panic, which Freud called "a gigantic and senseless fear," was, for Glick, itself a vexed term ranging from paralyzing phobia to uncontrollable tension.[41] Glick also could find nothing in the doctrine to warrant its use as a legal defense. The definition of the disorder, he states, "fails to take into account the other great instinctual drive (besides the sexual); that of aggression."[42] He argues for the possibility that the disorder could be attributed to an acute aggression panic in cases of men killing gay men. Glick's research illustrates a re-shaping of psychiatric articulation based not on empirical evidence but the need to find a rationale for a successful legal argument. As Comstock notes, however, because there is little further research on acute aggression panic, criminal lawyers have continued to employ the language of HPD in cases of violence against gay men. A "possible explanation," Comstock concludes, is that "defense attorneys perhaps assume that juries are more likely to sympathize with a defendant who claims to have killed because of confusion and rage experienced during a same-gender sexual attack than with one who claims to have difficulty controlling his violent behavior generally."[43]

---

40   See Comstock 93.

41   We find such a fear in Ennis del Mar, one of the central characters in Proulx's "Brokeback Mountain," treated at length in Chapter 4.

42   Comstock 88.

43   Comstock 89. As Peter Freiberg reported in his *Advocate* article "Blaming the Victim," one defense attorney told him he loved "former Marines [on his juries], because there is a strong element of antagonism toward homosexuals in groups like that." The defense easily convinces these jurors with a forceful story: "the kid panics, he doesn't know what the hell is going on ... They're down on the bed, and all he can think about is this guy

As the doctrine of HPD progresses from its first published account in a California case in 1967,[44] the law continues to turn Kempf's latent homosexual into an aggressive homophobe, allowing the victim's sexual orientation to justify his violence, in part through the sanction of insanity defenses as well as its official condemnation of same-sex desire in sodomy laws. Homosexual panic describes not the latent queer tortured by social restrictions but the justifiably enraged male protecting himself against displays of same-sex affection. Case law has moved further away from a careful reliance on expert testimony that shows how fear turns to violence and insanity, instead developing legal doctrines of provocation, justification, excuse, and self-defense. From a critical queer studies perspective, the out, gay male has emerged as the presumptive aggressor, threatening ordinary heterosexual men who cannot be expected to take unwanted sexual advances lying down. Jonathan Schmitz, for example, appeared with Scott Amedure on the Jenny Jones talk show in 1995, where Scott revealed that he had a secret crush on Jonathan. Schmitz, feeling "humiliated" and "embarrassed," bought a shotgun and put two shells through Amedure's heart three days later. Arguing that he had been objectified by homosexual advances, Schmitz claimed that his killing was justified. The jury agreed, finding the defendant guilty of the lesser offense of second-degree murder.[45] Schmitz had made no plea of insanity or latent homosexuality, but he did plead HPD. As Suffredini and others have argued, including Eve Sedgwick, "our legal system does not accept 'race panic,' 'gender panic,' or 'heterosexual panic' as culpability-reducing defenses to violence … In fact, our legal system frequently deals more seriously with acts of violence generally."[46] The continued hue and cry in state houses against adding sexual orientation to existing penalty-enhancing hate crime legislation that already covers religion, gender, and race gains a particularly trenchant irony in light of the existence of an extant legal doctrine that mitigates penalties for those who attack gays and lesbians.[47]

Although the temporary insanity or diminished capacity element of HPD continues to be viable, as evidenced by its use in McKinney's defense, Chen has noted that the de-medicalization of homosexuality by the APA in 1973 and the declassifying of HP in 1980 have rendered the latency argument specious from a psychological point of view.[48] Yet the panic moniker remains to describe

---

is going to ram his dick up my ass" (see Freiberg in Comstock 89). The presumed narrative of sodomy and the public panic that accompanies fears of penetration allow legal discourse to appropriate psychiatry to confirm the "convictions" of jurors.

44   *People v. Rodriguez*, 256 Cal. App. 663, 64 Cal. Rptr. 253 (Cal. Ct. App. 1967).

45   See Suffredini 280.

46   Suffredini 310.

47   Chen has also detailed the heterocentrism of HPD; as a practical matter, she demonstrates how the doctrine is the almost exclusive province of heterosexual males, since homicidal assaults by women are statistically low and attacks by gay men against solicitations by other men—if not impossible—are highly counter-intuitive (see Chen 211).

48   Chen 202.

what juries call excusable rage against unwanted sexual advances, even gestural solicitation. When used today, HPD has become a defense based on a heat-of-passion provocation, akin to the well-known cases of husbands justifying murders of their adulterous wives. The Nonviolent Homosexual Advance (NHA) employs a narrative logic that shifts blame from the closeted defendant to solicitous queers, who in the last half of the twentieth century have been making their love more visible. "Previously," Chin notes, "the external stimulus merely precipitated the homosexual panic and triggered the acute psychotic reaction and temporary insanity that caused the latent homosexual to kill."[49] Now a doctrinal shift has brought the "current provocation rubric," in which "the external stimulus—the homosexual advance—has been reformulated as the trigger or 'adequate provocation' for heat-of-passion killing." Whereas before homicide came about because of a "pyschogenetic" homicidal reaction, "now the reasonable and ordinary person provoked by a homosexual advance kills because the solicitation itself causes an understandable loss of normal self control."[50]

This move from inward to external causation, from the latently gay defendant to the provoking queer, represents both a denial and erasure of traces of latency in the straight male and a further demonizing of the queer trigger, whose mere gesture justifies violent panic on the part of the "disgusted," straight man. As Dressler argues, "the point is that an unwanted ... sexual advance is a basis for justifiable indignation" on the part of "ordinary, fallible human beings" whose actions are worthy of partial excuse in determining the degree of criminal culpability.[51] For Chen, however, this argument casts the ordinary, fallible human being as not only heterosexual but also one sufficiently homophobic to kill queers.[52] During our era of increasing visibility of gays and lesbians, criminal courts, in a discursive reaction, are still accepting the reasonableness of this irrational action and justifying this excusable panic, which the movement for gay equality, in social, political, and media arenas, has supposedly produced in the nostalgic "reasonable man." Robert Mison writes, "the defendant hopes that the typical American juror—a product of homophobic and hetero-centric American society—will evaluate the homosexual victim and homosexual overture with feelings of fear, revulsion, and hatred. The defendant's goal is to convince the jury that his [homicidal] reaction was only a reflection of this visceral societal reaction: the reaction of a reasonable man."[53]

The Nonviolent Homosexual Advance Defense, as it is now designated, articulates a narrative about 12 angry men that defies current social and legal advances in gay rights, including the federal overturning of sodomy laws in *Lawrence v. Texas*, 539 U.S. 558 (2003), as well as the striking down of anti-gay legislation in *Romer v. Evans*, 517 U.S. 620 (1996). But the anti-gay script

---

49   Chen 203.
50   Chen 203.
51   Chen 214.
52   Chen 215.
53   See Mison 158.

is a stubborn one, a "reaction" Mison calls "visceral": panic arises from fear—a fear that is usually groundless. By its very nature unreasonable but in "normal" eyes understandable—irrational but excusable, intolerable yet justifiable— HPD carves out a niche within criminal law for what Scalia in his *Romer* dissent called "legitimate animus" in relation to the ideological space of pure male heterosexuality, a fictionalized subjectivity devoid of latency, fiercely protective of any brush with gayness from the rising queer tide.[54] These complex narratives illustrate articulatory clashes between nostalgic ideology, social advances, and discursive knowledge (in the form of academic and psychological expertise), revealing how some legal discourse resorts to the body—its visceral emotion, its capacity for rage, its "natural" reaction—to rationalize the law's sanction of violence. While Chen notes that the provocation defense always requires some non-consensual physical contact beyond words, the bodily gestures and actions that justify violence are often unthreatening. Case scenarios where the defense is admissible include: (1) while they watch a pornographic movie at A's home, A put his hand on the defendant's knee and asked, "Josh, what do you want to do?"; (2) in an automobile, B put his hand on the defendant's knee, was rebuffed, and then placed his hand on the defendant's upper thigh "near [the] genitalia," and asked the defendant to spend the night with him; (3) at a party, C asked the defendant "something about gay people," held his hand for 15 seconds and later grabbed his right buttock while the defendant was walking through a doorway.[55] What conclusions might we draw from a system of criminal justice that recognizes such overtures of same-sex attraction as sufficient provocation for justifiable homicide? How does the legitimization of such panic complement a religious discourse that understands homosexuality as the potential downfall of civilization, a political discourse that outlaws same-sex marriage because it threatens the American way of life, a cultural discourse that continues to capitalize upon the clash of straight and gay cultures in mythical venues like the American West of Wyoming? If panic finds its motivation in groundless "fictions" about the aggressive, recruiting gay male, then the law's legitimization of that fiction reveals the serious dangers behind these narratives of prejudice.

The Laramie Project: **Aristotelian Tragedy or Transformative Theater?**

While studies by legal scholars have demonstrated the way discourses of law and psychology have intersected to legitimatize and even excuse violence against gay men through the workings of institutional knowledge, the non-recognition and erasure of statistics about this violence in parts of our current government stands as further evidence of what some lawyers might call reckless disregard. "Violence against gay men and lesbians," Kendall Thomas has observed, "on the

---

54   *Romer v. Evans*, 517 U.S. 620, 644 (1996).

55   See Chen.

streets, in the workplace, in the home—is a structural feature of life in American society."[56] Her observation is based in part on surveys taken in eight major cities in the United States, where 86 percent of those interviewed admitted they had been attacked verbally, 44 percent were threatened with violence, 27 percent had objects thrown at them, 18 percent were victims of property vandalism including arson, and 30 percent reported sexual harassment, many by members of their own families or by police. A Department of Justice study in the late 1980s concluded that "gays are probably the most frequent victims of hate crime today" including physical violence like torture and mutilation.[57] More recently, a FBI report released November 22, 2004, concludes "bias violence against gays is now the second most important category of hate-crimes in the U.S. after race."[58]

According to Allport's classic study, The Nature of Prejudice, patterns of rejection form a continuum from avoidance to verbal denunciation, from institutional discrimination to physical attack, from individual assault to organized extermination.[59] "Violence," Allport reminds us, is always an outgrowth of milder states of mind: "although most barking (allocution) does not lead to biting, yet there is never a bite without previous barking."[60] This axiomatic point about the genealogy of hate crime, though repeatedly made by experts, continues to have almost no effect on those who secure the coherence of their imagined identity by investing in an intense dislike of gays and lesbians, the most unpopular group in the country according to one American National Election Study.[61] The connection between rhetoric and violence finds one of its most virulent examples in Justice Scalia's famous dissent in Romer v. Evans, the 1996 Supreme Court case that overruled an anti-gay constitutional amendment in Colorado.[62] In responding to the majority's determination that the amendment was motivated purely by animus toward lesbians and gay men, Scalia stated, "I had thought that one could consider certain conduct reprehensible—murder, for example, or polygamy, or cruelty to animals—and could exhibit even 'animus' toward such conduct. Surely that is the only sort of 'animus' at issue here: moral disapproval of homosexual conduct."[63] The analogy between murder and consensual sex that this Supreme Court justice

---

56   Kendall Thomas, "Beyond the Privacy Principle," 92 *Columbia Law Review* 1431–1514 (1992).

57   Thomas 1463–1464.

58   See Ireland 2.

59   Allport's compendious study originally published in 1954 (500 pages) contains only one mention of homosexuality in a footnote, an omission that attests to erasure as one of the principle strategies of panic (Gordon W. Allport, *The Nature of Prejudice* [New York: Anchor, 1958]).

60   Allport 57.

61   Kenneth Sherrill, "The Political Power of Lesbians, Gays and Bisexuals," 29.3 *Political Science* 469–470 (1996); Andrew Koppelman, *The Gay Rights Question in Contemporary American Law* (Chicago: University of Chicago Press, 2002), 21.

62   See *Romer* 54.

63   *Romer* 644.

formulates evidences the continued willingness of many government officials, under the rubric of "moral disapproval," to align homosexuality with conduct that justifies violent retaliation, illustrating how civil and criminal law intersect to create the impetus for outlawing queers.

Although Russell Henderson and Aaron McKinney probably spent little time with the advanced sheets of United States Reports, one of them did attend the local Baptist church, where the minister was inheriting the wind of Wyoming—with his anti-evolutionary and anti-gay proselytizing. Besen's claim about "consequences of words" haunts the dramatic declaration by Laramie's own Baptist minister in *The Project*: "Now, as for the victim, I know that that lifestyle is legal, but I will tell you one thing. I hope that Matthew Shepard as he was tied to that fence that he had time to reflect on a moment when someone had spoke the word of the Lord to him—and that before he slipped into a coma he had a chance to reflect on his lifestyle."[64]

Into this spectrum of prejudice and panic and through articulations as varied as law and religion, I want in the second focus of this chapter to consider inserting another unlikely but common form of cultural discourse: the catharsis of Aristotelian tragedy—that quintessential narrative of anti-social conduct which results in a symbolic punishment leading to a return to a status quo of allowed discrimination along tolerated paths of the continuum. As Augusto Boal characterizes Aristotle, classical tragedy represents the counter-resistant world of a theater of the repressed, one near which *The Laramie Project*, I will argue, dangerously skirts.[65] In tragedy, the punishment of the anti-social hero returns order to the status quo, warning spectators, after their theatric experience of panic-like fear and pity, not to empathize too closely with those on stage who have acted on their aggressive impulses. From the perspective of the story of the murder of Matt Shepard, an analysis based on Aristotle's *Poetics* might posit that we can denounce, damn, ignore, maybe even beat up the faggot, but we cannot let ourselves exterminate him, for that would move beyond the boundaries of justice.

Kaufman's *Laramie Project* has become an "exemplar of the staged oral history," a fast-growing body of American docudramas that compile interviews, court transcripts, and other documents to create an on-stage dialogue.[66] Along with Emily Mann and Anne Deavere Smith, Kaufman's Tectonic Theatre Project in both this play and the earlier *Gross Indecency: The Three Trials of Oscar Wilde* (1997) has successfully turned law into theater by dramatizing historical trials.

---

64   See Kaufman 67–68.

65   "Let there be no doubt: Aristotle formulated a very powerful purgative system, the objective of which is to eliminate all that is not commonly accepted, including the revolution, before it takes place" (Augusto Boal, *Theatre of the Oppressed*, trans. Charles A. and Maria-Odilia Leal McBride [New York: Theatre Communications, 1985], 47).

66   Ryan M. Claycomb, "(Ch)oral History: Documentary Theatre, the Communal Subject and Progressive Politics," 17:2 *Journal of Dramatic Theory and Criticism* 99 (spring 2003).

Queer docudramas like *The Project*, Mann's *Execution of Harvey Milk*, and more recently Epstein's *Howl*, therefore, have created an intersection between legal and cultural articulation in ways that combine fiction and nonfiction, literature and law. Kaufman and nine members of his New Jersey company flew to Laramie barely a month after Shepard's murder, beginning to keep journals and interview residents. Fifteen months, five more trips, and 200 interviews later, the play was staged on February 26, 2000 in Denver. "Its form—open stage, minimal sets, direct address— harkens back to Greek tragedy, in which the outcome is known from the beginning and the play provides an opportunity for the community to talk about things that are on its mind."[67] The play is less a narrative than a series of voices that dramatize reactions to the murder of Shepard. Matthew himself is not a character in the play— but ministers, Laramie residents, lawyers, police officers, and students address the audience in the form of "Moments" that occur as part of the "Journal Entries" of the project actors themselves. As a model, Kaufman states he tried to use Brecht's notion of epic theater, a kind of witnessing of an event in which a drama launches into a dialogue "that brings to the surface how we are thinking and talking about … the difference between tolerance and acceptance."[68] Kaufman himself articulates a desire to explore "theatrical language and form" in his play.

The Laramie Project has emerged as one of the most successful pieces of progressive theater in decades, especially on college campuses where it generates discussion wherever it is performed.[69] In spite of the obvious queer-friendly perspective of the creators of the play, the text is careful to air views that run the gamut from those of Fred Phelps, the notorious Die-Fag Kansas minister, to Jonas Slonaker, a gay man in Laramie who criticizes the "live and let live" slogan of many residents as a mandate for continued intolerance. While difficult to measure the play's impact as a document of cultural transformation, its status as a representation of what Shewey calls "an American tragedy" raises questions about the political effectiveness of its generic structure.[70] To what degree does this play represent another form of institutional panic through the pity and fear generated by what one writer has called the crucifixion of Matthew, producing a contained form of cathartic sympathy that may be counterproductive to any progressive change the play may hope to create?

Amy Tigner has criticized *The Project* for molding its story into the structure of a western pastoral—"something that is generically fictional"—while at the same time tantalizing the audience with "inside, true information about the location" of "the crime."[71] Manipulating its "nonfictional content into a fictionalized form, [t]he company constructs a rhetoric of authenticity and truthfulness by portraying the

---

67   Don Shewey, "Town in the Mirror," 17:5 *American Theatre* 14–15 (2000).
68   See Kaufman ii.
69   See Claycomb 97.
70   See Shewey 15.
71   Amy Tigner, "The Laramie Project: Western Pastoral," *Modern Drama* 45:1 (spring 2002): 144.

'real,' while 'simultaneously manipulating the raw information of the 'real' into theatrical composition."[72] For Tigner, Matthew is the pastoral shepherd of Milton's "Lycidas," a heroic yet tragic figure, whose death at the hands of outlaws in the landscape of the American West shocks and titillates the public. Taking Kaufman's East-Coast acting company to task for turning this hate crime into a Wyoming phenomenon (when in fact, statistically, such violence is more likely in New York), Tigner—a Laramie resident at the time of the crime—speculates at the end of her essay that *The Project* may ultimately be as much a "universal tragedy" as a "tragedy of the West."[73]

Tigner's conclusion reveals the genre that underlies the development of her pastoral argument; even with its western setting, Shepard's death and its depiction in *The Project* may fall more squarely within the outline of Aristotelian tragedy, a genre that Brazilian drama theorist Augusto Boal calls "the theatre of the repressed" in his critique of "Aristotle's coercive system of tragedy."[74] For Boal, a student of Paolo Freire, the tragic genre, popular in American productions on stage and film, has the effect of upholding a powerful, intimidating, and stable social structure by staging the punishment and purgation of anti-social elements and allowing spectators to cleanse their aggressive tendencies through empathy with the punished protagonist.[75] Rather than fomenting change or promoting subversion, Aristotelian tragedy, for Boal, proffers a kind of contained outlet for emotional sympathy, and, I would add, panic, which has an effect of solidifying rather than challenging existing forms of "justice."

In the first section of *Theatre of the Oppressed*, Boal describes the trajectory of Aristotelian tragedy as a form of identification or empathy between the audience and the "hero" who makes a mistake (*hamartia*) in the face of some misfortune he or she encounters. This misfortune represents the conflict between the hero's ethos or values and the social situation the play posits, whether it is regicide, as in the case of Hamlet, or presumed adultery in the case of Othello. The spectator "enjoys the pleasures and suffers the misfortunes of the character, to the extreme of thinking his thoughts," Boal explains. The spectator also experiences "three changes of a rigorous nature: *peripeteia, anagnorisis*, and *catharsis*; he suffers a blow with regard to his fate (the action of the play), *recognizes the error* vicariously committed and is *purified of the antisocial characteristic* which he sees in himself."[76] Boal understands this process of empathy—pity for the flawed hero and fear that the spectator could himself commit the same error under such circumstance—as "a powerful system of intimidation."[77] While the structure of tragedy may vary "in a thousand ways," its basic task is the "purgation of all antisocial elements" and the return to a universe

---

72   Tigner 142, 144.
73   Tigner 154.
74   See Boal 40.
75   Boal 40.
76   Boal 40.
77   Boal 46.

of defined and accepted values, to a status quo that Aristotle refers to as the existing parameters of justice.

In a tack that throws Tigner's analysis into question, Boal maintains that the classic American Western invests our empathy not in the usually flawless good guy but the bad guy, who gains admired power through corrupt means—his *hamartia* or flaw. A Western begins "with the presentation of a villain" who "does all the evil he possibly can, and we empathize with him and vicariously we do the same evil—we kill, steal horses and chickens, rape young heroines, etc."[78] For Boal, what is missing in the Western is recognition (*anagnorisis*) that the villain is destroyed by the hero usually without the hero feeling regret. Still the audience is able to purge its aggressive tendencies, finish off the bad guy and return to their "square dances," the system functioning "to diminish, placate, satisfy, eliminate all that can break the balance—all, including the revolutionary, transforming impetus."[79]

In one of the final moments of *The Project*, we attend policewoman Reggie Flutie's barbecue after the arrest of the defendants McKinney and Henderson. She and her family are celebrating the news that her HIV test was negative, in spite of her handling of the bloody Matthew when she found him lashed to the deer fence. Though not a square dance, this "celebration" of what was more than a probable outcome given the difficulty of external transmission of HIV (which the play does not discuss), mirrors the washing of the hands that the participants in this tragedy must undergo as a catharsis. In *The Project*, as in original Greek tragedy, the townspeople are both actors and chorus, just as they were in the opening of the play in Denver and later when the real characters were invited to the Broadway debut of the play.[80]

While Boal's analysis of the American Western ignores Aristotle's insistence in *The Poetics* that the tragic hero cannot be wholly evil or wholly good and must rather occupy an admirable but not perfect status, his insistence on the villain as empathetic corresponds to the legal "tragedy" of HPD. Matthew Shepard, while portrayed as innocent, foolhardy, and amicable, is absent physically from the play altogether, and even in the recollections of him, there is little or no discussion of Matthew as a gay man with sexual relations. His iconic status draws from his appearance as boyish, idealistic, blonde, good-looking, but also strangely unattached to the real world of Laramie, fresh from his Swiss boarding school. McKinney and Henderson, on the other hand, however below average they may be, gain the socio-economic sympathy of characters in the play and commentators like Wypijewski. As townies or homeboys, they are not part of the snobby university crowd; they are roofers from broken, trailer-park families who have gotten into trouble with drugs and are struggling to survive in a town with little to offer them. In these ways, they are more integrally part of the town, and though the "natives" try to distance themselves from

---

78   Boal 47.
79   Boal 47.
80   See Tigner 153.

Aaron and Russell, they pity them, bursting into tears when they come to court for arraignment.[81]

With pity, comes identification; with identification the fear that any god-loving heterosexual could break under the pressure of an unwanted sexual advance. The power McKinney and Henderson hold when Shepard meets them at the Fireside Bar the night of the murder emerges, we could posit, from their erotic attraction for a gay man. Neither of them is overly heterosexual in appearance, both of a fairly slight build, both together alone in the bar, both aware of Matthew's difference. They use their status as viable trade to lure the slumming Matthew to their truck, where according to one version of their story, Matt "hits" on them, touching Aaron's legs and genitals.[82] The latter is disgusted—a response the predominantly straight audience, from Boal's perspective, can identify with, one they can conceive of having themselves—hence the sympathy that is a crucial part of both Aristotle's *Poetics* and a jury's determination that a reasonable man might face the misfortune of a recruiting queer and fly into an excusable panic.

The Project does complex cultural work that mirrors the work of jurors, who faced with HPD, must both convict the villain and excuse his rage. The play relives the crime through the eyes of the townspeople who for the most part cannot accept Matthew's lifestyle but also paradoxically must condemn the violence Shepard's immorality generates. As Tigner argues, actors and audience alike are "shocked" but "titillated" by the "crucifixion" of the queer, while most refuse to recognize the connection between their religious, social, and official opprobrium and the panic that McKinney initially claims motivated his rage. Moreover, the panic the murderers and their girlfriends plead come from a kill-the-fag narrative that already has a long history in the production of cultural discourse—from *Billy Budd* to *Suddenly Last Summer*, from Hollywood to grade-school tags—the scapegoating of homos makes the Shepard murder a re-enactment of a paradigmatic American story whose material consequences are already strongly embedded in the institutional regimes of legal, medical, and cultural truth.

Not surprisingly, the varied confessions of HP McKinney makes before the trial, according to Detective Debree, seem to be rehearsed, picked up from somewhere— school, the street, church, AM radio. In one of Aaron's statements as recorded by Beth Loffreda in *Losing Matt Shepard*, McKinney claims he beat Matt because "he tried to throw himself all over me. I don't know if he was trying to get away or what he was doing, but I just remember getting so mad ... He asked me once to stop, then he was just like all over me, trying to hug me and stuff like that. And I took my gun, and I was, like, 'Get away from me.'"[83] McKinney claims he does not hate gays; he just is aggravated when they "start coming on to me," though he admits Matt is the first gay man to hit on him.[84] Aaron confesses the greatest—and most groundless—

81   See Kaufman 49.
82   Kaufman 81.
83   See Loffreda 147.
84   Loffreda 147.

fear of every straight man, a fear that is the source of identification for audience and actors alike in tragedy: that they might lose their composure in the same way, might kill a king to gain a kingdom, or in this case, kill a queer to avoid facing the narrative fictions that have established the parameters of their own sexual identity.

Admittedly Kaufman's docudrama may engage in sufficient de-centering of character to make the tragic hero of this play the community itself, as Claycomb might argue, but the tenor of the play's tectonic archive of interviews is hardly one that embraces queer sexuality. Under the "live and let live" rubric of a western ethos, most interviewees labor to distance themselves from the murderers as well as Shepard without publicly recognizing their own fear and identification with the perpetrators. Jedadiah Schultz, the university student, whose parents refused to attend his performance in *Angels in America* but applauded his Macbeth, continues to think homosexuality is wrong throughout *The Project*, as does Aaron Kreifels, the Catholic student who finds Matt's body and struggles to know why God picked him to come upon the breathing scarecrow.[85] Others call Matt a barfly spreading AIDS who was half to blame for what happened to him. The treating physician the night of the murder feels compassion for McKinney and Shepard, both of whom he treated that evening, and Laramie residents are solemn as they watch their homeboys paraded into the courtroom in orange jumpsuits and shackles. These points of view demonstrate, from Boal's perspective, the subtle reaffirmation of prejudicial social mores that the cultural work of tragedy does, functioning as a form of extreme homeopathy in which the rage that has coalesced around the parameters of social disapproval is culturally produced for purposes of both acting out the causation inherent in prejudicial patterns and symbolically distancing that bigotry from the chain reaction it starts.[86] This homeopathy continues in the catastrophe, when the perpetrators are sentenced not to death but to a probable life of sodomy in prison, forced to make patent or un-repress the desire that may lie underneath their animus and fear. In one sense, the workings of tragedy undertake the therapeutic discovery of and rage against imagined or real homosexual experiences, allowing audiences to empathize with the reputedly abused childhoods of the murderers.

Tragedy, Aristotle states, is also a representation of justice; it imitates the actions of man's rational soul in the pursuit of happiness through virtuous behavior, "remote from the extremes, whose supreme good is justice and whose maximum expression is the Constitution."[87] Boal reminds us that justice, for Aristotle, consists of the laws that are made by those who have power—aristocratic men in Attic Greece—and that tragedy portrays the consequences of not obeying those laws, of moving beyond the legal parameters of moral disapproval. Boal's discussion of the ties between law and drama indicates how art often does the ideological work of reaffirming a legal system that is not only heteronormative, but often violently

---

85   See Tigner 145.
86   See Boal 31.
87   Boal 24.

hetero-imperative, as the success of HPD evidences. The staging of Henderson and McKinney's murder re-enacts a narrative of rage not to exorcise it, but in order to control and contain it, to present it as the grim alternative to a status quo of quiet homophobia and erasure. The legal and psychological logic of HP in the Shepard case, what Loffreda calls "a recent development in the ever-intensifying romance of jurisprudence and therapeutic culture," is thus embedded in the theatrical experience, especially the cathartic experience of tragedy, which re-produces in order to repress the violence that continues within social experience.[88] This intricate nexus between artistic and social fictions—between cultural and legal ideology—reveals the power of both the myths that inhabit legal discourse and the legal effects that cultural myths produce. [89]

As Sedgwick has argued in her trenchant analysis of HPD, one of its ironies comes from the assumption that hatred of gay men is so abnormal as to be classifiable as a psychological disorder, when in fact all the findings have shown that animus toward gay men is pervasive, public, and well within the boundaries of what politicians are calling family values.[90] For Sedgwick, the panic defense legitimates prejudice by entitling anti-gay assaulters under the protective rubric of a legitimate "heat of passion" defense, one that claims a *hamartia* that male jurors can identify with, an error which they both fear and pity. The defense, therefore, contains within it the strange logic of tragic catharsis, and the defendant, like McKinney, becomes a spectator in the dramatic fury of his other pathological self: "Blacked out. My fist. My pistol. The butt of the gun. Wondering what happened to me. I had a few beers and I don't know. It's like I could see what was going on but I don't know, it was like somebody else was doing it."[91] DeBree, the detective in the case, clearly thought McKinney and Henderson "knew their lines," and "had the gay-bashing script down cold," he told Loffreda, detailing the variations on their confessions.[92] Even if eventually ruled inadmissible by the trial court, the panic defense performed a justified narrative of "losing it" in the face of proposed gay sex and acting out a horrible reaction to a tendency that lurks in every soul, a reaction that can never be publicly condoned. "Being a verry [*sic*] drunk homofobick I flipped out and began to pistol whip the fag with my gun," McKinney allegedly wrote to a fellow inmate's wife, having honed the particulars of his tragic flaw, one that ironically assumes, as Sedgwick remarks, a kind of universal homoerotic impulse.[93] That "flipping out" is the socially sanctioned reaction to a cognizance of one's own desire, legitimating the sublimation of homoerotics through pistol whipping.

McKinney's aggression also masks a desperate attempt to protect what Lacan calls "the armor of an alienating identity," one whose history, according to his

---

88   See Loffreda 132.
89   Loffreda 132.
90   See Sedgwick 18–20.
91   See Kaufman 81.
92   See Loffreda 147.
93   Loffreda 14.

lawyers, included forced fellatio at the age of six, a liaison with his male cousin, and a mistaken entrance into a gay and lesbian church in Florida—apparently the ultimate trauma, loving the wrong Jesus.[94] That armor moreover assumes the metaphoric world of a gunfighter nation, in which our working-class Western hero must turn himself into Dirty Harry, toting a pistol that weighs over four pounds, and proceed to destroy someone whose countenance threatens cowboy mythologies of machismo and heteronormativity, thereby sacrificing himself to the Aristotelian myth of regeneration through violence.[95] McKinney and Henderson meet Shepard, the corrupt, effete East Coast pervert, dressed in patent leather shoes and drinking Heineken, take him out for a drive past Wal-Mart where they begin to bash his skull over 20 times with a pistol and tie him to a buck fence outside of town, rooting out the unnatural element from the wide vistas of the gem state. The legal panic defense McKinney rehearses in his confession, replays in his jailhouse correspondence, and returns to in the courtroom, has its roots in a Western mythos which expends its virulent misogyny and internalized homophobia on men who refuse to buy into the heteronormative ethos that is the presumed narrative of sexual identity. Shepard was out and that out-ness disrupted an economy of erasure and clandestinity that was intolerable for the likes of the wannabe toughs, Henderson and McKinney. They protected themselves by torturing him, taking part in a Western film script they had seen and wanted desperately to re-enact. Rid the queers from the land or at least put a lid so tight on them that they either move to San Francisco, get married, or stick it out at the rest stop.

Live and let live is the libertarian motto of Wyoming, a state where there is plenty of space between towns, one *Project* speaker tells us at the beginning of the play. "As far as the gay issue," Marge Murray claims,

> I don't give a damn one way or the other as long as they don't bother me. And even if they did, I'd just say no thank you. And that's the attitude of most of the Laramie population. They might poke one, if they were in a bar situation you know, they had been drinking, they might actually smack one in the mouth, but then they'd just walk away. Most of 'em said they would just say, "I don't swing that way," and whistle on about their business. Laramie is live and let live.[96]

Marge is the mother of Reggie Fluty, the deputy sheriff who was the first officer on the scene. Her folksy, down-home lingo reveals almost parodically how cinematic "us Westerners" have become, how seriously we take our fictions, how easily those fictions have moved into our courtrooms. Late in *The Project*, Jonas Slonaker, a gay man from Laramie, comments: "And it's even in some of the Western literature, you

---

94   Jacques Lacan, "The Mirror Stage," *Ecrits: A Selection*, trans. Alan Sheridan (New York: Norton, 1977), 4.

95   Richard Slotkin, *Gunfight Nation: Myth of the Frontier in Twentieth Century America*, (Norman, OK: University of Oklahoma Press, 1998

96   See Kaufman 29–30.

Figure 2.1   Still from *The Laramie Project*
Source: Image used courtesy of HBO.

know, live and let live. That is such crap. I tell my friends that … I mean basically what it boils down to: If I don't tell you I'm a fag, you won't beat the crap out of me. I mean, what's so great about that? That's a great philosophy?"[97] For Slonaker, the announcement of one's sexual orientation is a violent provocation, a public un-erasing that justifies panic, assault, and the tragic return of the repressed. From the perspective of Aristotle's *Poetics*, the communal flaw of the play is the expression of homosexual desire, one that justifies a violence that must also be condemned.

The HBO film production of Kaufman's docudrama, released in 2002, captures some of the strange admixture of pastoral idyll and internalized, dystopic panic that Proulx's "Brokeback Mountain" elicits. The Slonaker interview is wedged between two scenes of interviews with locals who comment on the Shepard phenomenon in Chapter 10 of the film, called "A Gay Lifestyle." In the scene prior to the Slonaker interview, a weather-beaten rancher and his wife sit in lawn chairs in front of a trailer, assailing the media's sensationalism, which in their view has treated the Shepard case as if "ten murders" had occurred instead of one. In a medium shot of the seated (and grounded) couple, they admit their disapproval of homosexuality but express their willingness to have a cup of coffee with queers as long as they don't wear their sexual orientation as a "banner."

The film cuts from the domestic scene of the elders to a long shot of a vast green field with blue sky and a few nimbus clouds framing two figures walking toward the camera. Though not as wild as the Canadian Rockies of *Brokeback*, this uncanny *mise-en-scène* bears a striking resemblance to the colors and setting Ang

---

97   Kaufman 60.

Figure 2.1   Still from *The Laramie Project*
Source: Image used courtesy of HBO.

Lee will use to portray Proulx's story years later (Figure 2.1). Slonaker's voice-over is punctuated by a break with the continuity of the camera's expected slow zoom, jumping twice to frame the figures in ever increasing closeness. Slonaker's repetition of the West's "live and let live" cliché concludes with a jump to a medium shot of the two men, the Tectonic Project interviewer and Jonas Slonaker, an outdoorsy man in his forties, who proceeds to translate the common laissez-faire slogan into its real threat to "beat the crap out" of any fag who has the gall to come out in public. His final rhetorical question—"what kind of philosophy is that?"—is voiced as the camera jumps again to a closer shot of the two figures, still walking across the stunningly beautiful setting (Figure 2.1). The jolting film editing captures the disjunction between the scene's visualized external paradise and Slonaker's description of the ugly landscape of social intimidation, between the wide-open West and the violent confinement of a mandatory closet. Slonaker's angry reproof of Laramie's hypocrisy adumbrates the internalized panic that will govern Ennis del Mar's consciousness in Lee's film, even as it defies the logic of students at the university who are interviewed in *The Project*'s succeeding scene—undergraduates who explain how their church upbringing has led them to disapprove of the "lifestyle"—to hate the sin even though they love the sinner. But "how can we tell the dancer from the dance," we are left asking, as the docudrama's pastiche underscores the gradations of panic—the spectrum of hate that runs from loving the sinner to crucifying him on a buck fence.

This sanctioned prejudice of homosexual panic resides not only in a mythic geographic consciousness that has filtered deeply into everyday idioms of school children as well as the rarefied language of dramatic art; it also slides across the spectrum of jurisprudence from criminal consciousness to legislative hearing. Shepard's murderers, like almost all high school kids across our country, are saturated with a reservoir of anti-gay epithets that exist as tools of ego-building, and their fear about their own queer desire is fed by discourses of religion, politics, and law. That potential for panic and passion, always on the brink of rearing its ugly head, becomes part of the trial of the heteronormative subject, a savage other he must exorcise, whether arrested and tried or not. Sedgwick has detailed what she calls the "endemic intimacy of the link between extra-judicial and judicial punishment of homosexuality" by reporting how state legislators—in spite of the statistics in front of them—have refused to enact sexual orientation hate crime legislation because such laws would condone the immoral acts of gay sex.[98] In other words, to protect queers from the violence that faces them would endanger the patterns of allowed prejudice that, by most accounts, causes that violence. Bias crime laws might jeopardize the rhetoric of hate that ministers depend upon for their control of their latent parishioners. Should we write laws to protect the Anti-Christ, one Wyoming legislator asked when the state unsuccessfully considered hate-crimes legislation in the aftermath of Matt's murder.[99]

Not surprisingly, the tragedy of the Shepard murder, and the incredible success of Kaufman's play across the country, has not directly led to any legislation beyond a sexual orientation discrimination policy at the University of Wyoming and as Loffreda narrates, a hard fought city ordinance mandating statistic gathering and police training more than a year after the trials. As Slonaker dramatizes in *The Project*:

> Change is not an easy thing, and I don't think people were up to it here. They got what they wanted. Those two boys got what they deserve, and we look good now. Justice has been served. The OK corral. We shot down the villains … The town's cleaned up and we don't need to talk about it anymore. You know, it's been a year since Matthew Shepard died, and they haven't passed shit in Wyoming … at a state level, any town, nobody anywhere, has passed any kind of laws, anti-discrimination laws or hate crime legislation … What's come out of it? What's come out of this that's concrete or lasting?[100]

This prophetic speech, which characterizes the so-called advances of the homosexual agenda, comes at the end of *The Project*, illustrating how the mythos of the West has deflated the Shepard murder into a HBO movie, while consequently posing the central question of the relation of culture to social reality. To test Kaufman's docudrama against the elements of Aristotelian tragedy and

---

98   See Sedgwick.
99   See Loffreda 53.
100   See Kaufman 87.

compare McKinney to Oedipus may indeed be far-fetched, but Boal's critique of the theater of the repressed at the very least subjects this story to a scrutiny that is crucial to one of the central questions I am asking. How do we use cultural representation not only to "pass shit," but to transform the social fabric; in Boal's terms, how do we move from a theater of the repressed to a theater of the oppressed, a theater that does not purge us of our aggressive impulses by punishing an individual but instead provokes us to transform those impurities in all spectators? How do we turn spectators into actors, performers that work to transform rather than accept a social fabric that endorses a modicum of hate?

Boal's legislative theater, in which the people perform their needs, desires, and dreams, out of which legislation is written, may seem utopian for us, but what it points to is the question of what a transformative theater might look like, and specifically how *The Laramie Project* at certain moments establishes a model that understands the murder of Matt Shepard as a crime not of a flawed individual but of a social fabric. "You and the straight people of Laramie and Wyoming are guilty of the beating of Matthew Shepard," one anonymous e-mailer wrote to the president of the University of Wyoming. "You have taught your straight children to hate their gay and lesbian brothers and sisters—unless and until you acknowledge that Matt Shepard's beating is not just a random occurrence, not just the work of a couple of random crazies, you have Matthew's blood on your hands."[101]

Conclusion

The Laramie Project was performed at University of Montana in 2003 in the wake of a still unsolved case of arson against two lesbians who had sued for the right to pay into the health insurance plan of the university. Fred Phelps, who promised to appear outside, canceled his trip to Missoula, but a two-hour talk back occurred after the performance of the play. The discussion was moving, but participants were also often quick—almost in panic—to distinguish Missoula from Laramie rather than draw comparisons. I was struck by the way in which Foucault's critique of the repressive hypothesis seemed to govern the production of talk in relation to the Shepard murder, talk that has taken the form of film, drama, essay, and media production and now perhaps this chapter. What strikes me as one of the dangers of airing differences and discussing tragic events is the capacity of discourse not to inspire but to defuse, to prevent change rather than foment it. The production of *The Project* in Missoula after all did not lead to any police training or legislation on a municipal or state level, though clearly most in the room after the production would have voted for it.

How can we, as citizens and commentators, distinguish a culture that justifies panic from one that promotes acceptance and non-discrimination? As legal

---

101   Kaufman 57.

critics, we must unmask fictional and ungrounded narratives that sometimes govern convictions by juries and jurists. HPD is one of those doctrines. As literary critics, we must discover narratives that inspire and facilitate change, rather than produce a contained form of sympathetic catharsis. *The Project* comes close to this material goal, especially in its re-production throughout schools, but for our narratives to evolve from those of repression to those of oppression, our dramas must come out of the closet of the theater into the streets, the courthouses, and the legislatures.

Chapter 3
Queer Torts: Gender *Trans*-gression in the Brandon Teena Case

Branding Brandon

On June 30, 2010, Patricia Dye, a 31-year-old Ohio resident, was arrested and jailed on three criminal misdemeanor charges, including "sexual imposition" and "contributing to the delinquency of minors" in connection with a series of relationships between Dye (under the name Matt Abrams) and a couple of teenage girls. After an initial not-guilty plea, Dye accepted the imposition charge, a six-month sentence, and a requirement of a 15-year registration as a sex offender.[1] The case garnered national attention, the Associated Press reporting the incident, and Reuters including a photograph of the shorthaired, round-faced Dye beside a shot from the famous film *Boys Don't Cry* with the caption "Life Imitates Art." Dye does bear an uncanny likeness to both a teenage boy and Brandon Teena, whose now admittedly "overexposed" life story has spawned an exhaustive amount of commentary and artistic treatment, though scholars have only glanced at the plethora of legal proceedings produced by what Judith Halberstam has aptly called The Brandon Archive.[2] Though I add another stone to this critical cairn with

---

1 *Denver Post* (October 7, 2010): 3A. Dye, who had no previous criminal record, initially pleaded not guilty and then bargained through a confession to the misdemeanor charge of sexual imposition, defined as sexual contact with another when the offender knows that the sexual contact is offensive to the other person or is reckless in that regard. Dye will spend six months in jail and have to register as a sex offender for 15 years. Her victim was a 16-year-old teenager, 5'5", who ran from a motel room where she had spent the last three days with Dye, who is 4'10". (The age of consent in Ohio is 16.) Warren County prosecutors allegedly lamented "not having the ability to charge Dye with a crime for pretending to be a boy" (See http://www.queerty.com/how-did-patricia-dye-who-pretended-to-be-a-boy-to-sleep-with-teenage-girls-only-get-6-months-in-jail-20101007/ October 7, 2010). "Life imitates art," read a caption under a shot from *Boys Don't Cry* included in a *Daily Mail* article (October 21, 2010). Age discrepancy and a lack of information about Dye distinguish this case from that of Brandon Teena, but the media's immediate analogy is germane.

2 Judith Halberstam, *In a Queer Time and Place: Transgender Bodies, Subcultural Lives* (New York: New York University Press, 2005), 54 ("the rude effects of overexposure"). A selection from the critical archive includes: Brenda Cooper, "*Boys Don't Cry* and Female Masculinity: Reclaiming a Life and Dismantling the Politics of Normative Heterosexuality," *Critical Studies in Media Communication* 19:1 (March 2002): 44–63; John M. Sloop, "Disciplining the Transgendered: Brandon Teena, Public Representation, and Normativity,"

some of the same trepidation about overkill voiced by others, the recent conviction of Dye on charges of "sexual imposition" and the concomitant media focus on Dye's transgenderism as tantamount to both a criminal offense and an *imposition* (in both legal and social senses) point to the ongoing ascription of illegality to queer subjectivity, an ascription that is necessarily maintained by both a prurient and policing spectatorship, including not only critics like myself but also a media readership that thrives on what Foucault has called *scientia sexualis*—the will to know about sex.[3] This will to knowledge—replete with its spirals of pleasure and power—inhabits not just the criminal and civil annals of law but also the aesthetic and social imaginations of the public—that great Aristotelian chorus destined to turn nonconformity into flaw, flaw into tragedy.

The existence of a transphobic continuum, which runs the gamut from liberal toleration to murder, requires that critical queer studies recognize the dangerous implications of participation in a tragic paradigm that understands justice as purely a matter of increased sentences for a few troubled individuals, like Brandon's killers, rather than as "a public and social disaster," as James Baldwin put it.[4] There is a kind complicity not only in a vilification of individuals that ignores the broader range of social opprobrium, but also in the assumption that any scholar or artist can presume to understand the Brandon Teena case in all its intricacies. The shaky ground we stand on by "studying" Brandon's rape and murder is mapped out by Foucault's comments about how knowledge, especially in relation to sexuality,

---

Western Journal of Communication 64:2 (spring 2000): 165–189; Ann Cvetkovick, *An Archive of Feeling: Trauma, Sexuality, and Lesbian Public Cultures* (Durham, NC: Duke University Press, 2003), 272–286 ("Epilogue"); C. Jacob Hale, "Consuming the Living, Dis(Re)Membering the Dead in the Butch/FTM Borderlands," *GLQ* 4:2 (1998): 311–348; from the mainstream media: Eric Konigsberg, "Death of a Deceiver," *Playboy* (January 1995): 92–94, 193–199; John Gregory Dunne, "The Humboldt Murders," *New Yorker* (January 13, 1997): 45–62; Donna Minkowitz, "Love Hurts," *Village Voice* (April 19, 1994): 24–30; from the film criticism: Ellis Hanson, ed. *Out takes* (Durham, NC: Duke University Press, 1999); Julianne Pidduck, "Risk and Queer Spectatorship," *Screen* 42:1 (spring 2001): 97–102; Danny Leigh, "Boy Wonder," *Sight and Sound* 10:3 (March 2000) (Interview with Kimberly Peirce); Jennifer Devere Brody, "Boyz Do Cry: Screening History's White Lies," *Screen* 43:1 (spring 2002): 91–96; Patricia White, "Girls Still Cry," *Screen* 42:3 (2001): 122–128; on the web: www.brandon-teena.tk. The story has given rise to two films: the documentary *Brandon Teena Story* (Susan Muska and Greta Olafsdottir, directors [Zeitgeist Films 1998]) and the feature film *Boys Don't Cry* (Kimberly Peirce, director [Fox Searchlight 1999]); Dinita Smith's novel *The Illusionist* (New York: Scribner 1997); and Aphrodite Jones's *All She Wanted: A True Story of Sexual Deception and Murder in America's Heartland* (New York: Pocket Books, 1996), an installment in her true crime series.

3   Michel Foucault, *The History of Sexuality, Volume I: An Introduction*, trans. Robert Hurley (New York: Random House, 1978), 53–73.

4   James Baldwin, *The Evidence of Things Not Seen* (New York: Henry Holt, 1995), 125 quoted in Halberstam 46.

is linked to power. "And so in the question of sex," he writes in his critique of the repressive hypothesis,

> (in both senses: as interrogation and problematization, and as the need for confession and integration into a field of rationality), two processes emerge, the one conditioning the other: we demand that sex speak the truth (but, since it is the secret and is oblivious to its own nature, we reserve for ourselves the function of telling the truth of its truth, revealed and deciphered at last), and we demand that it tell us our truth, or rather the deeply buried truth of that truth about ourselves which we think we possess in our immediate consciousness.[5]

In the case of sexuality, which is relegated historically to privacy and even to the unconscious, the drive to discover the truth about Brandon's "sex" gives any investigation, whether critical, legal or artistic, the nature of a pre-trial discovery process, one that necessarily must inform even a chapter like this one, which seeks to study how Foucault's notion of the will to know the truth about sex informs the Brandon Teena case. Both its legal and cinematic representations, I contend, participate in this "will to knowledge," a drive to confirm a tragic ideology that binds gender to anatomical sex in the service of a deeply entrenched heterocentrism—a cultural norm which must punish its transgressors.[6]

At the risk of engaging in the very dividing practices that Foucault himself questioned, I narrow the focus of my chapter by briefly reviewing the array of discourses—medical, psychological, cultural, and legal—that have arisen from this case of rape and murder of a 21-year-old outside Falls City, Nebraska, on December 31, 1993. Once newspapers reported that a triple homicide in the "heartland" of America involved not just an African American and a young mother, but also a woman masquerading as a man whose "charade" had been revealed (*The Des Moines Register*), Brandon Teena quickly drew the attention of national publications like *Playboy*, *The New Yorker*, and *The Village Voice*. Not long after, true-crime paperback writer Aphrodite Jones descended on Falls City to obtain exclusive rights to the story, eventually publishing *All S/he Wanted: A True Story of Sexual Deception and Murder in America's Heartland* in 1996. Films followed (the documentary *Brandon Teena Case* [1998] and the feature *Boys Don't Cry* [1999]), as did a novel called *The Illusionist* (1997), a Guggenheim Museum art website, and numerous critical essays in queer theory, film studies, communications, and cultural studies.

Falling along discursive axes of the popular and academic, the verbal and visual, the fictional and nonfictional, the Brandon Teena archive, through the example of its two award-winning films, illustrates how the discrete genres of documentary

---

5   Foucault 69. Though Foucault's use of the term "sex" has received some criticism for its imprecision, I understand the use in this quotation to refer to "sexuality," to the study of erotic practices, anatomy, gender, and the zones of knowledge they produce.

6   Sloop 172.

and dramatic biopic employ an admixture of fiction and nonfiction as part of their narrative endeavors. Muska and Olafsdottir's documentary (*The Brandon Teena Story*) has come under attack for perpetuating "bumfuck" myths about the fate of sexual minorities on the Nebraska plains when statistics have shown that most anti-gay attacks take place outside urban bars; on the other hand Peirce's feature film starring Hillary Swank has received criticism and legal challenges for turning Brandon and Lana into willing lesbians at the end of the film.[7] Influenced by Terence Malick (*Badlands*) and Gus Van Sant (director of the biopic *Milk*), Peirce unabashedly admits that she fell in love with Brandon after reading about the case. The photographer turned film director followed her Aristotelian impulses in limiting the action primarily to the Falls City period of Brandon's life, consciously seeking to turn this history into a *Romeo and Juliet* love tragedy (Cooper 58).[8] Muska and Oláfsdottir have also defended their country and western soundtrack and depiction of the Falls City way of life.[9] Confronting the inherent contradiction in telling a *story* that is also *true* (i.e. engaging in a selective version of the facts), these films necessarily plot their version of the truth about Brandon's life—their subjective approach to an objective set of events—thus dramatizing the way fact and fiction are intertwined and necessarily informed by ideological perspectives, a point worth extending, I think, to a discourse as objectively oriented as the law.

Legal processes permeate almost all facets of the history of Brandon Teena, including representation of the law within the story itself and legal actions spawned by the myriad efforts to capitalize on Brandon's sensational death through various cultural productions. Evidenced by a series of arrests for forgery and fraud, including a parole violation on December 15, 1993, which led to his incarceration in the women's section of the Richardson County jail, the law played a major role in Brandon's biography. These legal sequestrations led directly to the symbolic branding that followed Brandon through his life, an interpellation that also confirms, as Lacan argued, the arbitrary imposition of signification on the sexed subject. After the assault by Lotter and Nissen, Sherriff Laux of Richardson County would interview Brandon as a "female" rape victim, an audiotape of which, brilliantly woven into the fabric of Muska's documentary, became evidence in the wrongful death case brought by Brandon's mother.

In addition to the sensational murder trials which left John Lotter on death row and Tom Nissan serving consecutive life terms, this case has also involved two civil actions that broaden the scope of our law and literature inquiry from a concentration on easily "othered" criminal outlaws to an arena of tort law that demonstrates the workings of transphobic continuum among the unindicted

---

7   See Halberstam 89, and more generally, the chapter on the "Brandon Archive."

8   Cooper 58 and Brody 94.

9   J. Yabroff, "Trans America: Documentary Filmmakers Susan Muska and Greta Olafsdottir Talk About the Story Behind *The Brandon Teena Story*," *Salon.com*, in Cooper.

citizenry, some of whom were intimately connected to Brandon.[10] Although these two cases are not the only civil actions in this archive, they exemplify how the will to knowledge about sex has driven the engines of the Brandon Teena phenomenon, instantiating and problematizing the vexed intersections of sex (that amalgamation of hormones, anatomy, and chromosomes that make up the body), gender (the cultural assumptions that "attach" to that amalgamation), and sexual orientation (the trajectory of a subject's desire).[11] In the course of these two civil actions— one brought by Brandon's mother JoAnn and the other by Brandon's lover Lana Tisdel—damages allegedly arise as a result of deviation from the standards of heteronormativity, standards which act as the backdrop for what Victor Turner calls the "redressive machinery" that emerges when there is a breach in workings of social life.[12]

The first case, *Brandon v. County of Richardson* 261 Neb. 636 (2001), was a civil action for wrongful death, negligence, and intentional infliction of emotional distress brought by Brandon's mother, JoAnn Brandon, against Richardson County and Sherriff Laux in connection with the events leading up to the murder. The second civil action, *Tisdel v. Fox*—settled out of court in 2000—involves Brandon's lover Lana Tisdel's suit for defamation of character against Peirce and Fox Searchlight for *Boys'* portrayal of Lana as both "lazy white trash, a skanky snake," and a willing lesbian at the end of the film, a dramatic depiction that allegedly rendered the real Lana an object of "contempt and ridicule" in Falls City and led to both scorn and abandonment by "her friends and family."[13] These two civil cases dramatize how Brandon's attempt to live her life as a man met with obstacles of heterocentric surveillance in legal arenas—the will to impose a binary truth about sex and gender on the subject, an insistence that begins most notoriously with the medical "one body, one sex" rule which often governs the

---

10   See *State of Nebraska v. Lotter* 255 Neb. 456, 586 NW.25 591 (1998) and *State of Nebraska v. Nissen* 252 Neb. 51, 560 N.W.2d 157 (1997). Lotter is still on death row, maintaining his innocence. His petition for a new trial was denied, and he is now (as of May 2011) still awaiting a hearing on his appeal of the death sentence. Nissen has since recanted his plea, claiming he fired the shots.

11   Besides Lana's case against Peirce and Fox, three other civil actions have occurred. Aphrodite Jones sued Fox for breach of contract, alleging the studio had promised to film her version of the story, starring Drew Barrymore. The same alleged agreement led to a lawsuit by Diane Keaton and Bill Richardson—purported producers of the other planned film. Laurie Weeks, a writer, then sued to receive credit for writing some of the film's dialogue which *Boys* did not acknowledge. Lana Tisdel's suit, as well as Keaton's, were settled for an undisclosed amount.

12   Victor Turner, *From Ritual to Theatre: The Human Seriousness of Play* (New York: PAJ Publications, 1982), 10.

13   L. Barr, "The Other Woman," *Brill's Content*, in Cooper 60–61.

precipitous and now notorious use of anatomical surgery for interesex subjects at birth.[14]

The True Story of Brandon Teena: A Statement in Facts

There is no extant evidence, however, that Teena Renae Brandon, born in 1972, showed any signs of intersexuality.[15] Her father recently dead from a drunk-driving accident on the Cornhusker Highway outside Lincoln, Teena and her older sister grew up with their 19-year-old mother JoAnn in a series of trailer parks, both children reportedly the occasional victims of sexual molestation by one of their mother's male friends. JoAnn would later insist that these episodes had led to her daughter's sexual aversion to males, and she was vocal in her anger that Kimberly Peirce did not make that basis clear in *Boys Don't Cry*, upset as well that Hillary Swank, upon receiving the Academy Award for best Actress (*not* Actor), thanked Brandon Teena instead of Teena Brandon, pointedly employing the catachrestic alias Brandon adopted once Teena, after years of eschewing sexual dress and behavior codes, began cross-dressing with a sock stuffed in his jeans and dating girls. "He was so cute," interviewees remembered, but he was also, they admitted, a "cheat." Brandon stole ATM cards and forged checks, including one that paid for an engagement ring he bought for Gina, who broke up with him when she discovered Brandon had used her credit card to buy the gem—forging Gina's name in the same way, the media was quick to mention, Brandon forged his sex, showing the same cavalier disregard for private property as he did for private parts.

When push came to shove, the guy who knew just what a girl wanted, would often explain to his paramours that he was a "hermaphrodite" or had just begun to undergo the process of a sex-change operation, but there was little evidence in the history of Brandon's own self-formation that his "sexual identity crisis" was in fact a crisis or that his dysphoria was anything but euphoric. Brandon liked being a man and seducing girls, and he adamantly refused to have any truck with lesbians.

---

14   For the one-body-one-sex rule, see generally Alice D. Dreger, *Hermaphrodites and the Medical Invention of Sex* (Cambridge, MA: Harvard University Press, 1998); also Jeffrey Eugenides's novel *Middlesex* (New York: Farrar, Straus, and Giroux, 2002) broaches this very issue.

15   Some working definitions: *intersex* refers to a variation in sexual development attributable to anatomical, gonadal, or chromosomal atypicality, occurring in approximately one in every 1,500 individuals in some form. A *transsexual* is a person of one sex who identifies emotionally and psychologically with the other and often undertakes surgical or hormonal methods to accomplish a sex transition. *Transgender* is a signifier that applies to individuals or groups whose behavior varies from culturally conventional gender roles. As Butler and others have shown, these prevalent forms of sexual difference challenge the carefully guarded binary of sex. Brandon referred to himself as a hermaphrodite (intersexed), but there is no evidence of that variation.

His actions soon drew attention from the normalizing institutions of law, medicine, and psychology. After dropping out of high school and getting arrested, Brandon—like many queer and trans youth—tried to commit suicide. He swallowed a bottle of antibiotics and was hospitalized, diagnosed by psychologists as a "transsexual with a personality disorder." Discovering the truth about Brandon's sexuality, psychiatry branded him "disordered" because his birth sex and gender identity were not aligned.[16]

At first Brandon appeared to resist his psychiatric diagnosis. He avoided therapy, refused to avail himself of queer support services in Lincoln, and took no serious steps toward the operation that might or might not "solve" what he was told was his problem—even if he could afford it. Instead, Brandon continued his Don-Juan romp through a set of roller-skating girls who fell for long kisses and a dozen roses even if the flowers had been lifted from an unsuspecting florist. Convicted of forgery in March 1992, and put on probation for 18 months, Brandon broke parole often enough that a statewide warrant for his arrest was issued in the fall of 1993. Feeling the heat, Brandon left Lincoln, ending up in Falls City, a small town in southeastern Nebraska where he met Lisa Lambert, who admitted in interviews that she had had sexual intercourse with Brandon. (Lisa was changed to Candace in Peirce's film for—aptly enough—legal reasons.) Lisa was paying $150 a month for a little clapboard in Humboldt, a smaller hamlet outside Falls City where Lisa's new lover initially stayed.

In December, Brandon met Lana Tisdel—described in *The New Yorker* by John Gregory Dunne as a "femme fatale with a fitful sex-drive," a "Falls City itch that every local stud at loose ends felt impelled to scratch."[17] Dunne's tony prose—alliterative, allusory, and parodic—points to one of the crucial paradoxes that is central to this transgendered story. By casting Lana Tisdel as Lana Turner in his "cinematic" version of the story, Dunne does Lana as an itch, Brandon as a would-be stud—referencing a heterosexual paradigm as a way of fitting the history into a long line of Western outlaw legends like the James Brothers and Bonny and Clyde. Peirce in her feature film would also turn Brandon into a Hollywood Brando, slotting her film into the coded genres of the Western and love tragedy.[18] Yet much of the heterosexualization in these accounts serves not as an erasure of an "actual" queer or trans subjectivity but as an attempted depiction of Brandon's desire to be

---

16 Institutional dividing practice assumes first, that for those who are "ordered" gender is never in conflict with sex and secondly, that the categories of gender and sex are stable and objective—assumptions that largely ignore the innumerable variations on version of masculine and feminine gender as well as the variety of anatomical and biological variations among sexed subjects (see Kate Bornstein, *Gender Outlaw: On Men, Women and the Rest of Us* [New York: Vintage, 1995]).

17 Dunne 53.

18 See Pidduck.

recognized as a man.[19] For many male trans subjects, including probably Brandon Teena, masculine subjectivity is neither a closet, nor a form of passing, nor a performance; it simply fits the way they understand themselves in the world.

As Brandon began to fit into Lana's world, he met Linda Gutierres, Lana's divorced and alcoholic mother, who used her Falls City tract home as a crash pad for an assortment of party-downers, including her ex-con friends John Lotter and Tom Nissen. A young Lana had written to John in lock-up, and he grew particularly protective of her. Lisa, Lana, John, Tom, Linda, and Brandon drank a lot of beer together in December 1993, though according to Lotter, Brandon's gender was never a topic of conversation. Everybody assumed he was a guy in spite of his small hands and baby face, in spite of some *ex post facto* second thoughts. Tellingly, the intervention of legal process became the catalyst for the eventual discovery or, to use Aristotle's term, recognition of the true story of Brandon's sexuality, when, in attempt to make bail on a Minor in Possession citation, Teena Rae Brandon found himself in an orange unisex jumpsuit on the women's side of the prison for violating parole. The local newspaper announced the imprisonment of the female fugitive, publishing police arrests as a matter of community interest. Brandon had violated parole for conviction of the crime of forgery, but his remission into the prison system revealed that he had violated another form of parole—a temporary release from the surveillance of the law and its enforcement of gender divisions based on anatomy.

Lana visited Brandon in the women's section of the jail, asked for no explanation, and with the help of Tom Nissen and a blank check she got from her father for a new perm, made bail for her boyfriend. Once released, Brandon stayed with Nissen, a short ruby-lipped young man with fine features and a tapered haircut that ended in a bugger's grip. Nissen liked to burn things, having dabbled in arson and white supremacy movements. Shortly after Brandon's release, a Christmas Eve party among the usual suspects led to curiosity about the anatomy of the new kid in town. Lotter and Nissen wanted to know *what* Brandon was. They pantsed him and made Lana look directly at her boyfriend's vagina. Later that night they drove Brandon out of town and raped him vaginally and anally, angry that they had been duped by this "freak," as they called him.

The following day, Brandon filed a crime report with the Richardson County sheriff, but after examination, the nurse scratched out the previously "male" box and marked the "female" one. An interview with the victim by Sherriff Laux was described as "re-rape" by a "salacious, accusatory, derogatory" policeman, who in his defense claimed he was just trying to find out the truth about Brandon's sexuality. Sherriff Laux's "interview," as we shall see, demonstrated how the extraction of knowledge often functions as a violent and powerful tool of branding. This "criminalization" of the queer victim, caught on audiotape, captures the reality

---

19   Jay Prosser makes clear that the trans subject, like many intersex individuals, do not understand themselves as queer in any way (see Jay Prosser, *Second Skins: The Body Narratives of Transsexuality* [New York: Columbia University Press, 1999]).

of the negative social ethos of the state, to use Boal's term, a system of justice that projects its own flaws on to those who transgress its violently maintained standards of gender conformity—standards supported by ideological divisions.

On December 28, 1993, police records show that Lotter and Nissen were examined by the police but not arrested, in spite of the positive results of the rape kit. Prosecutors later claimed that the two men denied they had committed the sexual assault and reminded the police that Brandon was an inveterate liar. They were released on their own recognizance, and Brandon, who knew the men would come after him for reporting the rape, sought refuge at Lisa Lambert's house in Humboldt, deciding not to return to Lincoln or take off to other parts. Why didn't Brandon flee? Why did Lana and her mother, who had urged Brandon to report the rape, tell Nissen and Lotter where Brandon was hiding out on New Year's Eve? Why did they not alert Brandon when they knew the two men were on their way to Lisa's house? Had the objectification and designation of Brandon's sex by the law somehow broken a chink in the armor of Lana's imaginary love relation; had she suddenly become imprisoned by the specter of being known as a lesbian in Falls City, the willing lover of this female man—this hermaphrodite, this "it" as Lana's mother and Sheriff Laux called Brandon?

The next archival event in this tragedy was a report of a triple homicide on December 31 in the remote farmhouse south of Hill City. Together with Lisa Lambert and Philip DeVine, a 22-year-old African American Job Corps worker on vacation (who was excised from Peirce's film), police found the body of the stabbed and shot Teena Rae Brandon, alias Brandon Teena alias Charles Brayman—the body of a female dressed in male clothing. Brandon's gender transgression had followed him to the grave. The homicide indictment came to court in 1995. After a trial attended by queer and trans activists (including Kate Bornstein), Tom Nissen was convicted of one count of murder one and two counts of second-degree homicide. He later turned state's evidence against John Lotter, testifying that John had done the actual shooting and he had just stabbed Brandon after he was shot. Nissen's testimony led to the conviction of Lotter for first-degree murder, and Lotter presently sits on death row in Nebraska, while Nissen serves consecutive life sentences in the Lincoln Correctional Center.[20]

By the time of Lotter's trial, Aphrodite Jones had convinced most of the principals in the case to sign exclusive contracts for interviews and a share in the film rights. In 1996, Pocket Books came out with *All S/he Wanted*, the cover leader stating, "Brandon Teena: the girl who became a boy but paid the ultimate price." Criminal legal discourse now shared the stage with cultural production, both engaging similar dramatic vectors. Brandon had paid a tragic "price" for refusing to accept the arbitrary isomorphism of sex and gender, and his murderers had taken justice into their own hands, discovering the truth about Brandon's sex and redressing the breach that this rebellion against anatomy had produced. Now for

---

20   John Lotter remains on death row in Tecumseh awaiting the appeal of his capital punishment sentence.

only $6.99, America could find out the truth about Brandon's sex and participate cathartically in this story of reversal of fortune and recognition of the truth about sexuality. Three years after his death, Brandon had become a commodity, a fetish whose form (gender outlaw, transsexual menace, and hate-crimes victim) belied the particulars of his own homophobia, economic desperation, reckless romanticism, and heterocentricity.

Wrongful Death

JoAnn Brandon's legal action against the Falls City police department in Richardson County began in 1994, with a claim filed under the Political Subdivisions Tort Claims Act, an administrative law that protects sovereign immunity but allows a discretionary redress of claims.[21] JoAnn's action against the county and Sherriff Charles B. Laux alleged negligent failure to protect her deceased child and intentional infliction of emotional distress as a result of Laux's December 25, 1993 interview, an audiotape of which is part of Muska and Olafsdottir's award-winning 1998 documentary *The Brandon Teena Story*. JoAnn's initial claim was sparked in part by the reception given Tammy Schweitzer, Brandon's sister, when she arrived at the station to retrieve Brandon's clothes after the murder. Laux called Schweitzer a "bitch" and asked her "what kind of sister did [you] have?" (*Brandon* 646).

After the county let the six-month response period under the Tort Claims Act expire without reply, Brandon's mother brought a wrongful death action in district court. The lower court sustained the county's demurrer on the grounds that the government was immune from liability for failure to protect individual citizens from harm by criminal conduct. The Nebraska Supreme Court overruled the lower court, stating that given a sufficient evidentiary base, the plaintiffs could show that immunity was waived by a "special relationship" created between Brandon and the county "when Brandon went to law enforcement official and offered to testify and aid in the prosecution of Lotter and Nissen."[22]

The case remanded to the district court, JoAnn amended her complaint and the action went to trial in front of a judge instead of a jury on September 22, 1999, the same year of the release of the Muska documentary at Berlin and Vancouver film festivals. The audiotape of Laux's interview of Brandon on Christmas Day 1993, after a medical examination found evidence of sexual penetration, had become part of both the trial transcript and the documentary's screenplay. Deputy Tom Olberding conducted the initial interview with Sherriff Laux present, but Laux later took over the inquiry himself. His line of questioning of the recent rape victim included such queries as, "After they pulled your pants down and seen you was a girl, what did he do? Did he fondle you any?" (642). When Brandon said they had not, Laux followed up: "I can't believe that if he pulled your pants

---

21   *Brandon v. County of Richardson* 261 Neb. 636 at 646–647 (2001).
22   *Brandon v. County of Richardson* 252 Neb. 839, 566 N.W.2d 776 (1997).

down and you are a female that he didn't stick his hand in you or his finger in you." Laux's salacious exam proceeded unimpeded: "So they tried sinking it in your vagina?" he asked. "So then after he couldn't stick it in your vagina he stuck it in your box or in your buttocks, is that right? Did he tell you anything about this is how they do it in the penitentiary?" "Was he enjoying it, did he think it was funny?" Laux's crude prurience, caught on audiotape, indicates the way the discretionary license of criminal procedure allows law officers to participate in the erotics of interrogation, a "line of penetration" through examination that not only wills to know but derives pleasure in exercising that will. Laux's verbal "re-rape"—his intercourse with Brandon—derives its force from a certainty about Brandon's female gender, a truth that he impinges with a aggressive insistence, a truth derived from his own mythology about sexual practice.

Later Laux repeatedly asked Brandon, "Why do you run around with girls instead of guys beings [*sic*] you're a girl yourself? Why do you make girls think you're a guy? The girls that don't know about you, thinks [*sic*] you are a guy." When Deputy Olberding interrupted to tell Brandon he did not have to answer these questions, Laux stated that he needed an "answer" for the upcoming courtroom proceeding. Brandon whispered that he had a "sexual identity crisis" in response to Laux's examination, tentatively adopting the psychiatric "diagnosis" which had labeled him "disordered," but the sheriff, unsatisfied, continued to demand an explanation for "her" behavior which the traumatized Brandon said he could not "even talk about" (644).

Laux's equation of trans identity with deception and imposture effectively turned the victim into the accused, according to one investigator who testified at the trial (648). Like many rape victims, Brandon under this scenario is assumed to have provoked his reversal of fortune, not in this case because of some supposed feminine allure but because of the exact opposite—a masculinity that transgresses gender boundaries and threatens to usurp masculine power, as Judith Halberstam has pointed out.[23] In this context, Brandon's tragic flaw becomes a failure to conform to the regulatory isomorphism of gender and anatomy, a social deviance that invites punishment from both the legal and extra-legal forces of normativity. Brandon was destined for the coercion of tragedy.

On December 6, 1999, the district court issued its "Memorandum Finding" in the case, determining the county did have a duty to protect Brandon once he went to the police and agreed to testify against his assailants. The court awarded $6,223.20 in economic and $80,000 dollars in noneconomic damages to JoAnn for Brandon's "pre-death pain and suffering" (652). The judge, however, found Brandon one percent negligent himself, though court did not state how Brandon's conduct was unreasonable. Additionally Judge Coady reduced the negligence award against the county by 85 percent, ruling that Lotter and Nissen's own intentional torts were contributorily responsible for the damage. On the intentional infliction of emotional distress count, the district court denied recovery, finding

---

23   Halberstam 66–67.

that Laux's conduct was "not extreme and outrageous" and that there was a failure to prove that Brandon had suffered as a result of the sheriff's "locker room" language.

The district court's determination that Laux's conduct was not outrageous had the ironic effect of producing outrage nationally, resulting in a series of amicus briefs on appeal from the likes of the Lambda Legal Defense Fund, the ACLU, and the Nebraska Domestic Violence Assault Coalition. Two of the lower court's findings indicate the way queer subjectivity in general and in this case the reluctant trans subject (who is thrust under the queer umbrella) enters the socio-legal arena already indicted for a social transgression, a status that makes him from the outset a de facto outlaw, who is in effect asking for punishment. The district court judge's arbitrary finding that Brandon was one percent negligent *without explanation* speaks directly to the presumptive unreasonableness of the queer subject—as if the thing spoke for itself (or, to invoke another legal doctrine, *res ipsa loquitur*). Though the Supreme Court was quick to overturn this finding of Brandon's comparative negligence—the high court unable to ascertain how Brandon either failed to protect himself from injury or in some way conducted himself in a manner that contributed to his injuries—the court made no determination whether or not Brandon's transgender conduct alone served as the lower court's motivation for its finding.[24]

If the Nebraska Supreme Court avoided the legal question whether as a matter of law transgender identity could in itself be considered unreasonable for purposes of tort law, the higher court did take the trial judge to task for finding that the intentional assaults of Lotter and Nissen could somehow mitigate the misfeasance of the county for failure to protect. "[I]t would be irrational to allow a party who negligently fails to discharge a duty to protect to reduce its liability because there is an intervening intentional tort when the intervening intentional tort is exactly what the negligent party had a duty to protect against," the court wrote, citing its own precedent, as well as the Restatement of Torts (655). The trial court's error in this regard was not just egregious but also obvious and fundamental. Lotter and Nissen were the very individuals whose dangerous presence on the streets gave rise to the police department's duty to protect their victim; that the district court would have failed to understand legally that the murderers' action could not lessen the police's negligence is highly unlikely. This blatant error speaks directly to the way legal process often partakes in the methodology of what Boal calls tragic coercion, in this case manifesting as the court's participation in the transphobic

---

24   There was evidence that Brandon failed to return to the police department for a second interview between December 25 and New Year's Eve, but there was also testimony that he saw Lotter and Nissen outside the station as he approached and left. There was also some question about why Brandon did not leave the county after the incident, but JoAnn testified that Brandon did not want to return to Lincoln and jeopardize his mother. He was also allegedly unaware the Lotter and Nissen knew where Lisa Lambert lived (see Cooper 646, 666–667).

continuum. Whether consciously or not, the county and the district court system—as repositories of justice and social normativity—effectively displaced their own complicity in Brandon's murder on to the individual perpetrators of the crime, Nissen and Lotter, allowing the outlaws to enact, stage, and carry out the necessary justice that would return the community to a state of gender normativity. By ascribing 85 percent of the blame for Brandon's harm to the violence of the uncontrollable outlaws, the law was able to displace its own complicity on to the "villains" while maintaining the "integrity" of its own more quiescent forms of correction—through police interrogation, government immunity, and findings of facts that transferred justice from the community to a higher tribunal like the Nebraska Supreme Court, thereby washing its hands of responsibility for the higher court's correction.[25]

In handing down his decision to a brazen district court, Chief Judge Hendry found as a matter of law that Sheriff Laux's conduct was extreme and outrageous for purposes of infliction of emotional distress. He also ordered the court not to reduce the damage award of $80,000 for pre-death pain and suffering. His pointed decision reflects the degree to which an arguably obtuse district court remains entrenched in the social ethos of the community, one which was willing to endure this reprimand as a way of maintaining its solidarity with community standards of gender conformity. Under orders from superiors, in October 2001, District Court Judge Orville Coady awarded JoAnn Brandon an additional $12,000 dollars in damages for wrongful death and infliction of emotional distress, adding to the $80,000 the Supreme Court had reinstated.

The Nebraska Supreme Court's decision overturning Judge Coady's finding came down in 2001, well after the nationwide release of *The Brandon Teena Story* (1998) and *Boys Don't Cry* (1999), films that brought attention to Falls City in particular and transgender identity in general. Muska and Oláfsdottir spent four years making their documentary, attending both murder trials and at one point spending six weeks in the town. Both films shine a national spotlight on the events surrounding Brandon's death, giving rise not only to the amicus briefs filed on behalf of the plaintiff JoAnn Brandon on appeal, but also presenting a raw portrait of Richardson County and its inhabitants. In an interview in *Salon*, the New York documentarians told journalist Jennie Yabroff that they discovered that the people of Falls City just wanted to put the crime behind them. "In their eyes the murderers

---

25 Part of the displacement on to Nissen (who recanted his claim that he did not pull the trigger in 2007) and Lotter (who is still on death row) conveniently condenses social violence within the parameters of two scapegoated males, whose own histories of prison abuse and rape are largely ignored in legal and cinematic versions of the story, though the documentary gives some insight into their lives. As Carol Siegel states, "the film's [*Boys Don't Cry*] insistence that they struck out at Teena [*sic*] in a gesture of gender policing rather than as part of a perpetuation of the cycle of abuse within masculinity, in which they themselves were trapped, forecloses any useful examining of how and why masculinity in our time is so vexed" ("Curing Boys Don't Cry," *Genders* 37 [2003]: 25).

were nice guys," Muska stated, and, unlike Peirce's later dramatic film, *The Brandon Teena Case* spends considerable time talking directly to the defendants along with other inmates.[26] Given the amount of head-time the documentary gives to the prisoners and their families (especially Lotter's), *The Brandon Teena Story*, with its country and western soundtrack, reminds us of Boal's counter-intuitive observation that tragic empathy in Westerns often resides with the antagonists, those "bad guys" whom the audience really pities and fears, in part because these "homeboys" serve the Aristotelian purpose of "purging all the spectator's aggressive tendencies."[27] Like Henderson and McKinney in the Shepard case, these Falls City originals are put into context in Muska's film, understood as "down and out" ex-felons (probably sexually abused in prison), pitied as children of broken homes, as young men labeled "troublemakers" from the very first time they broke the law. When we learn from Lotter that he was not able "to get it up" during the rape and that Nissen turned state's evidence against him in order to receive life instead of the death penalty, Lottter arguably emerges as Boal's anti-hero, the man destined to set the record straight once Brandon's deception was revealed.

Muska's documentary intersperses interviews of the long-haired, big-eared Lotter and the eye-shifting Nissen with transcripts from the "extreme and outrageous" audiotape of Laux's examination of "it," as he later referred to Brandon. During the tape of the questioning, a black and white photo of the husky and bearded Laux appears in the upper corner of the screen while a photo of a reclining Brandon is situated at the bottom (see Figure 3.1). The audiotape of the interview, including both voices, provides the screenplay as the transcript is typed out beside the framed photos of Brandon and Laux. This format occurs three times during the documentary's unfolding of the events surrounding December 25, 1993, the faint nondiegetic soundtrack also playing in one slowed-down version. Brandon seems strikingly resilient, answering Laux's questions about Lotter's penis and her sex life with numbed objectivity. He even protests when Laux broaches the subject of Brandon's transgenderism. "I don't see why that is important," Brandon tells him. The *mise-en-scène* of these visualized transcripts includes a black background and crude typewriter lettering that duplicates the voice—imitating the work of a court reporter. Laux's prying questions are literally and figuratively domineering, skeptical, and dismissive in ways that make his demeaning words even more threatening than the "explanations" that the inmates Lotter and Nissen give to the documentary's interviewers, ironically transferring our pity to the more humanized prisoners.

The Brandon Teena Story by no stretch of the imagination, however, absolves the murderers of their violent action, though it does make an effort to understand

---

26   Peter Sarsgaard, who played Lotter in Peirce's *Boys*, wanted his character to "be likeable, sympathetic even," if not "charismatic." www.angelfire.com/film/petersarsgaard/ interview.html, 2003.

27   Augusto Boal, *Theatre of the Opressed*, trans. Charles A. and Maria-Odilia Leal McBride (New York: Theatre Communications Group, 1985), 47.

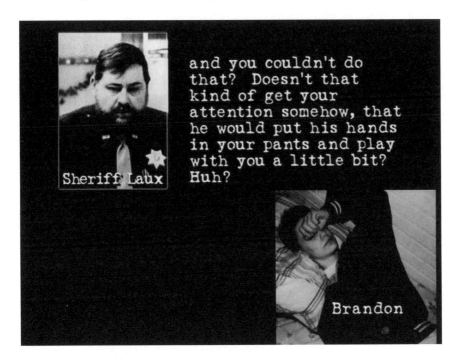

Figure 3.1   Still from *The Brandon Teena Story*

Source: Courtesy of Bless Bless Productions

them. Part of this humanization involves explaining the motivation behind their will to know the truth about Brandon. "It wasn't until everybody *started knowing* that Brandon was, underneath his clothes, a female," the filmmakers tell Yabroff, "that the homophobia came in to play, because then that meant [the girls who dated Brandon] were lesbians" (italics mine).[28] Time and again, the film and its makers mention Brandon's deception, his "lying," as the major concern of Falls City residents, even though Muska states that almost everyone in the town harbored his or her own lie or two. Underneath the anger about Brandon's "deception" was, in the filmmakers' view, a "homophobia" that may have belied Brandon's sense of himself as heterosexual but could not stop the townspeople from finding out "the truth" that was their truth (Falls City's truth, Main Street's truth)— the anatomical truth that Lotter and Nissen were finally fated to uncover, namely that Brandon was *really a woman* corrupting Falls City girls like Lisa and Lana, turning them into *unwitting* lesbians. "Once the town of Falls City found out that he was a

---

28   Jennie Yabroff, "TransAmerica," www.salon.com/entertainment/movies/int/1999/02/25int.html.

she, the whole town went ballistic," Leslie Tisdel (Lana's sister) told reporters.[29] Lotter and Nissen—in spite of their own bugger tails, ruby lips, and history of imprisonment—emerge in this documentary as the unlikely and unlucky enforcers of the social balance, a heteronormative standard that required a rooting out of the "homosexual agenda."

The L Word: Libel and Lesbianism in Peirce's Biopic

Critical queer studies requires a frank assessment of the contradictions that exist within the range of positions along the spectrum sexual minorities inhabit. Under the acronymic umbrella LGBTIQ, orientations and categorizations not only differ but also clash at the far end of the rainbow. Queer subjectivity, dedicated to resisting identitarian positions, necessarily critiques the out and proud stances of gays and lesbians, while transgendered, transsexual, and intersexed subjects, as we have noted, often resent being touted for making gender trouble, and in many cases are, if not homophobic like Brandon Teena, at least not prepared to share the stage with lesbians and gay men. Brandon was no exception. He could not stand being touched by men, and yet he refused to associate with lesbians. His lover Lana Tisdel brought a lawsuit for defamation of character when Kimberly Peirce's biopic, *Boys Don't Cry*, suggested that Lana was willing to have sex with Brandon even after she became fully aware of Brandon's female anatomy. These individual responses to public interpellation, exemplified by Lana's and Brandon's attitudes, indicate that the sexual minority coalition, though fraught with internal antinomies, has as its common ground a socio-legal opprobrium that attaches to anyone who deviates from regulatory regimes of gender, sex, and sexual orientation. While some are born queer and some achieve queerness, most of us, to borrow Shakespeare's adage, have queerness thrust upon us—an imposition that requires a greater attention among queer critics.

In 1999, Lana Tisdel filed suit in a Los Angeles federal court through her attorney Charles Coate, alleging that defendants Kimberly Peirce and Fox Searchlight invaded her privacy and used her name and likeness in *Boys Don't Cry* without her authorization. The complaint sought an injunction against distribution of the film and was settled for an undisclosed amount in March of 2000, shortly before the Academy Awards ceremony in which Chloe Sevigny was nominated for Best Supporting Actress in her portrayal of Lana. *Tisdel v. Fox* alleged, among other things, that Lana's "loss of reputation" continued to bring her "humiliation, embarrassment, hurt feelings, mental anguish and suffering." Besides the skanky portrayal of Lana as "white trash," the complaint claims damage as a result of the film's depiction of Lana having sex with Brandon after it was determined that he

---

29   Eric Harrison, "A Filmmaker Fictionalizes to Get at Difficult Truths," *Los Angeles Times* (February 6, 2000), http://articles.latimes.com/2000/feb/07/entertainment/ca-61809.

was "anatomically and chromosomally" female, causing Lana to be scorned in her community as "a lesbian who did nothing to stop the murder."[30]

Peirce's film portrays Brandon and Lana having sex on New Year's Eve at the location of the murder before Nissen and Lotter arrive, even though police reports did not put Tisdel at the scene of the crime and Nissen later retracted his testimony that Lana was present. In defense of her sex scenes—which Peirce had to edit to prevent the MPAA (Motion Picture Association of America) from rating her film NC-17 instead of R—the director reminded reporters she had "spent five years bringing Lana to the screen in a way people could love."[31] "Somebody got to her," Peirce speculated about Lana and her civil action. Tisdel had, after all, already signed a release, and the story was by that point in the public domain. Even though Peirce flew Lana out to London to see the film before its debut, Tisdel did not drop the lawsuit, pursuing it through her attorney until a settlement legally acknowledged Lana's damages for being depicted as, among other things, a lesbian. Later, in discussing the question of cinematic authenticity in relation to a recent rash of Hollywood biopics, Peirce staunchly maintains that "factual accuracy should never be the goal of art," and that the power of film comes from "the value of myth, of dreams, to illuminate truth, in art as well as life."[32]

Peirce's insistence on the autonomy of fiction even when it employs history joins a controversy that began at least as far back as Shakespeare's vilification of Richard III and cinematic depictions of Oscar Wilde, yet the popularity of her *Boys*, bought for five million dollars by Fox after its entry in the Sundance Festival, produced a national reaction that not only led to new calls for hate-crime legislation but also spotlighted the Falls City community in a way that rendered art and life inseparable, suddenly treating the mirror of Peirce's camera *as* nature. People wanted to know the truth about Brandon and Lana, and they wanted to know if Peirce's fictional film was faithful to that "truth."[33] In fact, Brandon Teena's followers demanded it. They created websites, compared Peirce's film to the documentary, measured it against interviews and *All S/he Wanted*, instating a standard of fidelity to reality that brought lawsuits and critique. Peirce had betrayed Brandon's transgender identity by creating a lesbian love scene; she had ignored race by dropping Philip DeVine from her film.[34] Her fictional film was not just *based on* fact; through the sheer magnitude of its dissemination it had come to *replace* the facts themselves.

---

30   Philippa Hawker, "Seeing Doubles," *The Age* (March 1, 2002), www.theage.com.au/articles/2002/03/01/1014704987942.html.

31   Leigh 20.

32   Harrison.

33   In film adaptation of literature, the myth of fidelity assumes that the value of a cinema is dependent on its accurate depiction of the details of the novel. In this case, the measure of fidelity came from Brandon's history.

34   Halberstam 89 ("Peirce suddenly and catastrophically divests her character of his transgender look and converts it to a lesbian and therefore female gaze"); on race see Brody.

As Philippa Hawkins states in an article about biopics, unlike public figures "private individuals such as Tisdel ... who get caught up in biopic narratives, find that their lives are being made into history. The film converts into fact, and there are no alternative versions in circulation."[35] Tisdel's lawsuit, no matter how groundless legally, points to the material effects of fictions like Peirce's film, effects which include not just defamation actions in court, but the creation of revisionary histories which in turn have the potential to shift social viewpoints in ways similar to the coercive force of the law itself. Peirce sought to turn Brandon's life into a love story with an "emotional truth" the audience could understand, and through that understanding, discover the "truth" of Brandon's transgender desire. Her aesthetics echo those of the Renaissance, in which artists sought not to replicate reality but to represent the essence of it. Yet the public—in Falls City, in academia, in courts, and in the media—wanted their truth, one that did not necessarily give credence to Peirce's Romeo and Julietization of this two-week affair between Brandon Teena and Lana Tisdel.

Ironically, both Tisdel's lawsuit and Halberstam's extensive analysis of the case in her *Queer Time and Place* share this displeasure with the film's romantic conclusion. While Halberstam sees the lesbian love scene as a sell-out of the transgender gaze the film had cultivated up to that point, Lana's defamation suit treats Brandon's gender passing as the means by which the deceived Lana maintained her heterosexual reputation and avoided the societal homophobia that was triggered once Lana and others discovered the truth about Brandon's anatomy and were no longer victims of Brandon's transgender "fraud."[36] As long as Lana could contend that she believed she was in a heterosexual relationship, she was free from the "humiliation" that her complaint alleges she suddenly experienced once *she discovered of the truth about Brandon's sex*. As soon as Lana is portrayed, even in a fictional cinematic rendering, as aware of that "truth," she falls into the scorned position of the lesbian, suffering damages for loss of reputation in a community of reasonable men and women who equate same-sex love with mental anguish and suffering. Though truth is a defense to libel and in this case Lana's sexual behavior was not in dispute, the film was allegedly defamatory because it falsely portrayed Lana of having sex with Lana *after she knew the truth* about her lover's anatomy, making the tort tantamount to intentional imposition of lesbianism. The distribution of *Boys Don't Cry*, her attorney maintained, necessarily interpellated Lana into a legal status that is actionable on its face as a civil wrong. Analogous in

---

35   Hawker, "Seeing Doubles."

36   Part of Lana's civil suit against Fox also claimed invasion of privacy, a tort similar but distinct from defamation. As Kendall Thomas and others have argued, claims to a right to privacy in regard to sexual orientation, like that of Lana Tisdel, have the effect of enshrining an anti-queer animus in the social arena by bolstering a presumption that homosexual behavior—whether true or not—is sufficiently egregious to warrant damage for loss of reputation (see Kendall Thomas, "Beyond the Privacy Principle," 92:6 *Columbia Law Review* 1431–1516 [October 1992]).

some ways to Henderson and McKinney's use of the homosexual panic defense, Lana and her lawyer found a way to capitalize upon the law's inscription of the tragic homosexual paradigm. The film's false accusation of lesbianism, even in a fictionalized romantic love story, carried with it an opportunity to collect material damages for what Lana's lawyer knew was the crime that dare not speak (or in this case acknowledge) its name.

If Tisdel's opportunistic suit builds on an ideology of homophobia embedded in the law, it nonetheless evinces one of the tensions that inhabit the array of positions within the LGBTIQ penumbra. Lana's lawyers, after all, were not claiming that their client's initial ignorance of Brandon's anatomy was damaging to her reputation; they were not arguing that her continued use of the male pronoun to describe her lover after Nissen stripped Brandon in the bathroom necessarily impugned their client's reputation. Their argument rests on a clear division between a willing hetero misrecognition, as Halberstam calls it, and a change in Lana's *cognition* that suddenly crossed the line into the otherness of homosex.[37] From one perspective even the sex scenes in the film that take place *before* Brandon lands on the women's side of the prison are played ambiguously, as Lana outside the factory, for example, looks into Brandon's shirt with uncertainty. What the end of the film does, however, is unclothe both the lovers—in a moment of anatomical truth that Peirce presents as part of an ongoing revelation between the two lovers, one that transcends anatomy and gender. The filmmaker states:

> I interviewed a number of butch lesbians and pre-op transsexuals about their histories, because I wanted to understand why they dressed as boys. And I started seeing wonderful divisions within the queer community where you get transsexuals who pass as boys to align their bodies with their true selves and butch lesbians who pass as performance. I learned Brandon was all that and neither, and what I didn't want to do was characterise him in any way he wouldn't have characterised himself. I wanted to get in touch with Brandon and his desire.[38]

But Peirce's attempt to abrade the trans categories—her desire to "queer" Brandon through non-characterization—had the boomerang effect, at the end of her film, of re-characterizing him—at least in the eyes of Tisdel and Halberstam—turning Brandon into a woman and a willing lesbian, Lana into a true lover of women. While for Halberstam what is co-opted in this scene is the success of Brandon's transgenderism and for Tisdel what is undermined is Lana's reputation as a heterosexual, both understand the end of the film as a reinstatement of dividing practices based on sexual orientation; both react to Peirce's final lesbian love scene in a way that renders them strangely homophobic bedfellows.

---

37   Halberstam 89.
38   Peirce in Leigh 18.

Foucault cites what he calls "dividing practices" as one of the epistemological modes through which "human beings are made into subjects."[39] Through these methods of medical or social classification, "the subject is objectified through a process of division either within himself of from others," a division that uses the power of knowledge to control and compartmentalize the subject.[40] Though Foucault argues that these techniques of subjectification belong increasingly to the realm of the social sciences and not the law, in the case of *Boys Don't Cry* a form of cultural representation (the biopic) appears to function as a technique of manipulation, or, if you will, a way of classifying Brandon and Lana which shifts their perceived sex/ gender status from a woman in love with a (transgendered) man to a woman in love with woman (or more precisely, with a transgendered man who reveals his anatomy to his lover). These classifications have material effects on the social subject— ones that run the gamut from legal damages for "humiliation" in the community to what Halberstam calls a failure to maintain a "nonfetishistic mode of seeing the transgender body." Peirce's film, according to Halberstam, replaces that mode with "a tired humanist narrative" of two lesbians in love who become victims of a "kind of homosexual panic" that turns them into tragic subjects.[41]

Halberstam sees the genius of Peirce's film in her early depiction of a female man who has the ability to "hijack the male and female gazes, and replace them surreptitiously with transgendered modes of looking and queer forms of visual pleasure" (83). From this critic's perspective, *Boys Don't Cry* revises Mulvey's famous formula for visual pleasure in film as dependent on a male gaze that idealizes and domesticates the female, thereby allowing the audience to idealize and narrativize by means of a look from a transgendered subject, through a queer gaze that "reveals the ideological content of the male and female gazes" and "disarms, temporarily, the compulsory heterosexuality of the romance genre" (86). While it is unclear how exactly this disarming takes place, part of what Halberstam sees in the film is a combination of the usurpation of the male gaze by the transgendered (f to m) subject (what she calls a "suturing") but also a concomitant empowerment of Lana's female gaze. "The transgender subject [is] dependent on the recognition of a woman," one who recognizes the incompleteness of the male subject but accepts it anyway, in a "power sharing" that presumably questions rigid gendered modes of viewing as proposed by Mulvey.

For Halberstam, the transgender look, with its mobile and queer positioning, is catastrophically undermined by the sex scene that takes place in the shed before the murder, when "the double vision of the transgender subject gives way to the universal vision of humanism; the transgender man and his lover become lesbians, and the murder seems to be simply the outcome of a vicious homophobic rage" (91). For Halberstam, Peirce displays a "lack of nerve" that leads her to

---

39   Paul Rabinow, "Introduction," *The Foucault Reader* (New York: Pantheon Books, 1984), 7–8.

40   Rabinow 8.

41   Halberstam 92, 90, 91.

conclude the film with "a humanist scene of love conquers all" (91). Once the "naked embodiment" replaces the "credible masculinity" of Brandon as man, the true female subject appears before "the judge and jury"—the cinematic audience. Halberstam's exercised argument attempts to draw a clear dividing line between the multidimensionality of the queer gaze at work before the final sex scene and the return to a dominant homophobic male gaze once the two "women" make love. Yet this critic's romanticization of the "shared power" between Brandon and Lana before the exposure of Brandon belies a dynamic of considerable inconsistency between the two lovers from the outset of the film. How can Brandon's earlier careful, fully dressed seduction of Lana, replete with her willful misrecognition, fall into the "beautiful, desirable, and special relation" that Halberstam ascribes to their fantasy? (89). And is not Halberstam's sanguine view of the "queer" mobility of their transgender affair—a word that Brandon would, by the way, probably never adopt for himself—fraught with the same universal "humanism" that the critic ascribes to the filmmaker's final sex scene? If Peirce's scene clearly does in fact stage a move from a transgender affair to a lesbian liebestod—which, I think, may be worth re-considering—in what way can we possibly align a cinematic portrayal of sex between two women—heavily censored by the MPAA and grounds for a defamation lawsuit—as universal and humanist?

In discussing an interview with Peirce in which the filmmaker claims that Lana had told her about this last encounter, Halberstam decries Peirce's sudden commitment to "authenticity," tying Brandon's "humanity to a particular form of naked embodiment." But the critic's own argument is also based on an ascription of authenticity and accuracy—even humanity—to the earlier non-embodied relation between the two lovers. In many ways, Halberstam wants to exact her truth about the Brandon story just as Peirce has presented hers, but she comes to that truth, like Lana, by demanding that art live up to her version of the facts of life—facts that themselves are stitched with the fictions of narrative selection and epistemological standpoint.

Halberstam's belief that the unveiling of Brandon's anatomy in the film functions as a teleological revelation of an objective, realistic truth about the two characters—one that allows for the tragic homophobic denouement—not only overlooks the ambiguities of the film's full narrative but betrays the way anatomy does *not* necessarily function as destiny in the case of Brandon and Lana. Their relationship—a complex combination of misperception, fantasy, bodies, and genders—a configuration of subjectification and objectification—is not suddenly transformed by their "getting naked" in the final "sex" scene, especially since this scene actually situates Brandon in a "masculine" time and space, on an old couch in a darkened shed where the down-and-out Brandon hides the bruises on his face in a hoodie. The slow zoom into the dark aperture of the old white shed as the scene opens certainly adopts Lana's point of view as she approaches the man she loves, but the camera soon reverses angle when we get to the doorway and see Lana's body framed and backlit by the moon.

While Peirce's sequence engages in few of the formalistic elements—the blue filtering and time-last fast-forwarding—that characterize the cinematography of the film as a whole, this sequence has a careful admixture of two-shots and reverse angles that avoids producing a prominent point of view. Lana is clearly the seducer in this scene—femmed up with red nail polish, jewelry and long flowing hair—as she approaches the pale, and grimacing Brandon, asking him "can I sit by you?" and "do you hate me?" and remarking "you're so pretty," a comment that oddly contradicts the scowl on Brandon's pale and bruised face. Brandon is anything but "pretty" in this visually heterosexualized sequence. The cinematography insists on the continuance of Lana's imaginary fantasy, until the screenplay interrupts the girl/boy approach as Lana asks Brandon what "you were like" before all this. Lana wants to know if Brandon was "like her"—was he a "girl girl"? As a two-shot catches the lovers on the old couch, Brandon moves into a confessional mode that gives Halberstam fodder for her assessment. He was a "girl girl" then became a "boy girl" and then became a "jerk" who "felt right" being with Lana, who is nervous about "how to do it," now that she has been made to know her lover's anatomy.

This edited sex scene contains no frontal nudity except for a quick side shot of Lana putting on her jacket as she leaves to pack her things for Lincoln. (The frontal nudity that created trouble for Peirce from the MPAA remains in the earlier scene when a clothed Brandon brings a naked Lana to orgasm.) When in this final sex scene Lana removes Brandon's sweater, the camera shoots from an angle behind Brandon's back as we watch Lana watching Brandon's exposed chest, no longer bound.[42] The complicated camera angle of this scene has both figures in its medium shot, but the viewpoint is primarily Brandon's. We look with him at Lana looking at him, revealing his "true" anatomy, as low-volume organ music intersperses with diegetic crickets in the moonlight. Peirce's use of a double-exposure sequence provides insight into the way this scene is established to portray on the one hand the "figuring it out" of sex between "women" and on the other the "universalizing" love gesture that Peirce seeks to invoke in this reconciliation scene. Although the sequence works, like those in *Brokeback*, through the limited license of allowable Hollywood depiction of same-sex desire, the use of double exposure provides the film with its formalistic method of sequencing the unsequenceable. The slow move from shirt removal to higher angle shot of the two lovers on the couch allows the camera to superimpose the face of each figure on the other's body. First Lana's face appears imposed on Brandon's back, and then in the subsequent frame that superimposition is preserved along with an overlay of Brandon's face on Lana's body. This doubling and mirroring create a palimpsest, an imprint of self on other, one which is complicated but not determined by two anatomies that are similar by one standard of characterization (sex) but wholly different within the gender spectrum of that category, in so far as Lana is overly feminized in the scene, and Brandon, at least in dress, masculinized. As Warner has noted in his critique of homo-narcissism, the equation of homosexuality with narcissism mistakenly

---

42   Fox Searchlight owns the rights to *Boys Don't Cry* but requires permissions of the actors before granting the right to reproduce them. Hilary Swank was unwilling to allow these particular shots to be reproduced for this work.

assumes that two individuals with the same genitals are somehow the same.[43] The feminized Lana and masculinized Brandon in this scene bear out Warner's point. Though the girl/girl, boy/girl "right feel," as Brandon calls it, finds its momentary fit in the collapse of self and other in love-making, a strong anatomical difference continues to overlay this romantic merging even as the figures recognize their affinity with the inexact and multiple category of female. Peirce's fantasized breakdown of dividing practices in her depiction of the lovers' willingness to overlook the difference between transgender and lesbian sex, takes place, notably, in a lightless run-down shed, a hideout where Brandon is licking his wounds after the violent attack of Lotter and Nissen. If the scene buys into an *amor vincit omnia* ideology, it foregrounds that ideology through cinematographic formalism and an initial self-conscious cut to a romantically coded moon shot outside the shed. In this scene, the film seeks to capture a desire between two subjects that not only overcomes the categorizations that will lead to the "death of a couple of dykes" as Lotter puts it, but also shows how subjectivity can resist the imposition of sexual classification which the will to knowledge persistently implants on the social and psychological subject.

In the scenes that follow, Lana agrees, after their love-making, to leave Falls City with Brandon, return to Lincoln, and live happily ever after, but while Lana is packing, she suddenly gets cold feet. Brandon's hair looks different, she tells him, and though he tries to fix it, the arbitrary action of an unbrushed forelock comes to symbolize a closeted homosexual future for Lana, even if Brandon successfully passes. Lana declines to accompany him, and he accedes to her misgiving, telling her to come later. Lana, suffering from a moment of internalized homophobia, then tries to stop Lotter and Nissen but is forced to accompany them to the house where Brandon and Candace are murdered. The lesbian sex scene between the overly effeminized Lana and the bruised, sweat-shirted Brandon has produced not a "humanist narrative" but a story of deeply conflicted sexual experience, Lana recoiling finally from facing her lover as a boy girl—afraid of the social reality of becoming Brandon's lover, a public shame symbolized by the material object of the suitcase she is packing when Brandon comes in and begins dancing with her before she changes her mind.

Peirce's representation of Lana's "recoil" would certainly have militated against her case of libel against Fox, and the "suitcase" scene definitely complicates any reading of the film as ultimately portraying the two lovers as lesbians, in spite of the way that label would be thrust upon them by the community and critics alike after release of the film. Yet with the removal of Brandon's shirt in the shed scene, the L word arises to impugn the "authenticity" of Brandon's persona and defame the purity of Lana's heterosexual consciousness. By delving into the history of Brandon's sexuality, Peirce's art has taken a life of its own, one that in many ways has had greater material effects than life itself. *Boys Don't Cry* not only

---

43   Michael Warner, "Homo-Narcissim; or Heterosexuality," *Engendering Men: The Question of Male Feminist Criticism* (London: Routledge, 1990) 191–206.

spawned the will to know but also created an outcry that demanded—in critical and legal circles—a return to heterocentricity and the defined boundaries created by its litany of LGBTIQ otherness—boundaries that relegated Brandon's story to the exile of a pervasive tragic paradigm.

Conclusion

Kate Bornstein, the transexual actress and author who came to Nebraska to attend the murder trials, writes, "[i]n living along the borders of the gender frontier, I've come to see the gender system created by this culture as a particularly malevolent and divisive construct, made all the more dangerous by the seeming inability of the culture to *question* gender, its own creation."[44] The myriad cultural and legal stagings that have erupted in relation to the Brandon phenomenon illustrate how the malevolent divisiveness Bornstein enumerates retains its stubbornness through the linking of gender to anatomy and sexual orientation. Not only do laws and outlaws in the Brandon Teena narrative police the regulatory alignment of sex and gender; they undertake that surveillance in the service of a compulsory heterosexism that is necessarily violated by a transgender subject whose anatomy comes under such surveillance. This power of enforcement or branding, I have argued, provides ironically enough the glue to hold the LGBTIQ continuum together, in spite of a set of internal contradictions within the coalition itself, and it is my contention that this collective discrimination against the queer subject can create a coalitional unity that struggles for change.

Do the cultural and legal documents that have arisen in conjunction with the story of Brandon Teena merely underline the divisiveness Bornstein laments, or might they reflect the beginning of a cultural and legal inquiry into our continued imprisonment by a gendered ontology, one which prescribes only one acceptable trajectory of desire? The troubling techniques of gender knowledge that this case history has produced—ranging from defamation lawsuits to Hollywood love tragedy to critical inquiry—attest on the one hand to the commodification of and capitalizing on this curiously queer but true crime. At the same time the explosion of discourse that has accompanied Brandon's story, including Supreme Court decisions and ground-breaking essays like those of Halberstam and Bornstein, also indicates that not every form of understanding is necessarily contained by a larger matrix of power.

"Resistance to power," Foucault wrote later in his life, "does not have to come from elsewhere to be real, nor is it inexorably frustrated through being the compatriot of power."[45] Brandon Teena herself was determined to be a man; that determination, however complicit with a notion of fixed heterosexual orientation

---

44   Bornstein 12.

45   Michel Foucault, *Power/Knowledge: Selected Interviews and Other Writings: 1972–77*, Trans. Colin Gordon et al. (New York, Pantheon, 1980), 142.

and male gender identity, had the very real effect of subverting gender boundaries. At times, Brandon had to lie about his body in order to perform the truth of his masculinity, a truth that gave him the power to seduce, love, and legitimate his love of women. Yet this lie—which for Brandon is the only truth—necessarily produced a vigilant investigation and subsequent Hollywood quest narrative—an apparatus of legal and cultural inquiry that investigated and discovered the truth about Brandon, a social and legal truth that branded him as tragic gender outlaw, "freak," and finally "dyke." Nissen and Lotter became the unlikely and pitiful tools for returning Falls City to social normativity, a status quo which Aristotle calls "justice," by impinging the paradigm of coercive tragedy on to Brandon's story—a scripted narrative that informs both fact and fiction, law and film.

Complicit at some frightening level with the quest to discover the truth about Brandon's sex, to undress him and find out what is between his legs, is a cultural fascination that is piqued by the boundary-crossing hybridity that Brandon Teena represents. Relegating this violent policing of gender to the rural "heartland" of Middle America (Falls City, population 4,000) has allowed the mainstream media both to distance this story from its own internal workings and to study it, to produce text and images about a "true story" that has captured the imagination of audiences who vicariously partake of this gender thriller in the privacy of their home and the darkness of theaters. Applause and an Academy Award have gone once again to that most challenging role of all, the performance of gender—in this case, a female who can convincingly act like a male, astonishing us with her ability to cross a boundary whose material entrenchment consistently produces a desire to see it overcome within the secure circles of cultural representation. The heterosexuality of Hillary Swank, the Academy's Best *Actress*, assures us that the commercial success of *Boys Don't Cry* stays contained within the parameters of entertainment and brilliant *acting* in all senses of that word—a compartmentalization that has its dark parallel in the neat and tidy imprisonment of Lotter and Nissen. Two repositories of our own unacknowledged shame about a persistent legacy of queerphobia continue to be the halls of justice and film.

Chapter 4
"The Imagined Power:" The Specter of Hate Crime in *Brokeback Mountain*

The opportunity to be threatened, humiliated and to live in fear of being beaten to death is the only "special right" our culture bestows on homosexuals. (Diane Carmen, *Denver Post*)[1]

Gay Spaces

On September 22, 2010, Tyler Clementi, a freshman at Rutgers University, jumped to his death off the George Washington Bridge a few days after his roommate Dharun Ravi and fellow student Molly Wei disseminated a live webcam recording of Tyler kissing another man in his dormitory room. When Tyler asked to have their dorm room to himself for a couple of hours on September 19, Ravi went to visit Molly, remotely accessed the webcam on his computer, and began to watch Tyler kissing another man. Ravi then tweeted his discovery and set up a live feed of the intimate encounter. Three days later Clementi left a short Facebook message ("Jumping off the gw bridge sorry") and then committed suicide. Wei and Ravi were subsequently arrested for invasion of privacy. Ann Woolner's editorial on this "tragedy" for the Bloomberg Report noted that there were actually three "crimes" involved in the tragic cyber event: Ravi's failure to shut off his camera, Ravi's dissemination of the kissing, and lastly, the "crime of shame"—the psychological impetus that somehow led a talented freshman from a relatively progressive and urban university in the "post-gay" East to kill himself as a result of being outed on cyberspace.[2] After all the *Ellens* and *Will and Graces*, after Van Sant's *Milk* and *Lawrence v. Texas*, after passage of the federal hate crimes Shepard Act and Judge

---

1   Diane Carman, *Denver Post* (October 10, 1998): B01 (editorial).

2   Ann Woolner, *Bloomberg News* in *The Denver Post* (October 3, 2010): 2A. "We don't know whether Clementi thought of himself as gay or was merely experimenting. But it's obvious he believed it shameful to be seen engaging in sexual conduct with another man. And for that crime, the guilt is more diffuse." A follow-up article, "Suicides Highlight Gay Teens' Torment" (Jesse McKinley, *The New York Times*) appeared in *The Post* (October 4, 2010): 4A, detailing several other gay suicides in the week surrounding the Clementi death. The Rutgers incident is also inflected by race, the alleged perpetrators being people of color. Ravi was found guilty of some counts of bias intimidation, invasion of privacy, and tampering with evidence on March 16, 2012 (http://www.cbsnews.com/8301-504083_162-57397991-504083/dharun-ravi-verdict-guilty-of-bias-invading-privacy-in-rutgers-clementi-spycam-case/). For a revisionist view of the case, see Ian Parker, "The Story of a Suicide," *New Yorker* (February 6, 2012) 37–51.

Walker's decision overturning California's Proposition 8, the shock that followed the initial reports of the Clementi suicide—even before all the facts in the case are uncovered—speak forcefully to what Gail Mason calls the "spectacle of violence," namely the way in which "for many lesbians and gay men, the knowledge that they may be targeted for homophobia-related violence ... becomes a variable in the mapping of safety, whether they have directly encountered violence or not" (84).[3]

Mason's interest in what she calls the "spatialisation" of personal safety, specifically the way "knowledge of violence" persuades lesbians and gay men to alter the parameters of their private and public movements, clearly has ramifications for the increasingly populated but as yet unregulated expanse of cyberspace. The Clementi case points not only to the effects of an ever-increasing use of "cyber-bullying," but also to the persistence stigmatization of homosexuality across geographic, communicational, and generational lines, in spite of the many legal and cultural advances since the 1960s. If Tyler Clementi did commit suicide wholly or in part because of the imagined consequences of being labeled "queer" at Rutgers University in 2010 and the virtual locales of Facebook and Twitter, his death confirms the enduring power of heterosexual conformity, most tellingly in the consciousness of the closeted queer himself.[4]

Clementi's "shame" as Woolner calls it, has its historical legacy in the state-sanctioned vilification of same-sex relations from thirteenth-century faggot burnings through the current stonings under Sharia law. The *Lawrence* case, which held the Texas sodomy law unconstitutional, overturned ages of legal and religious precedent that subjected gays and lesbians to torture, mutilation, and castration, and more recently terms of imprisonment—a legal heritage still extant in the religious and social discourse in congregations, student bodies, board rooms, and courtrooms.[5] The Clementi case dramatizes the internal and external power of a persistent ideology to control and even eliminate the nonconformists, a power that finds its engine in the peculiar ability of the queer minority, unlike others, to hide their love in the vast social and paranoiac expanse of the closet. The epistemology of that closet, to use the late Eve Sedgwick's terminology, has as its foundation a fear of exposure, a fear that may or may not be grounded in reality, but one that maintains its grip on the subject through the processes of imagination which are

---

3   Gail Mason, *The Spectacle of Violence: Homophobia, Gender, and Knowledge* (New York: Routledge, 2002).

4   "*Heterosexism* is defined here is an ideological system that denies, denigrates, and stigmatizes any nonheterosexual form of behavior, identity, relationship, or community. Like racism, sexism and other ideologies of oppression, heterosexism is manifested both in societal customs and institutions, such as religion and the legal system ... and individual attitudes and behaviors (referred to here as *psychological heterosexism* ...)" (Gregory M. Herek, "The Social Context of Hate Crimes: Notes on Cultural Heterosexuality," in *Hate Crimes: Confronting Violence Against Lesbians and Gay Men*, ed. Gregory M. Herek and Kevin T. Berrill [Newbury Park: Sage, 1992], 89).

5   Herek 1.

fostered by the ability to pass as straight. The closet gains its strength through a paradoxical combination of denial of sexual practice and a fabrication of the dire consequences of publicity—of being found *out*, literally and figuratively.

The unrelenting evidence of gay shame in the 2010 Clementi case establishes a crucial link to the tragic trajectory of Ennis del Mar, one of the main characters in Annie Proulx's now famous short story, "Brokeback Mountain." Ennis is also a figure who is paradoxically hemmed in by a vast expanse of space, in this case the ranges of the Rocky Mountain West, a space that mirrors the open range of the protagonist's epistemological closet. Ennis, who meets Jack Twist in 1963 on a sheep drive, avoids the suicidal narrative that *The Celluloid Closet* has documented and current high school statistics still bear out, but his awareness of the spectacle of homo-violence in rural Wyoming—as evidenced by his childhood trauma of viewing the mutilated body of Earl and his later assumption that Jack was bludgeoned to death by a tire iron—is sufficiently overwhelming to fence Ennis in emotionally and physically for his entire life. As he admits to Jack, Ennis is "caught in [his] own loop," one that shuttles from the practice of high-altitude fucking to denial of gayness to an imagination of the brutal death that will face him if he is outed (14).[6] The impetus for Proulx's short story, first published in *The New Yorker* in 1997, as the author has famously stated, was not to tell "a tale of two gay cowboys" as urban critics have suggested, but to unfold a "story of destructive rural homophobia" in a western state like Wyoming, where although some gay men do "live in harmony with the community," Matthew Shepard, a year after the story's publication, "was tied to a buck fence outside the most enlightened town in the state, Laramie," a state where the highest suicide rate in the country finds its statistical preponderance in elderly single men (130–131).[7]

In spite of Proulx's counter-intuitive insistence that her short story is about destructive rural homophobia but not about gay cowboys, her narration does not in any depth depict anti-gay antagonists; its plot contains no McKinney and Henderson, no Lotter and Nissen, no Dan White. In fact, her story's failure to explore the hate crimes that frame the narrative—the death of Earl and imagined murder of Jack—suggests the opposite of the author's purported thematic. Rural anti-gay violence in the story is not investigated but presented from the outset as

---

6   Annie Proulx, "Brokeback Mountain," in *Brokeback Mountain: Story to Screenplay* (New York: Scribner, 2005): 1-28. Citations come from this version of the text. My reading of the influence of the Earl hate crime on Ennis's attitude is indebted to Michael Gorton's "The Hate Crime," *The Gay and Lesbian Review Worldwide* (May–June 2006): 13 and Antonio R. Gamboa's Letter to the Editor, *The Gay and Lesbian Review Worldwide* (September–October 2006): 7. Although *The Brokeback Book: From Story to Cultural Phenomenon* (edited by William R. Handley [Omaha: University of Nebraska Press, 2011]) was published after this chapter was drafted, I will reference relevant essays. Colin Carman's "American Eden: Nature, Homophobic Violence, and the Social Imaginary" (123–136) is the most closely aligned with the connection between homophobia and the imagination.

7   Annie Proulx, "Getting Movied," in *Brokeback Mountain: Story to Screenplay* (New York: Scribner, 2005) 129-138.

a given—gratuitous, assumed, unprosecuted, almost etched into the landscape of her narrative as indelible. The only measurable antagonist Proulx's story develops is Ennis's own consciousness, the internalized voice of a father who has convinced his son that queer visibility equals death—not just any kind of death, but one that entails mutilation, as the statistics on hate crimes in fact bear out.[8] This "knowledge" instilled in the young queer consciousness makes Ennis certain that the same tire iron that turned Earl's skin into "pieces of burned tomatoes" is the weapon that kills his lover Jack Twist on a Texas roadside at the age of 39 (15).[9] According to Hannah Arendt, violence is a tool used by those in power to silence "difference," and for Kendall Thomas "homophobic violence" in particular constitutes "a mode of power" or "institution" that "serves to construct LGBT identity as subordinate and devalued."[10]

In many ways, the author's refusal to recognize the almost inevitable imbrication of the gay cowboy story and anti-queer oppression (whether internalized or not) reflects the tragic flaw that inhabits the *Brokeback* phenomenon as a whole. If, as Augusto Boal maintains, the Aristotelian tragic paradigm represents a "powerful form of intimidation" that warns both spectator and character of the consequence of action that does not conform to the law, Ennis del Mar has by the end of the story not only gone gently into the closet once he learns his lesson from his imagined assessment of Jack's "accident," but he also recognizes that his own self-coercion stems from the intimidation that has governed his failure to face the contradictions of his own denial and left him in the end separated from the love of his life. Ennis's insistent erasure of his own queerness haunts not just Proulx's central character, but the entire *Brokeback* phenomenon—the story's film adaptation, its criticism, and, I will argue, the un-narrated trajectories of the two hate crimes that bookend Proulx's plot.

At the end of this striking short story, anthologized in the author's collection *Close Range*, Ennis visits Jack's childhood bedroom in Lightening Flat and finds two shirts "one inside another" in "a slight hiding place," a jog at the "north end of the closet." He presses the fabric to his face in hopes of catching "the faintest smoke and mountain sage and salty sweet stink of Jack," but realizes "there was

---

8   Elizabeth Birch and Paul Weyrich, "Symposium—Debate for Specific Hate Crime Legislation Protecting Homosexuals," *Insight on the News* (July 24, 2000), http://findarticles.com/p/articles/mi_m1571/is_27_16/ai_63692894/?tag=mantle_skin;content. "A survey by the National Coalition of Anti-Violence Programs reports that in antigay hate crimes in 1998, guns used during assaults grew 71 percent; ropes and restraints, 133 percent; vehicles, 150 percent; and blunt objects, clubs and bats, 47 percent. The alarming statistics show that the intent of perpetrators is not simply to kill their victims, but to destroy and punish what their victims represent" (1).

9   See Gamboa 7 and Alex Hunt, "West of the Closet, Fear on the Range," *The Brokeback Book*, 146 for further discussion of the symbolism of the tire iron.

10   Sally Kohn, "Greasing the Wheel: How the Criminal Justice System Hurts Gay, Lesbian, Bisexual and Transgendered People and Why Hate Crime Laws Won't Save Them," 27 *New York University Review of Law and Social Change* 257 at 277 (2001–2002).

no real scent, only the memory of it, the *imagined power* of Brokeback Mountain of which nothing was left but what he held in his hands" (26, italics mine). In this closet within a closet, where Jack's bloodied shirt covers Ennis's, Proulx's uncanny imagery captures the inestimable melancholy that will haunt Ennis for the rest of his life, a stubborn obsession that attests to the power of the imagination to determine the outcome of this story. The "magic" of Brokeback Mountain represents simultaneously the compelling passion of same-sex love and the intensity of a closet that represses, condenses, and regulates queer subjectivity.[11]

Like Earl, whose fate "scares the piss" out of him, Ennis is also a "tough bird," one who, as the spooning metaphors that pervade this story show, loves to fuck and get fucked by men, but one whose insistence that "he ain't no queer" signaling a devotion to a power of intimidation and denial that creates a mental torture which leaves him pissing into a sink and gazing at a postcard before he reaches 40. At the end of the story in Ennis's dream, Proulx's spooning metaphor seems to represent the barebacking that Jack and Ennis enjoy as well as the "artless, charmed happiness in their separate and difficult lives" as symbolized by Ennis's inability to embrace Jack face to face (22). But the spoon suddenly morphs from a handle jutting out of a can of beans with a "lurid shape" of "comic obscenity" into a tool "that could be used as a tire iron" (26–27). This symbolic transvaluation from phallic tool of sustenance to violent weapon attests to the way in which a heterosexist social ethos and its concomitant internalization necessarily turn this "obscene" romantic comedy into a gay *Romeo and Juliet*, where the ancient grudge of homo-hate kills the joy that Ennis and Jack experience, leaving the former in the end with an occasional wet pillow, an occasional stiff sheet (28).

Proulx ends her acclaimed story with a reference to "an open space between what he [Ennis] knew and what he tried to believe," but, the narrator concludes, "nothing could be done about it, and if you can't fix it you've got to stand it" (28). While the author's reference to "open space" alludes to the way the wilderness of the Rockies shapes the relationship the story unfolds—from one recent perspective, as "a vast field of homoerotic possibility" or, if you will, a pastoral idyll—the story's reference to open space in this context also refers not just to the outdoors but to Ennis's inner landscape, to a consciousness that has "known" and internalized his father's queer jokes, Earl's unprosecuted murder, Alma's reference to Jack Nasty, and his lover's questionable demise. But, as the text suggests, Ennis tries to believe something else, namely that Jack remained deeply in love with him to the very end, in spite of Ennis's frequent unavailability— emotionally, physically, publicly.[12] That open space between knowledge and

---

11   See Andrew Holleran, "The Magic Mountain," *The Gay and Lesbian Review Worldwide* (March–April 2006): 13. As Chris Freeman discusses, Tom Gregory bought the two shirts in the film at auction for $101,100 ("'Jack I Swear:" Some Promises to Gay Culture from Mainstream Hollywood," *The Brokeback Book*, 105).

12   For wilderness as a space of homoerotic play, see Catriona Mortimer-Sandilands and Bruce Erickson, eds. *Queer Ecologies: Sex, Nature, Politics, Desire* (Bloomington:

belief, at a more basic level, evidences the catastrophe that this closet has brought about, the estrangement and death of the man with whom Ennis "never had such a good time" in his life (6), the man Ennis's panic-stricken consciousness has to relegate to "'hell out in the back a nowhere'" (15)—that vast public expanse of their closeted wilderness. The hypermasculine space of their "fishing trips" also facilitates, according to the editors of *Queer Ecologies*, "the story's effective disarticulation of same-sex love and desire from gay identity, the former of which is presented as natural—masculine, rural, virile—in opposition to the latter's spectral invocation of historical and ongoing discourses of *perversion*."[13] The "it" which Ennis must "stand" because he cannot "fix"—the impersonal pronoun that *stands for* Ennis's love of the "brilliant charge of their infrequent couplings"—this crime that dare not speak its name—also refers paradoxically to the open space of the rural closet, the imagined and real power that the spectacle of violence perpetuates—the power of intimidation that pervading the open and close ranges of Ennis's circumscribed life.[14]

Incapable and unwilling to overcome the implacable landscape of compulsory heterosexuality, our tragic hero, like the-down-and-out Oedipus, ends up blinded by the dreams that both haunt and sustain him. We pity Ennis, but we also know that socio-geographic law and custom have led inevitably to the destiny of his laconic melancholy. We know he has a right to fear being queer. Look what happened to his friend Jack, whose catastrophic death—whether real or imagined—has led to the purgation of any impulse we or Ennis may have had to challenge the necessity of the down low in Wyoming. "If you can't fix it, you got to stand it," Proulx's story of oppression concludes, supplying little hope of release from the loop that has hobbled Ennis—the specter of sanctioned violence that both reigns him in and reigns over him.

Homo-hate

If, as Shoshana Felman has posited, legal and literary meaning necessarily inform and displace each other, then the framing of Proulx's plot around two unprosecuted hate crimes—the dick dragging murder of Earl and the imagined bludgeoning to death of Jack by a tire iron—necessarily tells us something about the social ethos of Aristotelian "justice" in the West during the last half of the twentieth century when these fictionalized acts took place. This ethos continues to control the "tragic" narrative of proposed and rejected hate-crime legislation in western

---

Indiana University Press, 2010), 3.

   13   Mortimer-Sandilands and Erickson 2.

   14   Carman discusses the "it" at 123–124. David Leavitt writes, "In the end, *Brokeback Mountain* is less the story of a love that dares not speak its name than one that doesn't know how to speak its name, and is somehow more eloquent for its lack of vocabulary" ("Men in Love: Is *Brokeback Mountain* a Gay Film?" *The Brokeback Book*, 30).

legislatures through a repeated process during which hearings are held to determine if the queer subject is worthy of the negative and positive effects of these statistic-gathering and penalty-enhancing laws.[15] Even after the federal Shepard and Byrd Hate Crimes Prevention Act was signed into law by President Obama in 2009, states like Wyoming and Montana repeatedly consider and reject the statistical evidence of LGBTI oppression, deciding after testimony from experts, victims, and religious institutions, that the flawed homosexual is not worthy of protection by the state, that the state has a greater interest in coercing tragic queers to stay in the closet than in prosecuting those who attack them. As terrifying and pitiful as Earl and Jack's deaths are, these fictional characters remain reminders of the dangerous consequences of flaunting one's perversion in a conservative atmosphere. Up to this point, these legislative debates have done nothing but affirm the paradigm of Aristotelian tragedy—replaying a legal theater of oppression that maintains the status quo in spite of a growing trend in the country to include sexual orientation in these criminal statutes. Whether or not the mainstream initiative to pass these laws in states like Wyoming and Montana will ultimately be successful, the debate over their value as well as the arduous endeavors to pass them highlight the central question underlying Boal's attempt to turn a theater of oppression into a *"poetics of the oppressed,"* into a poetics and politics of liberation (155).[16] Does the passage of hate-crimes legislation transform the coercive paradigm of the tragic queer or merely enshrine the LGBT subject in a legal box that is tantamount to another closet?

Predictably, the debate about the efficacy of hate-crime legislation in general suddenly grew more strident once legislators agreed to consider adding sexual orientation as a new category to a set of race and religion statutes that had passed years before without much hullabaloo. When gays and lesbians wanted bashers to pay a price, commentators became convinced that all crimes were hate crimes—an erasive gesture that in some ways adumbrated the way the media instantly saw Ang Lee's film adaptation of Proulx's work as a universal love story rather than a queer one.[17] When conservatives complained about the "special rights agenda" of the LGBT lobby, Critical Legal Studies scholars began to question the validity of using law as the major means to overcome bias, a debate fostered initially by law professors like Mary Ann Glendon, whose book argues that "an undue emphasis on rights unduly privileges the judiciary" and creates a "strident legalism" which impedes "'a grammar of cooperative living.'"[18] "Rights must not be confused with equality nor legal recognition with emancipation," Wendy Brown warned in *States*

---

15   Shoshana Felman, *The Juridical Unconscious: Trials and Traumas in the Twentieth Century* (Cambridge, MA: Harvard University Press, 2002), 8.

16   Augusto Boal, *Theatre of the Oppressed*, trans. Charles A. and Maria-Odilia Leal McBride (New York: Theatre Communications Group, 1985), 155.

17   See Roger Ebert in *Chicago Sun-Times* (December 16, 2005) and *Roger Ebert.com*, http://rogerebert.suntimes.com/apps/pbcs.dll/article?AID=/20051215/REVIEWS/51019006.

18   Mary Ann Glendon, *Rights Talk* (1991) quoted in Wai Chee Dimock, *Residues of Justice: Literature, Law, Philosophy* (Berkeley: University of California Press, 1996), 182.

of Injury, pointing trenchantly to Foucault's analysis of the way legal recognition functions as a form of control.[19] The work of Brown, Glendon and others has led to further critique of neo-liberal notions of liberation through judicial process. Authors like Ruthann Robson have detailed the way LGBT lawsuits create ideal "but-for" queers, subjects who are in all respects the same as heterosexuals except for what they do in the bedroom, thereby establishing assimilated subjects and ignoring queers of color, economic disadvantage, and trans subjects.[20] Except for Ennis's ongoing economic issues, Robson's profile of the ideal gay litigant bears an uncanny resemblance to the closeted, family men of Proulx's short story, indicating how the struggle for legal recognition necessarily flirts with the dangers of normalization.

Though the addition of sexual orientation to enhanced penalty hate-crime statutes hardly confers affirmative "rights" on the queer subject, the repeated failure of many states to add sexual orientation to the categories of race, religion, and gender continues to send a signal that the queer body has not yet reached a status of social being or acceptance. But does the LGBT population really want the conferral of that social status to become the special province of police and district attorneys? These legislative initiatives, according to some scholars, fail to take into account the dubious value of allowing a historically homophobic criminal justice system the discretion to determine what crimes fit under a codified notion of queer bashing. While right-wing legislators hold hearings about the dangers of legitimating sodomy and impingement upon the supposed First Amendment right of religions to preach homosexuality as a path to hell, left legal scholars maintain that hate-crime statutes add legitimacy to social hierarchies by codifying them, i.e. by acknowledging the queer subject as stigmatized.[21] Instead of promoting a fairer application of prosecutorial discretion in the criminal justice system, hate-crime statutes backfire, according to some experts, leading to prosecutions against queers for coming on to straight males under "sex discrimination," resulting in the "cooptation" of political power by "those who have control inside the sphere of politics"—namely district attorneys, police officers, and courts—those very institutions that have historically either erased queerness altogether or prosecuted same-sex practitioners as more criminal than those who actually use violence against LGBT subjects (Kohn 271). By struggling to join a long list of targets of social opprobrium (such as ethnic Americans and women), gays and lesbians, these scholars argue, are rushing to establish themselves as abject subjects, ignoring the more important arenas of social engagement in favor of expensive

---

19   Wendy Brown, *States of Injury* (Princeton: Princeton University Press, 1995), 87–88.

20   Darren Rosenblum, "Queer Intersectionality and the Failure of Recent Lesbian and Gay 'Victories'," 4 *Law and Sexuality* 83, at 93 (1994). Ruthann Robson coined the phrase during the Address at The Conference of National Lesbian and Gay Lawyers Association (NLGLA), October 24, 1992.

21   Kohn 261.

legal battles, investing in the corrupt American prison system as a remedy, and assuming naïvely that these laws will somehow secure deterrence.[22]

Against these anti-categorical arguments about the deleterious effects of criminal statutes that establish the lesbian or gay subject as bashable, the Human Rights Campaign's Elizabeth Birch and others have defended their drive to pass these laws (now existing in 45 states and more than a dozen countries) as a way of redressing historical discrimination and sending a message that these once anti-gay governments are now prepared to prosecute those who commit crimes with a motive of homo-hate. As Birch maintained in 2000, alarming statistics recently revealed a 47 percent increase in the use of blunt objects in the perpetration of anti-gay hate crimes, a fact that shows

> the intent of perpetrators … not simply to kill their victims, but to destroy and punish what their victims represent. In a sense the victims are not the real targets but convenient outlets for those who hate and wish to unleash their bigoted rage and fury against an entire group … [H]ate crimes are forms of domestic terrorism that threaten the very fabric of our nation.[23]

While debates persist about the collective versus individual goals of activism, about resource allocation, and about the pitfalls of co-optation by a suspect legal system, sexual orientation hate-crime bills continue to find their way into the theater of the legislative hearing in western state houses, a line-up of folks waiting their turn to testify that such laws will establish a "terrible lifestyle" and lead to recruiting in the public schools.[24] Pentecostals like Jack Twist's folks swear that "gay men think they are doing children a favor by sodomizing them" even though we all know "homosexuality is a sin and a crime" in the eyes of God.[25] On the other side of the aisle, lesbians and gay men tell stories of the history of police and community brutality, stories that range from bullying in school to arson, from hurled objects and name-calling to death threats and beatings—stories not unlike the incidents that bookend Proulx's narrative. Pastors claim laws that prevent them from condemning the gay lifestyle will abrogate their freedom of speech, while human rights advocates insist that LGBTIQ individuals deserve equal protection under the law. The repeated defeat of these laws in committee points to a constituency unwilling to turn the theater of oppression into a theater of

---

22   For a summary of some of the critiques of hate-crime legislation, see "A Compilation of Critiques on Hate Crime Legislation" (2009), www.blackandpink.org/revolt/a-compilation-of-critiques-on-hate-crimes-legislation/; scc also James B. Jacobs and Kimberly Potter, *Hate Crime: Criminal Law and Identity Politics* (New York: Oxford University Press, 2001) and Andrew Sullivan, "What's So Bad About Hate?" *New York Times Magazine* (September 26, 1999).

23   Elizabeth Birch, "Interview," *Insight on the News* (July 24, 2000).

24   *Montana Human Rights Network News* (February 2003).

25   *Montana Human Rights Network News* (May 2008), 3.

the oppressed, unwilling to change a form of justice that in many states refuses to recognize the status of the abnormal and abject queer.

Rarely do we find Critical Legal Studies scholars lining up to testify in the legislative chambers of Laramie and Helena; their absence attests to the ongoing staging of the legal drama of LGBT rights in spite of the trenchant critique of identity politics from scholars like Wendy Brown. In her recent essay "Suffering the Paradoxes of Rights," Brown eloquently outlines the way the pursuit of rights claims leads to re-inscription and a de-emphasizing of the larger collective goals of progressive politics, but in the end she acknowledges that the pursuit of rights, though flawed, still may be able to "gain a political richness when it is understood as affirming the impossibility of justice in the present and as articulating the conditions and contours of justice in the future."[26] Through a pluralistic approach to activism and resistance, scholars like Patricia Williams and Wai Chee Dimock have also recognized the value of rights movements that coincide with political organizing, cultural production, and social interaction. Williams insists, for example, that "for the historically disempowered, the conferring of rights is symbolic of all the denied aspects of their humanity: rights imply a respect that places one in the referential range of self and others, that elevates one's status from human body to social being."[27]

Though Boal's 1960s vision of the transformation of tragic paradigms from oppressive to liberatory through legislative theater does not, of course, take into account what Brown calls the "immobilizing features of designation" through codification, a poetics of the oppressed nevertheless envisions cultural drama as a method for citizens to demand the kind of respect that Williams envisions (422). "The spectator is less than a man," Boal writes, "and it is necessary to humanize him, to restore to him his capacity of action in all its fullness. He too must be a subject, an actor on an equal plane with those generally accepted as actors" (155). The Ennis del Mars who testify at legislative hearings, for Boal, move from witnesses of trauma (spectators) to social beings who demand "a referential range," to use Patricia Williams's terms, within the legitimating if interpellating institution of justice. The struggle for hate-crime legislation, under Boal's vision, creates a ritualized space of transformation from the coercion of tragic fatality to the mobilization of narrative in the service of political change. The repeated failure of LGBT activists to gain legislative ground, at least in western state houses, reminds us of an almost willful amnesia in regards to violence against queers, a concerted erasure that sanctions continued dehumanization of the Earls and Jacks of the world and reinforces the walls of the queer closet—barriers which cannot, however, be broken down without a commitment to activism.

---

26   Wendy Brown, "Suffering the Paradoxes of Rights," in *Left Legalism/Left Critique*, ed. Wendy Brown and Janet Halley (Durham, NC: Duke University Press, 2002), 432.

27   Williams is quoted in Dimock 190. For a discussion of the "bare life" of the societally unrecognized, see Giorgio Agamben, *Homo Sacer: Sovereign Power and Bare Life*, trans. Daniel Heller-Roazen (Stanford: Stanford University Press, 1998).

Within this theater of hate, the ACLU defends the rights of Fred Phelp's Baptist Church to blame war deaths in the Middle East on the homosexual agenda while gay men and lesbians, in hopes of gaining a legal status akin to other minorities, testify to the indelible genetics of their same-sex attraction, a homo-biology many admit they would gladly disown if they could become straight. Like a tragic chorus, these players enact their drama, seeking recognition through a law that does little more, from the perspective of many, than increase prison sentences. The risk of hate-crime legislation backfiring must be weighed against the immeasurable but nonetheless material effect of the passage of laws like the Shepard Act—an effect which may in large part be symbolic but is not therefore unreal. Legal processes not only engage fictional constructs like the impartial juror, equal protection, and blind justice, but these fictions, I maintain, are instrumental in the construction of social consciousness. They instill what Drucilla Cornell, in her book *The Imaginary Domain*, calls "minimum conditions of individuation," even though they engender a trade-off between the confines of equality and the utopia of liberty through an embrace of the problematic but compelling struggle for legal recognition. For Ennis del Mar, this imaginary domain is Brokeback Mountain, the imaginary location of a utopian West that embraces the love between men.[28] This imaginary power is paradoxically also a back country that doubles as a closet, hidden from everyone except the occasional voyeuristic pair of binoculars.

Proulx's story dramatizes the tragedy of Ennis's social consciousness even as the narrative avoids any detail about the consequences of the murder of the castrated Earl—the hate crime that conditions Ennis's make-up and presents homo-violence as an unimpeded fact of life. But what if a hate-crime law were in effect at the time this narrative? Would Ennis or Jack even have known about it? Would that statutory mandate have entered into the domain of their imaginations, contending with the spectacular force of Earl's body; would that law have made a difference in the circumscribed lives of these two ranch hands, the trajectory of which ironically spans such epic events as Stonewall (1969) and the election and assassination of Harvey Milk (1978–1979)? Brokeback's plot takes no notice of the tumultuous gay movement transpiring during this closeted romance even as it assumes the perpetrators of hate crime will go unprosecuted. When Jack's off-handedly suggests that they move to Denver or Mexico, the parochial Ennis finds his friend's proposal inconceivable, impracticable, and even dangerous, saddled as Ennis is by child support payments and a dying ranch economy.

Proulx's story takes place in a landscape that "disarticulates" its characters not only from historical social activism but legal advancement as well, even as it conditions Ennis to internalize the unwritten law that the only good queer is a dead one. Though the story's publication in 1997 occurs at a time of increasing

---

28   See Peter Boag, *Same-Sex Affairs: Constructing and Controlling Homosexuality in the Pacific Northwest* (Berkeley: University of California Press, 2003) for a discussion of same-sex traditions in non-urban settings. James Morrison discusses the pastoral in "Back to the Ranch Ag'in: *Brokeback Mountain* and Gay Civil Rights," *The Brokeback Book*, 81–100.

demands for queer legal protections nationwide and internationally, it takes place in a region that has actively rejected those demands, even after *The Laramie Project*. Proulx's story looks forward to Matt Shepard even as it looks back to Earl and Jack, reminding the reader of the stubbornness of heterosexism and anti-gay bias psychologically, geographically, culturally—a tenacity that will require more than law, film, and fiction to uproot. The success of hate-crime legislation and the passion of Ennis and Jack must, as Patricia Williams suggests, work inside and outside the subject to elevate the queer to a level of social being. That elevation must take place in multiple venues—the domains of courthouse, publishing house, movie house, and even the house of the imagination—a house where, in the case of the queer subject, there is the added hurdle of stuck closet doors.

The Spectacle of Ang Lee's *Brokeback*: A Gay Cowboy Movie

Reality's never been of much use out here. (Proulx, *Close Range*)[29]

Larry McMurtry and Diana Ossana optioned Proulx's story after reading it in *The New Yorker* in 1997. When they circulated their screenplay, in no time at all it "had acquired the reductive and spurious tagline 'a story about two gay cowboys.'"[30] They finally sold it seven years later to James Schamus at Focus Features. *Brokeback* the movie went into production in spring 2004, Ang Lee directing the late Heath Ledger and Jake Gyllenhaal on location in Alberta, Canada.[31] The film cost 14 million dollars and opened to a limited urban release (New York, San Francisco, and Los Angeles) in December, 2005, expanding its market over the holidays, eventually running for 133 days, and grossing over 83 million dollars— the top box office success of Focus Features and the fifth highest grossing Western of all time. *Brokeback* was banned in Utah (in a Salt Lake suburb), China, and parts of the Middle East, while remaining a number one box office success in London and Paris for many weeks. In a Bonus Feature DVD entitled "Sharing the Story, The Making of *Brokeback Mountain*," director, producers, and actors go to considerable length to tell interviewers that Lee's film is not a "gay cowboy movie," but just an extraordinary story of two men who fall in love.

As critics have noted, the film adaptation heterosexualizes Proulx's story— adding marriage scenes and Thanksgiving dinners while subtracting pissing and

---

29   Epigraph to Annie Proulx, *Close Range: Wyoming Stories* (New York: Scribner, 2000). "Brokeback Mountain" became part of this collection, though it originally appeared in *The New Yorker*.

30   Diana Ossana, "Climbing Brokeback Mountain," in *Brokeback Mountain: Story to Screenplay* (New York: Scribner, 2005), 147.

31   For a discussion of Alberta's capitalization on the *Brokeback* phenomenon through tourist promotion and gay erasure, see Jon Davies, "Alberta, Authenticity, and Queer Erasure," *Brokeback Book*, 249–266.

semen from the gritty text, presumably as part of the necessary requirements of Hollywoodization. The film leaves out the italicized opening scene of the text, which frames the narration as a remembered "panel" sliding forward when Ennis wakes up in his trailer years later, urinating "in the sink," pouring stale coffee into a stained cup, and feeling "suffused with a sense of pleasure because Jack Twist was in his dream" (1). Unlike the handsome stars cast for the film, Proulx's protagonists are a "pair of deuces going nowhere," not particularly attractive, intelligent, or well off, even though later Jack marries into money. The final scene, which also recalls a dream in Proulx's text, is replaced in the film by a wedding announcement from Ennis's daughter. The movie also spares the viewer from watching Jack's uncut father (played brilliantly by Peter McRobbie) piss on his circumcised son to teach him to aim better into the toilet. The fastidious Lee reduces the male sex scenes to cigarette-smoking head-and-shoulder shots for the most part, an occasional shirt removed. (He makes up for this Puritanism in his succeeding film, *Lust, Caution.*) Viewers are also not allowed to fully witness Ennis as "he shoved his pants down, hauled Jack onto all fours and, with the help of the clear slick and a little spit, entered him," nor do we see him fully "spread eagled" and "still half tumescent" at the Siesta Motel four years later (7, 12). Lee's mainstream film sanitizes, upgrades, and domesticates Proulx's gritty piece, in effect closeting the narrative by turning it into a heterosexual tragedy, whose protagonist is not just the failed family-man Ennis but also his poor wife Alma Beers and later his frustrated girlfriend Cassie. "It's because of you, Jack, that I am like this," Ennis complains to his lover, in a screenplay addition that epitomizes the admixture of heterocentricity and queer bias, which, some critics note, facilitates the transformation of short story into blockbuster movie.[32]

Brokeback the movie gains its cash and cache from an attempt to appeal to all audiences—straight and gay alike—but in seeking to cross this important cultural and capital divide, it tells the story of a couple of what Ruthann Robson has called "but-for" queers instead of sticking to Proulx's portrayal of a more randy pair of what we might coin as "butt-for" queers. In neither work are Jack Twist and Ennis del Mar radical fairies, however, for the premise of the story, like that of Forster's posthumously published novel *Maurice*, is the creation of a couple of nondescript dudes who happen to fall head over boot heels in love with one another. It's a "one-shot thing," Ennis tells his friend, which is "Nobody's business but ours" (7). The screenplay lifts this dialogue straight from the story, but instead of repeating Ennis's subsequent "I'm not no queer," the screenwriters' Ennis del Mar states, "You know, I ain't queer" (7, 20). This seemingly minor change may be attributable to Ossana and McMurtry's sense of dialect, but the shift from double to single negative has the effect of undoing the irony of Ennis's over-protestation in the original text, which turns his solecism into an unconscious admission (Ennis is *not* a "no queer"). The screenplay erases Proulx's linguistic irony, just as the

---

32   The screenplay is available in *Brokeback Mountain: Story to Screenplay.* This rewriting takes place on page 83.

film as a whole shifts the point of view from the gaze of an omniscient and more neutral narrator to a tear-filled Alma, a miffed Cassie, a jealous but voyeuristic Aguirre, a homophobic rodeo clown.[33]

The additional irony in this morning-after scene—replete in the film with a slaughtered "scape lamb"—in case we needed further symbolism of the characters' dereliction of heterosexual duty—comes from Ennis's unique use of the "q" word, the only time an identity category is vocalized in film or text, where even language must remain metonymically hidden under the headings of "Old Brokeback" (13), "what you like to do" (16), and "them guys you see around sometimes" (14).[34] The usual signifiers—gay, homosexual, even faggot—are carefully avoided in favor the single albeit archaic use of the word theorists have appropriated to abrade categorization, even though Ennis sees the noun as classificatory, as establishing an identity that the new definition of queer eschews.

At some strangely paradoxical level, Ennis *is* very queer, since text and film gain their most subversive quality from a Trojan-horse portrayal of two butch protagonists, who, from one critic's perspective, take their homosocial bonding to the next logical step.[35] Contradictory as it may seem, *Brokeback* packs its greatest punch through a strategy of hyperbolic assimilation. Piggybacking on the tropes of the Western and Proulx's earlier work in the *Field and Stream* genre, this story by a heterosexual woman brilliantly turns (or "twists," if you will) the screw on the intense male-bonding of an American homosocial literary and cinematic genre that ranges from *Deerslayer* to *Deer Hunter*, turning John Wayne into a potential sodomite and carrying Leslie Fiedler's famous essay to its logical conclusion: "Come back to the tent, Ennis, honey."[36] Set in the burly environs of the backcountry, Lee's prudish direction may turn away from the earlier precedent of *Desert Hearts*, the steamy lesbian Nevada film of the 1980s— it may also avoid the kind of *Last Tango in the Tetons* gay critics desired—but the very premise of its big-screen depiction—two very lonesome, very romantic, and very "straight-acting" cowboys going at it day and night (admittedly in a series of very open shots)—was sufficiently unsettling to stir the conservative teapot in ways tellingly analogous to the maelstrom over the legal push for hate-crime laws

---

33   See D.A. Miller's trenchant review, "Brokering *Brokeback*: Jokes, Backlashes, and Other Anxieties," *Film Quarterly* (spring 2007): 50–60. "Only the fictive surveillance intrinsic to our spectatorial position," Miller writes, "allows us to diagnose the 'paranoia' of Ennis's belief in the fictive surveillance that he imagines to know about him. We are his paranoia" (9). Miller does not acknowledge how the male gaze disrupts the economy of Laura Mulvey's famous feminist essay on visual pleasure and narrative cinema.

34   "Scape-lamb" is Christian Draz's term. See "Lost in Adaptation," *The Gay and Lesbian Review Worldwide* (May–June 2006): 12.

35   Judith Halberstam reminds us that the cowboy movie genre was always already homoerotic ("Not So Lonesome Cowboys: The Queer Western," *Brokeback Book*, 190–204).

36   Morrison discusses Fiedler in his essay in *The Brokeback Book*, and Holleran mentions Fiedler's famous phrase as well.

and gay marriage. Major motion pictures circulate in a public space sufficiently widespread to produce a policing of their messages in a manner analogous to the theatrical circus during hearings on LGBT legislative proposals.

Predictably, when Lee's film was widely released in 2006, it not only warranted censorship internationally; it spawned a reaction from the Christian right and members of the Academy of Motion Pictures that mimicked the testimony of god-hates-fags lobbyists who regularly line up in state houses to crusade against sodomites. While *Brokeback* did not stir the civil unrest that Mehta's *Fire* fomented in India, commentators like David Kupelian of Fox News were eager to claim that the film was part of a liberal Hollywood's agenda, "geared towards making homosexuality seem like … a wonderful lifestyle," turning "the adulterous relationship of these two men, which destroyed both their marriages and left their children bereft of a father, into something like a wonderful, magnificent love story."[37] Kupelein's critique fails to notice, on the contrary, how McMurtry and Ossama's screenplay actually domesticates this gay story, enhancing the consequences of a clandestine love affair for family values by turning Ennis's wife Alma Beers, played by Michelle Williams, into a major character. Kupelein's commentary also ignores the way the film turns Jack and Ennis into loving parents.

Was the release of *Brokeback* "a Christmas gift for conservative Christians," a "docudrama" of the "depressing, damaged lifestyle" of the gay cowboy, as Michael Cobb argues in "God Hats Cowboys (Kind Of)," or was it as "universal tragedy" of star-crossed lovers, whose gayness seems secondary to the passion that overcomes and dooms these two souls, as Daniel Mendelsohn summarizes the mainstream media's attempts to de-queer the film?[38] A critical closeting of the film, insisting that its strength lies in its subtle appeal to *all* audiences, is of course another assimilationist gesture—one that replays the familiar rhetoric at legislative hearings that all crimes are hate crimes—an argument which gains its greatest strength when it serves to erase the statistical evidence of prevalent gay bashing in the home of the free.[39]

While it should come as no surprise that Roger Egbert would try to turn *Brokeback* into *West Side Story* (a much queerer film in many ways), Gene Shallit's infamous quip that Jack Twist was a sexual predator who marred Ennis's happy home life created a much greater stir among the LGBT cognoscenti. Universalization and heterosexualization are rhetorical strategies of erasure that relinquish any chance for subversion because they refuse to recognize the particularity of Ennis's hand on Jack's "erect cock" (7). By the same token, Ennis's insistence that his love

37   David Kupelein in Eric Patterson, *On Brokeback Mountain: Meditations about Masculinity, Fear, and Love in the Story and the Film* (Lanham: Lexington Books, 2008), l–li.

38   Daniel Mendelsohn, "No Ordinary Love Story (*Brokeback Mountain*)," *Gay and Lesbian Review Worldwide* (May–June 2006): 10.

39   Recent statistics show 14 percent of reported hate crimes involve sexual orientation, a percentage that does not reflect the proven reticence of LGBT individuals to contact historically homophobic authorities (see Randy Hall, CNSNews.com [May 3, 2007]).

affair with Jack ain't nobody's business but his own engages in a particularism that is more hypocrisy than deconstruction. Although Shallit's reduction of Jack, the gay Romeo, to a stalker—a comment he later retracted at the behest of his gay son after much drama—relies on a serious misreading of Ennis's investment in the affair, the commentator must be lauded for at least talking about the protagonists as gay lovers struggling with a long-distance relationship. The eponymous Jack Twist, whose black hat and last name seem to perform the etymology of queer twistedness, is, after all, the man who "has been riding more than bulls," though he denies it to Ennis. But Jack is also the romantic who wants to settle down to a "little cow and calf operation," the guy who "can't make it on a couple of high-altitude fucks once or twice a year," the one who finds himself crossing the border for some Mexican sex (13, 14, 21). It should come as no surprise that Ang Lee's attempt to show Jack picking up a striped-shirt *puto* to the soundtrack of "Quizás, Quizás" is possibly the most contrived scene in the entire film, its clumsiness highlighting the almost exclusively straight production values of this picture.[40] Under the interpretive hands of heterosexual screenwriters, director, and actors, *Lonesome Cowboys* was destined to become *Lonesome Dove*. If there is a grain of truth in Shallit's controversial observation, it comes from Jack's status as a character who fights the closet as best he can, a man who needs but hardly ever gets it (21).

Jack wants to make it real, but Ennis, who is literally sick to his stomach when Jacks leaves and has "wrang it out a hundred times thinking about" his lover, exhibits a passionate attachment that is unquittable and reciprocal (12). No one can watch Gyllenhaal's performance as he drives back to Texas after finding Ennis unavailable without realizing how deeply unpredatory Jack Twist is, how hard he has tried to turn these fishing expeditions into a life together: "What Jack remembered and craved," Proulx writes in a moment of narrative pause, "in a way he could neither help nor understand was the time that distant summer on Brokeback when Ennis had come up behind him and pulled him close, the silent embrace satisfying some shared and sexless hunger" (22). Lee films this flashback with a subtle realism that easily can escape the viewer's eye; we only know we are seeing an earlier moment by the change of clothes and Jack's lack of a mustache. Gyllenhaal's performance as the "outer" of the two men achieved less critical acclaim precisely because it is less laconic, less closeted, less conflicted.

The *Brokeback* adaptation and media spin on a story "in which love feels almost as if it were being reinvented" undertakes the ideological work of folding queer sex into the deepest bastion of the masculinist ethos. So too the insistence—even by the likes of Gyllenhaal himself—that this is not a gay cowboy movie but a movie about two cowboys who happen to be gay rehearses the central paradox of identity politics: namely that the opposing goals of equality and liberty, acceptance and recognition, sameness and difference are necessarily antonymous even though

---

40   Compare the Mexicanization of Jack's lust for gay sex to the scapegoating of Harvey Milk's Latino lover, Jack Lira in Van Sant's *Milk*.

central to a social movement that seeks to turn its abjection into social viability.[41] Culture and law are agents in constructing social consciousness, and an industry as influential as Hollywood necessarily partakes in some of the same social dramas that are staged in the arenas of state rotundas, wood-paneled courthouses, and even the halls of academic and non-academic think tanks. As the quixotic quest of the producers of *Brokeback* to shift the focus in the film from "high altitude fucking" and "drowning" in one's own blood to a new and improved version of *Love Story* met with roadblocks in the Academy Award ceremony in 2006, an underdog film about class and race in Los Angeles called *Crash* "stole" the award for best picture from the front-running *Brokeback*, a film that had previously won Best Picture accolades from the Golden Globe, the British Academy, and the Critics Choice.[42] In her funny, self-deprecating account of her night at the Kodak Theatre, "Blood on the Red Carpet," Proulx describes "the hordes of the righteous" on the sidewalks outside, delivering "their imprecations against gays and fags" while the red carpet was rolled out to deliver the overdressed to a three-hour "butt-numbing" ceremony in which the "home-town favorite" *Crash* was announced by Jack Nicholson as the best picture to a collective "gasp of shock" from an audience, which included Proulx herself, planning what she calls her "Sour Grapes Rant."[43] *Brokeback* garnered three awards, putting it on "equal footing with *King Kong*," she quips, while Seymour Hoffman gained the best actor award for mimicking a "once-living celeb" (the flamboyant and queer Capote) and actors like Ledger and Gyllenhaal, who had to construct their "character from imagination and a few cold words on the page," were given short shrift.

Journalists would later discover that old members of the academy like Ernest Borgnine and the late Tony Curtis (who played next to Olivier in the famous oysters scene in *Ben Hur*) refused to impugn the memory of Gene Autry and others by even watching the film.[44] The celluloid closet is alive and well in Southern California, home of the John Birch Society, but also home of the film *Crash*, which employed an Iñárritu trope (*Amores Perros*) to tell the story of a single car accident that develops into a *choque* of class and ethnicity. The film only slightly brushes the queer end of this multicultural spectrum in a scene of a failed liaison between two cops, one of whom might be queer. *Crash*'s unwillingness to include the LGBT contingent in its pastiche of the multicultural southern landscape and its inclusion of rap music, which in itself has a checkered history of homophobic

---

41   See Iris Marion Young, *Justice and the Politics of Difference* (Princeton: Princeton University Press, 1990) for the conflicts between equality and liberty in identity politics. Owen Gleiberman's trailer (love reinvented) comes from his review in *Entertainment Weekly*, "The Searchers" (December 9, 2005): 59–60.

42   See Kenneth Turan, "Breaking No Ground: Why *Crash* Won, Why *Brokeback* Lost, and How the Academy Chose to Play It Safe," in *The Brokeback Book*, 101–103.

43   Annie Proulx, "Blood on the Red Carpet," *Guardian* (March 11, 2006) in http://www.guardian.co.uk/books/2006/mar/11/awardsandprizes.oscars2006.

44   Patterson xlviii.

lyrics, points to the continued uneasy intersection of ethnic and sexual minority politics.[45] Not only does mainstream LGBT activism often fail to recognize the hierarchies of gender, class, and race within its own movement; feminist and ethnic constituencies reciprocally have enduring anti-gay traditions. Like the "cloistered" and segregated lives of the LA film industry, the inclusivity of multiculturalism often runs into a telling obstacle when homosexuality—with its ambiguous closetry, its Kinsey-scale non-essentialism, and its radical queer theorists—attempts to crash the masculine, heterocentric party. When it came to acknowledging the amazing success—emotionally, commercially, and socially—of the *Brokeback* phenomenon, the Academy balked in a way reminiscent of the ideological antagonism fostered by the hate crimes debate. What Proulx does not state plainly is that no amount of romantic whitewashing can take the barebacking out of *Brokeback*. We have the Academy to thank for reminding us that anti-gay bias still persists in institutions like the liberal media, the liberal academy—as well as conservative western state houses—in spite of attempts from left and right to usher in a post-queer age.

Queer critics of Lee's film have also participated and illuminated the ideological antagonism of the *Brokeback* phenomenon. Like the hate-crimes controversy, this picture has produced an explosion of discursive commentary from both left and right, generating a book-length homage by Eric Patterson, two anthologies of essays, and dedicated issues of journals (*GLQ*, *Film Quarterly*, *Intertext*), including D.A. Miller's essay, which sets the tone for much of the ground this chapter covers.[46] Miller attributes Lee's lauded "craft" to a "covert figure of the Closet itself: that well-made piece of cabinetry where homosexual desire, far from generating an overt politics, lives quietly with heroic restraint" (4). Queer criticism has run the gamut from novelist Andrew Holleran's assessment of the film as a magical Aristotelian tragedy that portrays the clash between pastoral ideal and homophobic real world to other commentators who have decried the de-eroticization of Proulx's text, the turning of Ennis into a bitter and trapped Jack addict, as well as the de-gaying of a story about an overwhelming and doomed passion *à la* Anna Karenina.[47] What

---

45   See E. Patrick Johnson and Mae G. Henderson, eds. *Black Queer Studies: A Critical Anthology* (Durham, NC: Duke University Press, 2005). The down-low phenomenon, dramatized by recent allegations of homosexuality against Atlanta's Baptist minister who has called publicly for the death of sodomites, has established important connections to the "don't flaunt it" mentality of the west. (The same minister was later discovered to be having same-sex relations, not surprisingly.) See also Patricia Nell Warren's "Real Cowboys, Real Rodeos," *The Gay and Lesbian Review Worldwide* (July–August 2006): 19.

46   Patterson; *The Brokeback Book*; and Jim Stacey, ed. *Reading Brokeback Mountain: Essays on the Story and the Film* (Jefferson: McFarland, 2007). Scott Herring edited *GLQ* 13:1 (2007); Rob White edited *Film Quarterly* 60:3 (2007), which includes the D.A. Miller essay, to which I am indebted in this chapter. Many essays and letters also were featured in *The Gay and Lesbian Review Worldwide* (March–April 2006, May–June 2006, and September–October 2006).

47   See Holleran for the story as love tragedy; Draz and Mendelsohn discuss the heterosexualization of the film.

this panoply of critical reaction to the *Brokeback* phenomenon reveals finally is the power of cultural capital and the concomitant struggle to appropriate and use artistic representation to promote one's own code or, from a law and literature perspective, one's own legislative agenda.

"The Family Plot": Ashes to Ashes, Shirt to Shirt

> I only felt the full strength of my attachment to her when she was out of my sight. (Rousseau)[48]

If the measure of love is loss, as Jeanette Winterson wrote in the opening of her novel *Written on the Body*, then Jack's absence assumes a presence in both story and film, one which temporarily drives Ennis out of his closeted loop and gives Ang Lee an opportunity to turn Proulx's cold metaphors into a visual archive of feeling, to borrow Ann Cvetkovich's phrasing.[49] Even though *Brokeback* teeters on the brink of morbidity as it engages the "only good queer is a dead queer" trope made famous well before *A Single Man* and *The Hours*, Lee's film dramatizes the way the phenomenon of death paradoxically underscores the abjection of the queer subject. The jealously heterocentric law has used marriage as a means of preventing queer subjects and their "families" from visiting bedsides, burying their dead, attending one another's funerals, and inheriting. Tom Ford, in his recent adaptation of Isherwood's novel, changes his source to highlight the injustice that haunts the queer subject at the time of death when George receives a phone call informing him of his lover's fatal car accident and dis-inviting him to the funeral. The law refuses to recognize LGBT subjects as social beings not only by denying the existence of violent bias against them when they are alive but also by policing their remains after death. In the case of Earl, the abject queer body is left to rot in a dried-out irrigation ditch in a fate reminiscent of Antigone's brother, while in the case of Jack, the proper burial of his ashes brings Ennis face-to-face with not only the pure intensity of his feelings but also the complete erasure of them in the heterocentric sphere of Jack's nuclear family.

When at the end of the film Ennis's postcard comes back stamped "DECEASED," the shock of the symbolic red capital letters edges him out of his panoptic cell and leads him to dial Jack's phone number for only the second time in his life. After the "huge sadness of the northern plains" rolls down on him when he hears that his lover is dead, Ennis has the courage to ask the snow-cold Lureen where Jack is buried.

---

48   Rousseau's *Confessions* (New York: Penguin, 1954) at 152 is quoted in Jacques Derrida's *Of Grammatology*, trans. Gayatri Chakravorty Spivak (Baltimore: Johns Hopkins University Press, 1974) at 107.

49   Ann Cvetkovich, *An Archive of Feelings: Trauma, Sexuality and Lesbian Public Cultures* (Durham, NC: Duke University Press, 2003). Jeanette Winterson, *Written on the Body* (New York: Vintage, 1992).

"We put a stone up," she replies, and even though Jack asked to have his ashes scattered on Brokeback Mountain, his wife (Anne Hathaway heavily jeweled and coiffed with a frosted flip on the screen) informs Ennis that half the ashes were kept in Texas, half sent up to Jack's parents in Lightning Flat. Lureen suggests that Ennis get in touch with Jack's folks. "I suppose they'd appreciate it if his wishes are carried out" (24), Lureen assumes; she herself apparently never made the effort. Like the rights of queer men and women everywhere, Jack's wishes are ignored by his wife, in favor of a cemetery stone that commemorates his status as heterosexual husband.

Ennis's trip to his lover's biological family meets with a frigidity that renders Lureen warm and fuzzy by comparison. Lee casts the old house on Lightning Flat, not as Proulx's " tiny brown stucco" but as a chipped, white-paint clapboard bathed in the same washed-out light that bleached the scene of Earl dead in the ditch. Ennis begins his discussion with Jack's father, John C. Twist, the "stud duck in the pond," by employing a series of circumlocutions indicative of the rhetoric of the closet, the open secret, which confines the queer to a set of metonymies that stand in for the unmentionable. "I feel awful bad about Jack," Ennis begins, "Can't begin to say how bad I feel. I knew him a long time" (24). The inside of the house is also painted white, but the camera's blue filter gives the Spartan furnishings a dirty look in spite of years of scrubbing. Of course, in this stark and stolid environment, Ennis is unable to disclose his passionate attachment nor describe how well he has "known" his lover, so he couches his love in generic feelings of sorrow and knowledge as a way of saying what he cannot say. John Twist is nonplussed. "Tell you what," he says, spitting into his cup, "I know where Brokeback Mountain is. He thought he was too goddamn special to be buried in the family plot" (24).

Proulx's dialogue is both naturalistically real and highly symbolic, the word "special" of course directly echoing the anti-gay legal rhetoric, which the old man throws out vituperatively, then telling the story of Jack's "half-baked idea" of bringing Ennis up to the ranch and building "a log cabin" for the two of them to live in. The father's allusion to Jack's imagined life together with Ennis as "half-baked" not only references Ennis's failure to pull himself out of the closet but also baldly denigrates the queer quest to gain the right to social being, the right to domestic equality in spite of difference. Ennis confirms his fear of the imagined power of homo-violence when he interprets John Twist's mention of another of Jack's friends coming up to the ranch as an indication of the inevitability of Jack getting caught and killed. For Ennis, Jack's decision to leave him was a death sentence, an assurance that his lover faced the fatal tire iron. This "imagined power" is oddly complicit with the "family plot" (in all senses of that word) where John Twist insists his son's ashes must rest in dubious peace. Ennis passes the country cemetery on his way out; it is surrounded by "sagging sheep wire" and "a few graves bright with plastic flowers" (27). Ennis "didn't want to know Jack was going in there, to be buried on the grieving plain" (27).

Both deeply figurative and unrelentingly literal, the family plot on Lightning Flat buries Jack and his vision in its entrenched narrative of queer oppression and compulsory heterocentricity. That plot, relentlessly retold, blows with the force of the Wyoming wind which strikes Ennis's trailer like a load of dirt in the beginning of Proulx's story. This plot, flat and plain, erases its queers, turning them into sexual predators, failed fathers, dead meat in a ditch, scared men who have sex with men. Ennis does not want to know this story even though it is his, and not until Jack dies does he have to face the reality of an ongoing refusal of anyone, including himself, to fully acknowledge his relationship. This plot, where queers are buried in "tiny fenced squares on the welling plain," is the same unhallowed ground as the halls of justice and state legislatures where LGBT activists cyclically introduce hate crime bills that are repeatedly dismissed, a narrative re-run of the story of the powerless and tragic queer.

Brokeback interrupts this plot cycle by instilling in Ennis another imagined power—the grandeur of the mountain as a commemorative space that contrasts the flat plots of Texas and Lightning Flat. Ennis taps into the primacy of his senses— the sight of bloodstains and the smell of the spooned shirts—to recall a place that becomes a visceral memory, a memory that is also a memorial—a symbolic but real camp site where two young men fell in love. The ashes and cemeteries—the burial grounds of queer subjectivity—are replaced by the shrine Ennis creates in the closet of his trailer, where their shirts, now in reversed order, hang below the postcard of the mountain which Ennis touches in the final scene of the movie (Figure 4.1).

Ang Lee's close-up of the inside of Ennis's closet door, which appears shortly before the end of the film, memorializes the gaze and emotion behind the main character's whispered "Jack, I swear"— the last words of the screenplay. Ennis has just finished toasting the upcoming marriage of his daughter after asking her if she loved the roughneck whom she wants to marry, a question that evokes in the laconic Ledger a memory of his own love. Alma Jr. leaves her sweater behind in

Figure 4.1   Still from *Brokeback Mountain* **(2:07:50)**

Source: © 2005 Focus Features. Courtesy of Universal Studios Licensing LLC

Ennis's rundown trailer, and he folds it and takes it to his armoire to store, opening the door to reveal his same-sex shrine on its inner panel. Gustavo Santaoialla's sparse guitar solo has already begun to prepare us for the symbolic move to the hidden interiority of Ennis's solemn oath to preserve his mourning and melancholy for his dead lover.

The close-up triangulates the reversed shirts—replete with a spot of blood on the plaid of Ennis's shoulder. Both held up by a symbolic wire hanger in the lower part of the frame, the layered shirts are juxtaposed to a faded postcard in the upper right, tilted and thumbtacked to the door. Ennis's thumb on the left side of the frame is about to straighten the crooked postcard of Brokeback Mountain—a still picture within a motion picture that captures the condensation and obsession of Ennis's lament into this long shot of a distant range. The blue filtered postcard tellingly depicts an almost blackened set of foothills that highlight the alpenglow of the higher mountains, giving the viewer a sense of the censorious lowlands of Aguirre and homophobic Wyoming towns in contrast to the stunning beauty of the snow-covered peaks where the lovers were free to consummate their unforgettable passion. Symbolically, in the film adaptation Ennis's shrine remains tacked to a closet door, its appearance triggered by the intrusion of heterosexual marriage. Ennis's tearful gaze at the memorial he must both hide and pay homage to symbolizes the melancholy that arises as a result of the gay lover's inability to publically mourn the loss of his lover.[50] Unable to resolve or "fix" his grief, Ennis is stuck within his tragic melancholy, even though his memorial, no matter how hidden or unceremonious, creates a place of resistance to the heteronormative burial rites he has encountered in his visit to Jack's relatives. As Ennis swings the door closed, the cinematographer zooms quickly into the faded postcard, simulating the gazer's inevitable focus on the place and time that preserves his indelible and haunting memory.

Can Ennis's memorial, akin to the repeated screenings of *Brokeback* and readings of *Close Range*, create a transformation in social consciousness? Can these repetitions lead to the passage of equal protection clauses, act as a catalyst for the recognition of the queer as social being? Can the impact of this fiction, the imagined power of *Brokeback*—through dissemination, citation, and reiteration—bring about a fix for the legal and social bias that underwrites suicide and closeted lives? Or do these cultural plots just help us "stand it," allow us to cope with the implacable monuments of hate? If cultural production is an agent in the production of society's sense of itself—if this story tells us about who we are—then it is incumbent upon the audience, the tragic spectators, not just to pity and fear, but to use *Brokeback* to clarify, as one definition of catharsis has it, the inequities of a justice system that continues to sanction hate.

---

50   Judith Butler discusses the protracted role of melancholy for the queer subject in *Gender Trouble* (*Gender Trouble: Feminism and the Subversion of Identity* [New York: Routledge, 1990], 57–66), a reading of Freud's famous work, *Mourning and Melancholia*.

Chapter 5

Queer Exposures: Making the Real Reel in Van Sant's *Milk*

[E]very act is to be construed as a repetition, the repetition of what cannot be recollected, of the irrecoverable, and is thus the haunting spectre of the subject's deconstruction. (Butler, *Bodies That Matter* 244)

Out at the Center: San Francisco's City Hall Plaza

Gus Van Sant's critically acclaimed *Milk* had its initial release on October 28, 2008, only a week before a general election in California saw the passage of California's Proposition 8, a constitutional amendment that banned gay marriage. After the law took effect on November 5, freezing the licensing of marriages in San Francisco, the Supreme Court of California agreed to hear a challenge to the amendment.[1] Oral argument took place at the Supreme Court headquarters in San Francisco's Civic Center, a big screen television set up in the plaza where the public viewed the proceedings in March 2009. The *Strauss* decision upheld the amendment, holding that existing domestic partnership legislation insured that Proposition 8 did not violate the state constitution but only carved out a "limited exception" to equal protection based on differing terminology. The existing 18,000 same-sex marriages, the court ruled, would remain valid under California law.

Concurrent with this legal drama in the plaza, Van Sant's film *Milk* was garnering eight Academy Award nominations in another California city, including Sean Penn's successful bid for Best Actor. The cultural drama playing in movie houses across the globe (except in Samoa where it was banned) told a different story than the *Strauss* case, a narrative that also had as one its central locations the very same plaza where a screen projected Judge Carlos Moreno's cross-examination of the experts in that case.[2] *Milk* depicts the tragic story 30 years earlier of the rise

---

1   *Strauss v. Horton* 46 Cal.4th 364; 93 Cal.Rptr. 951, 207 P.3d 48 (2008).

2   Moreno dissented in *Strauss*, claiming that Proposition 8 violated equal protection. In the subsequent federal challenge to Proposition 8, *Perry v. Schwarzenegger* (704 F.Supp. 2d 921 [N.D. Cal. 2010]), Judge Walker ruled that the ban on same-sex marriage in California violates the due process and equal protection clauses of the Fourteenth Amendment of the United States Constitution. Walker's decision is currently on appeal in the Ninth Circuit, where a three-judge panel has referred the case to state court for a determination whether or not the appellants (the sponsors of the initiative) have standing, since the attorney general of California elected not to participate in the appeal. When Vaughn Walker retired in 2010, appellants also brought an additional challenge, arguing that Walker should have recused

and fall of Harvey Milk, one of the first openly-gay elected officials in the United States; the film finds its apogee not only in his historic election to office in 1977 but also in Milk's address to thousands in the same plaza during the 1978 Gay Pride Parade, where he began with his signature opening: "I am Harvey Milk and I am here to recruit you."

The action of Van Sant's biopic shuttles at key moments between the Castro—the gay colony in a once working-class neighborhood of Eureka Valley—and the grey brick expanse of City Center Plaza a mile down the hill. In the film, gay activists march down to the plaza three times: first after a police raid on gay bars, again after defeat of gay rights ordinances in the 1970s, which was spawned by Anita Bryant's Save Our Children campaign, and finally in a candlelight vigil that takes place after Supervisor Milk's and Mayor Moscone's assassination on November 28, 1978. Though the film ends with the vigil, San Francisco's Civic Center Plaza would again become the site of queer history after Dan White's manslaughter verdict spawned one of the most violent queer uprisings in United States history—the White Night Riots of May 21, 1979.

Although the Stonewall Inn in Greenwich Village, now a historic monument, has rightly garnered considerable attention as the symbolic location of the beginning of the gay rights movement, San Francisco's Civic Center Plaza represents a public space that has also seen innumerable iterations of queer activism since 1972, when Harvey Milk, the Long Island Goldwater Republican, tuned in, turned on, and came out (west), moving to San Francisco and giving up his Wall Street career to open a camera shop and run endlessly for public office as the unofficial Mayor of Castro Street.[3] Milk's migration, a kind of queer Horatio Alger story, has as its commemorative backdrop the plaza outside Arthur Brooks's 1915 architectural masterpiece, a Beaux Arts city hall with the fifth largest dome in the world, the location where we witness Milk's transformation from hippie to polyester-suited legislator, from populist to Boss Tweed insider, from Harold-Stassen laughing stock to gay martyr.[4] Yet the central role of the plaza in the ongoing struggle for

---

himself from the case because he is gay. In response, the retired Vaughn told reporters, "If you thought a judge's sexuality, ethnicity, national origin, (or) gender would prevent the judge from handling a case, that's a very slippery slope" (Bob Egelko, "Vaughn Walker, Retired Judge, Reflects on Prop. 8," *SFGate.com* [April 7, 2011]). A hearing on the bias charge took place in federal court June 13, 2011 (see Scott Shafer, "When a Gay Judge Rules on Gay Rights, *NPR.org*). I discuss the *Perry* at length later in this chapter.

In February, 2012, the Federal Court of Appeals held Proposition 8 unconstitutional on narrow grounds; they also ruled that Judge Walker did not need to recuse himself from making his original ruling because he was a gay man (http://latimesblogs.latimes.com/lanow/2012/02/gay-marriage-prop-8s-ban-ruled-unconstitutional.html). The case could reach the United States Supreme Court as early as 2013.

3   For the most recent publication on Stonewall, see David Carter, *Stonewall—The Riots that Sparked the Gay Revolution* (New York: St. Martin's Griffin, 2010).

4   Unlike Alger's young heroes, however, Harvey went from "riches" to "rags," nor did he, like Alger's characters, end up married.

queer recognition does not stop with the White Night Riots in 1979; the plaza re-emerged in 2009 as the location of the televised marriage debate, a location that moviegoers, through a historical palimpsest, were simultaneously revisiting in the screening of Van Sant's biopic at the multiplex in nearby Civic Center Plaza.

The uncanny simultaneity of these two broadcasts—one legal (*Strauss v. Horton*) and the other cinematic (*Milk*)—as well as their substantive and temporal differences cast San Francisco's Civic Center as a performative and charismatic site of queer acts and activism. In his discussion of the symbolics of power and charisma, Clifford Geertz develops his notion of centers as "concentrated loci of serious acts" or "points in a society where its leading ideas come together with its leading institutions to create an arena in which the events that most vitally affect its members' lives take place."[5] Though Geertz claims such centers have "little to do with geography," his examples encompass not only charismatic figures but also the set of actions, ceremonies, and formalities that appertain to symbolic power, including processions and parades analogous to the many marches from the Castro to City Hall in the 1970s as well as the subsequent 2009 march on the Day of Decision, after the California Supreme Court upheld Proposition 8.

I want to shift the focus in this chapter from the charisma of the performative subject to the charisma of geographical location, as exemplified by the role San Francisco's City Hall Plaza plays through its repeated citation as the stage of queer drama. Employing Derrida and Butler's theorizing of the performative as sedimented repetition of precedent, this chapter seeks to transfer the application of these ideas from human subject to geography. While such a displacement requires, admittedly, a capacity to imbue place with an unlikely epistemology, such a transference allows us to shift our inquiry from individual identity to political act, from doer to deed, and, more radically, from the cult of the individual to the symbology of place. San Francisco's Civic Center Plaza—a flat open collection of bricks, lawns, and trimmed poplars surrounded by City Hall, the Public Library, and the Civic Auditorium—exists as an open and now often homeless-oriented liminal space that represents neither the safe homolocale of Castro Street nor the heterocentric interiors of the courtrooms and legislative offices in City Hall.[6] The plaza is open, public, unstructured, yet at the same time bounded by historic architecture, adjacent to the

---

5   Clifford Geertz, *Local Knowledge: Further Essays in Interpretive Anthropology* (New York: Basic Books, 1983), 123–124.

6   See for example Nancy Oswin, "Critical Geographies and the Uses of Sexuality: Deconstructing Queer Space," *Progress in Human Geography* 32:1 (2008): 89–103; also Pat Califia, "San Francisco: Revisiting the City of Desire," in *Queers in Space: Communities, Public Spaces, Sites of Resistance*, ed. Gordon Brent Ingram, Anne-Marie Bouthillette, and Yolanda Retter (San Francisco: Bay Press, 1997), 177–196; Lawrence Knopp, "Sexuality and Urban Space: Gay Male Identity Politics in the United States, the United Kingdom, and Australia," *Cities of Difference*, ed. Ruth Fincher and Jane M. Jacobs (New York: Guilford, 1998), 164–168 (a section entitled "Urban Spectacle, Social Democracy and the Management Success" discusses Sidney's gay pride parade); see also David Bell and Gill Valentine, eds. *Mapping Desire* (New York: Routledge, 1995).

populist Market Street that runs diagonally across the city's grid, a street that divides classes and runs its railway up the hill to Castro Street.

San Francisco's Civic Center Plaza has over the last 30 years staged enactment after re-enactment of queer performances—political, social, and discursive—in ways that demonstrate what Judith Butler calls the paradox of subjectivation, the processes through which LGBTIQ activism both resists and defines itself in relation to what she calls enabling norms. In "Critically Queer," the last chapter of *Bodies That Matter*, Butler examines the history of the word "queer" from its origin as slur to its re-appropriation by activists and academics as a way of showing how re-signification allows the "abjected" to "make their claim through and against the discourses that have sought their repudiation" (224). The term "queer," she argues, acts as a "deformation" of the performative marriage vow in part by revamping the repeated invocation of a "shaming taboo" into a designation for those who resist the social norm of heterosexual marriage (226). Relying on Derrida's critique of Austin in his essay "Signature, Event, Context," Butler reminds us that though performatives may create material effects through their enunciation, they only gain that force by virtue of their precedent, their pronouncement within a historical context, their echo of "prior actions" that gain *"the force of authority through the repetition or citation of a prior, authoritative set of practices. What this means, then, is that a performative 'works' to the extent that it draws on and covers over* the constitutive conventions by which it is mobilized" (227). Most famously in Butler's work, gender binaries act as performatives to the degree that they gain authority through a repeated claim to the natural that has as its authority nothing more than the mobilization of the process of repetition or citation itself. The re-signification of the term queer "derives its force precisely through the repeated invocation by which it has become linked to accusation" while at the same time claiming a "collective contestation, the point of departure for a set of historical reflections and futural imaginings" (226, 228).

Butler's use of the "power of citation" as a formula for the binding force of speech acts invokes the legal discourse of citation as the prevailing metaphor for the way a set of queer acts at the San Francisco Civic Center have emerged "in the context of a chain of binding conventions" (225). These acts—ranging from demands for equal rights, criminal justice, and marriage equality—dramatize a temporal progression of queer activism that replicates the collective amnesia of the effective performative. The demand for marriage equality, I contend, as symbolized by the broadcast of *Strauss* and more recently by Judge Walker's federal court decision in *Perry v. Schwarzenegger* both *draws on and covers over* the checkered domestic legacy of Harvey Milk, as dramatized in the cultural replication of his biography in Van Sant's Focus Features film. The simultaneous "broadcasting" of the California marriage cases and the commercial dissemination of *Milk* the movie exemplify a conflict between normative assimilation and queer resistance which characterizes what Butler calls the "paradox of subjectivation" in the struggle for queer rights. Ironically, access to the most cited speech act of all time, "I now pronounce you man and wife," underpins the current lesbian and gay claim to same-sex marriage rights, a claim that ignores the messy domestic life of Harvey himself, even as it builds on his legacy to legitimate its claim to a place at the marriage table. "To what extent," Butler asks, "has the performative 'queer' operated alongside, as a deformation of, the 'I pronounce you …' of the marriage ceremony?" (226).

In this chapter, I examine the simulcast of the Milk story and the Proposition 8 cases as a way of engaging in a queer critique of the history of gay politics in San Francisco's Civic Center Plaza, a critique that will show how the gay marriage movement both cites and disowns its Castro heritage in its quest for equality. The juxtaposition of the identitarian Milk years, replete with their pre-AIDS public sex and utopian gay ghettos—against the quiet domesticity of two mommies in search of a certificate of approval underlines the way the marriage quest necessarily *covers over* a part of queer subjectivity even as it stages its quest for equal rights under the law.

Milk's Citations: The Reel and the Real

"Not only is *Milk* about politics," Andrew Holleran writes, "so is its release."[7] Focus Features delayed general dissemination of the film until after November 4 because the studio wanted to avoid its picture being labeled a purely political one like Oliver Stone's *W*. Ironically, however, Van Sant's biopic became "edited by history" regardless of its timed release, the successful passage of the Christian and Mormon-backed Proposition 8 that November bringing an alarming setback to the very gay rights movement the *Milk* screenplay celebrates. In 2008, the successful campaign of the ProtectMarriage.com forces against same-sex marriage invoked the same appeal to child brainwashing that Anita Bryant had deployed in Dade County 30 years earlier, a tactic that almost succeeded for Senator Briggs in California until Harvey Milk organized a campaign to defeat the 1978 ballot initiative, known as Proposition 6. That initiative would have banned lesbian and gay teachers from public schools.[8] Given the ability of the Christian right to revive and cite the Anita Bryant legacy with success in 2008, the regressive political context of *Milk*'s release gives its queer populist message an uncanny tinge of datedness, even as the reminder of Harvey's legacy has fostered perseverance on the part of the marriage equality movement.

Van Sant's film details Milk's crusade against Proposition 6 at length, engaging in the marvelous "interweaving of real and reconstructed scenes" that marks the picture's unique blend of fiction and fact, but the reiteration of Harvey's message of hope in the screenplay, echoing the campaign rhetoric of the Obama victory, is

---

7   Andrew Holleran, "'If They Know Us …'," *Gay and Lesbian Review Worldwide* (April–May 2009), www.glreview.com/article.php?articleid=148.

8   B. Ruby Rich, "Ghosts of a Vanished World," *Guardian* (January 16, 2009), www.guardian.co.uk/film/2009/jan/16/harvey-milk-gus-van-sant.

thrown into question by this expensive and disheartening defeat for gay rights, as illustrated by the line of pickets protesting the passage of Proposition 8 as viewers emerged from the premiere of the film at the famous Castro Theatre.[9] "A new sense of loss and betrayal," one critic remarks, cast a metaleptic pallor over Van Sant's upbeat rendition of Milk's rise and fall in the aftermath of the decisive passage of Prop 8, whose signature campaign featured a mother complaining that she didn't want her daughter coming home and announcing it was perfectly acceptable for her to marry another princess. The specter of the potentially pedophiliac queer had once again seized the ideological imagination of the heteronormative populace, Milk's ironic message of recruitment—as if queers were missionaries—resurfacing as the irrational motive for renewed discrimination.

If Van Sant's retelling of the tragic and historic Milk narrative coincides "eerily" with the politics of 2008, Harvey's message of hope also resonates dissonantly with the 2010 challenges of a déjà vu Republican landslide, replete with the defeat of three Iowa Supreme Court judges who voted to legalize same-sex marriage.[10] The 2010 Tea Party backlash took place at the same time as a rash of gay teen suicides, including a dramatic leap off the George Washington Bridge by Rutgers' freshman Tyler Clementi, who was outed on the Internet by his roommate. Harvey's perennial message, "come out, come out wherever you are," laced with its liberationist idealism, has since come under attack by those who have analyzed the exclusionary and pigeon-holing properties of minority politics and instead have championed the intentionally indeterminate qualities of "queer."[11] "For whom is outness a historically available and affordable option?" Judith Butler asked 15 years after Milk's assassination, 15 years before Van Sant's film dramatizes a phone call from a disabled gay teen in Minnesota, who announces his plans to commit suicide rather than attend a reform school where his parents want to send him.[12] Harvey convinces the young Midwesterner to hold off and recommends he get on a bus for San Francisco or Los Angeles. Years later, during election night, Harvey hears from the same teenager, now

---

9   See Rich, Nicholas Rapold, "Come with Us," *Sound and Sense* (February 2009): 28–30; Harry M. Benshoff, "*Milk* and Gay Political History," *Jump Cut: A Review of Contemporary Media*; A.O. Scott, "Freedom Fighter in Life Becomes Potent Symbol in Death," *The New York Times* (November 26, 2008), http://movies.nytimes.com/2008/11/26/movies/26milk.html; Johnny Ray Huston, "*Milk*," *Cinema Scope*, www.cinema-scope.com/cs37/cur_huston_milk.html. Holleran criticized the film for being neither "fish nor foul, neither documentary nor feature film." Others criticized the fluffy soundtrack of the movie, and its failure to capture the "darkness and craziness" of the period (Rich), while other gay critics have commented on the subdued depiction of sex scenes.

10   "Eerily" is from Benshoff.

11   "As much as identity terms must be used, as much as 'outness' is to be affirmed, these same notions must become subject to a critique of the exclusionary operations of their own production" (Judith Butler, *Bodies that Matter: On the Discursive Limits of "Sex,"* (New York: Routledge, 1993) 227.

12   Butler 227.

safe and sound in what we assume is West Hollywood. This poignant scene in the film dramatizes the paradoxes of the contemporary queer subject—*constituted by a past* history of opprobrium that faces continual *reiterations* even as the movement dodges the boomerangs of backlash.

Though inspirational politically, *Milk* also fits, ironically, into the only-good-queer-is-a-dead-queer genre that *The Celluloid Closet* examines in its history of LGBT cinema (epitomized best perhaps by Williams's *Suddenly Last Summer*). This genre finds its most recent commercial successes in *The Hours* and *Brokeback Mountain*—even Ford's *Single Man*.[13] If the tragic *Brokeback*, which like *Milk* takes place during the 1960s and 1970s, concerns itself with internalized homophobia, one commentator has suggested, then the narrative of *Milk* depicts its external counterpart—both stories ending in the demise of its queer hero whose sexual orientation complicates his status as protagonist and renders his demise as either a triumph of the Aristotelian status quo or a demonstration of Boal's theater of the oppressed.[14] In either case, unlike most of the films in this genre, *Milk* relates a story of political stamina and optimism even as it complies with the generic requirements of queer erasure through its aesthetic rendition of the slow-motion slaying of Harvey by Dan White, a poster for Puccini's *Tosca* at the War Memorial Opera House in the background. Van Sant's film thus foregrounds the queer tragic paradigm that its biographical content necessarily unfolds, even as it frames Harvey's martyrdom as an event fraught with cultural and social symbolism. Though the film ends on an implausible note when Harvey's friend and ex-lover Scott Smith and Anne Kronenberg (the only female character of substance in the film) walk into a poorly attended memorial in City Hall before realizing that a candle-light vigil of thousands is on its way (once again) down Market Street to the plaza, this march at the close of the film nevertheless dramatizes Milk's status as a populist—an *out*sider whose support came from the streets, not the courthouse.

Milk inevitably cites and as a result carries forward this tragic queer paradigm, but it also twists that story into a celebration of coming out—politically, socially, and geographically. Van Sant chooses not to depict the aftermath of Milk's assassination, including the famous "Twinkie Defense" trial of Dan White and the subsequent riots detailed in *The Times of Harvey Milk*, the 1984 award-winning documentary that serves as one source for the filmmaker (see Chapter 1). Instead the queer auteur Van Sant focuses on the metaphoric candle-lighting of the progressive LGBT movement and Harvey's resounding and simplistic call for a universal coming out as a solution to discrimination. Harvey's message sounds a pre-Foucauldian note that is both utopian and liberationist, but also one that has come under recent attack as imperialist and precariously ill-advised for queers in Uganda and Nigeria.[15]

---

13   See Vito Russo, *The Celluloid Closet* (New York: Harper & Row, 1987).

14   See Holleran for external/internal.

15   See Martin Manalansan and Arnaldo Cruz-Malave, eds. *Queer Globalization: Citizenship and the Afterlife of Colonialism* (New York: New York University Press, 2002) and Jasbir Puar, *Terrorist Assemblages: Homonationalism in Queer Times* (Durham, NC:

The film incorporates some of this critique through a telling conversation between Harvey and Scott in an alley after a campaign meeting during which Harvey hands a phone to one of his aides and enjoins him to call his parents and come out. Scott reminds Harvey of his own hypocritical personal history, recalling the closeted phone calls Harvey made to his mother in Long Island during their relationship. Harvey never *did* come out to *his* family, even as his taped testament—made prophetically in the event of his assassination—asked that the bullet of his death break open closet doors around the world.

The film's narrative begins with a shot of Harvey in the kitchen of his apartment tape recording his life story, and the screenplay will return to this table scene throughout the unfolding of Harvey's history. In his recording, Milk acknowledges the risks that accompany the speech act of coming out, but he is even more aware of the material consequences of silence—aware of the long-term impact of the closet. On the one hand, for example, a queer politician, teacher, or Walmart worker who proudly pronounces that "we are everywhere" while working and living beside those who fear homos does the important work of breaking down boundaries; on the other, an assimilationist announcement that "we are just like you" incites resistance from a heterocentric world order that defines itself in part through homo-exclusion. In his tense relationship with Dan White, Harvey Milk not only recognized but also seemed to cultivate the dangerous supplement that haunts the act he championed— the way queer subjectivity both adds to the normative world and replaces it through a constitutive outside seeking to find a place within.[16] At the table where gays and lesbians seek a place, knives are often sharpened. Yet for Milk, the closet was an even more dangerous enemy; silence a more painful, if slower, death.

Van Sant's version of the Milk story—even as it strikes the major key of progressive politics—does not ignore the history of external and internal oppression that necessarily attaches to any historical account of the queer subject. His biopic announces its ties to gay history in its masterful opening montage of black-and-white footage of police bar raids in Los Angeles and Miami. The newsreel footage features men in thin ties and 1960s suits hiding their faces from the public camera, then cuts to newspaper headlines about bar raids, including a New York newspaper article about the Stonewall Riots. Setting the context for the Castro migration a decade later, this opening of the movie ends with the closing of the door on a police paddy wagon as it drives off to the station—queer men criminalized for gathering in a bar. Van Sant's prologue not only establishes a backdrop for Milk's amazing transformation from New York insurance broker to

---

Duke University Press, 2007). Puar's recent critique of Dan Savage's It Gets Better (IGB) campaign can be found at www.guardian.co.uk/commentisfree/cifamerica/2010/nov/16/ wake-it-gets-better-campaign (Jasbir Puar, "In the Wake of It Gets Better," *Guardian* [November 16, 2010]).

16   See Barbara Johnson's discussion of Derrida's notion of the dangerous supplement in her "Translator's Introduction" to Derrida's *Dissemination* (Chicago: University of Chicago Press, 1981) x-xiii.

Castro hippie; it foregrounds the shift in gay culture from a pre-Stonewall fear of the camera's interpellating lens to a Castro Street celebration of it, from avoidance of the cinematic gaze to Van Sant's saturated use of it in his retelling of the story of a famous camera-store owner.

As one critic describes his experience of watching *Milk* in the Castro Theatre, he realizes how much "harder and harder" it became, "to separate the world of the screen from the one we lived in"—a trenchant observation that speaks to the film's insistence on mixing reality and fiction, on interspersing, as it does, newsreel with on-location shooting of the feature film.[17] In the first half of the picture, Van Sant's homage to the news film genre emerges in the careful splicing of shots of the burgeoning Castro into scenes of Harvey and Scott opening their camera store, weaving news interviews after bar raids into re-created riots as the filmmaker attends to details like replacing Milk's visage with Penn's in actual campaign posters. This reconstruction, a dizzying splice of the real and the reeled, represents more than Van Sant's playful post-modernism; it establishes an intimacy between culture and social reality that understands the camera as chronicler of the world, as agent in constructing our sense of reality.

If Van Sant's formalism asks the viewer to recognize the visual constructedness of history, Lance Black's screenplay emphasizes the way Milk's biography borrowed from the operatic drama he championed. From soap-boxing at Market and Castro to bull-horning after the repeal of gay rights laws in Wichita and Eugene, Harvey staged his endless campaigning through charm, wit, and lime-lighting that was nothing if not theatric and scripted. After the initial archival footage shows a police wagon full of bobby-socked and Vitalised Paul-Drake clones, the film cuts to Milk in 1978, hunched over the kitchen table taping an account of his political legacy— one that disdained the queer good old boys like *Advocate* owner David Goodstein and his attorney sidekick Rick Stokes. The tape, which ironically was recorded only 10 days before Harvey's murder, was made, Milk states, in the event of his death by assassination. It introduces the audience to Milk's reminiscences—from rallies in the Castro to meetings with unions—but the recording is soon interrupted by Van Sant's cut to live coverage from City Hall after White's murders, a close-up of Supervisor Feinstein announcing the assassination of Moscone and Milk. The early inclusion of this famous newsreel, which opens Epstein's 1984 documentary as well, establishes Van Sant's indebtedness to his documentary source and foregrounds *Milk* as a remake, a homage, a reiteration of the ensuing and oft-told Aristotelian tragedy. Van Sant's interest in recapture and retelling has its own precedent in the use of citation in his other films: *Henry the Fourth Part One* in his *My Own Private Idaho*, Hitchcock in his remake of *Psycho*, the Columbine murders in *Elephant*, and the Kurt Cobain biography in *To Die For*.[18]

As *Milk* progresses, the gaps between the narrative framework of Harvey in his kitchen and the depiction of the story line grow longer, but in the opening sections

---

17   Rich 3.
18   On Van Sant's retellings, see Rapold.

of the movie, the director carefully foregrounds the camera as both his narrator and to a certain extent his subject. Through his mixture of black and white snapshots, grainy 1970s footage, re-created home-made videos, and realistic re-creation of Milk and Scott Smith settling on Castro Street, the filmmaker features visual representation as an a-temporal archive, a time-capsule device that loses its context through dissemination. Van Sant mixes and matches his borrowed and created shots, his historical and fictional frames, creating a post-modern effect that simultaneously situates Harvey in history while at the same time presenting his story as recaptured in the film's "take" or version of the now iconic biography. A-chronologically, the film moves from its opening 1960s gay arrest prologue to the kitchen narrator in 1978, then moves forward to the assassination and back to 1970 in the New York subway before Harvey lands in San Francisco where he and Scott eventually open Castro Camera in the early 1970s. Milk's taped voice-over accompanies the famous footage of police swarming the corridors of City Hall after the murders, his declaration "we have broken down major prejudice" ironically juxtaposed to the violence between queers and the police in the Castro after the murders, by most accounts egged on by Dan White's anger about "degenerates" taking over the city. Yet in Van Sant's version of Milk's life, the celebratory continuously vies with the brutal: the deep pessimism Harvey's death could have produced in a cinematic retelling is countered by the film's carefree 1970s soundtrack, its colorful depiction of the excitement and novelty of the Castro revolution, its punctuation of police brutality with birthday parties and the opening of Mom and Pop (or Pop and Pop) enterprises.

Van Sant's hand is not a heavy one, and his technique, at least for the first hour of the film, eschews the unflinching realism of an Ang Lee. As the camera shoots Harvey taking pictures with his SLR, the snapshots serve as cuts from color to black and white; in one instance the clicking of a Castro Street scene results in a cut to grainy archival footage of the Golden Gate Bridge, in homage to a city that has swayed the American social imagination from the days of flower children in the Haight Ashbury to the out-and-proud sidewalks of Upper Market Street in the 1970s. As Harvey casts his eye on the plate-glass storefront that will become his shop in the middle of the first block of Castro, a scene called The Kiss epitomizes the film's preoccupation with the paradox of camera work: the way it preserves even as it interprets. The scene begins with Harvey and Scott hanging their new Castro Camera sign in the store window, the camera angled level and shooting from the shadowed interior of the store, where it will stay for the duration of the initial episode, gazing through the plate glass on to Castro Street, superimposing the dark Castro Camera sign on the red liquor store sign across the street, where a baggy-sweater owner emerges to converse with the new jean-clad renters.

Harvey's *camera* store gives Van Sant his *Blow-Up* metacinematic license—his narrative ground for thinking about queer history as pictorial, stagey, and visual. After the sign is hung, Scott leaves the store to gaze with Harvey at the sign and thus directly at the camera and us. They stand in the street and kiss as the liquor merchant emerges from his store and crosses towards them. Harvey introduces himself as a new shop owner, a Jew but not, he hopes, an interloper in the fast-changing Irish

Catholic neighborhood. The liquor storeowner informs the gay couple that the police will revoke their business license if they try to open the store. "There's god's law and man's law," Mr. McConnelly tells Harvey, "and the San Francisco Police are happy to enforce either." As he walks away from the new queers on the block, he tells them to have a nice day. Harvey sarcastically thanks him for the "warm welcome" to the neighborhood and calls him a schmuck under his breath as he and Scott walk into the store and Harvey stoops to put the "Yes, We Are Open" sign in the window while a scruffy queer couple walks by on the sidewalk and looks in.[19]

The other form of law this scene does not articulate explicitly emerges as the law of economics, a form of power that eventually if begrudgingly prevails in the Eureka Valley, as subsequent scenes of gay commerce demonstrate. Further in the narration, we encounter the inside of the same liquor store where gay men are lining up to buy booze, some shirtless on a summer day. Harvey enters to ask Mr. McConnelly how business is, to which the homophobic but now moneymaking shop owner replies "fine, Harvey." With his characteristic sardonic edge, the shirtless and long-haired Milk asks the shop owner if he is still upset about doing business with "homosexuals," smirking and withdrawing his comment, then instructing the gay customers to "spend away," sending his regards to McConnelly's wife. This subsequent scene captures the chutzpah of Milk's in-your-face approach to the gay takeover of the Castro, but the film leaves open the question whether or not the law of economics, and in this case capitalist economics, trumps the law of God. The proximity produced by the steady stream of queer customers may or may not have influenced McConnelly's point of view, but we do know that his accumulation of capital gave him the power to contribute to the campaign, if he wished, of Dan White, a supervisor from a southern part of the city, who harbored the very resentments McConnelly voices earlier. In an era when stores like Target can cater to gay clients and at the same time give hundreds of thousands of dollars to the passage of Proposition 8, the laws of economics are hardly guarantors of queer acceptance.

Conversely, the film depicts David Goodstein, the fired financier turned owner of *The Advocate*, as a queer Uncle Tom who stands in the way of the populist Milk. Goodstein is portrayed as the subaltern gay capitalist whose behind-the-scenes efforts are criticized as too little too late, ineffectual beside the straightforward assertiveness of the Long Island Jew turned Mayor of Castro Street. Through Scott's critique of his lover's Republican past, the film glances at Harvey's conflicted social development as small business owner turned equal rights advocate, as Teamster's Union ally who helps with the Coors boycott but at the same time cultivates his image as a neighborhood merchant. Harvey's un-ideological capitalism would eventually give way to his efforts to protect seniors, unions, and victimized queers, his ears deaf to White's pleas to keep the

---

19   According to Randy Shilts (*The Mayor of Castro Street: The Life and Times of Harvey Milk* [New York: St. Martin's, 1982]), Castro Camera's homemade wooden sign read, "Yes, We Are *Very* Open" (65). Van Sant left out this detail.

delinquent boys' home out of his working-class neighborhood—for economic as well as social reasons.

To return, "The Kiss" scene follows and underscores the bristling encounter of old and new merchants in the middle of Castro Street. The cinematographer's camera continues to hold its gaze from the dark interior of the store until it cuts to a shot of Harvey's butt inside the story as he stoops to flip up the open sign in the window. The lens moves quickly to an oblique bird's-eye angle above the street, which lightens the grit of the previous scene and blithely captures the romantic couple now framed on the bench outside the store in their faded jeans, Penn on his knees leaning between his lover's legs as the latter sits on the bench. Scott (James Franco) bends to kiss the kneeling Harvey, the couple framed by the high angle shot against the plate glass window where their embrace is reflected above the symbolic "Yes, We Are Open" sign and below the Castro Camera logo at the top of the window—now illuminated with an orange tinge that takes on the color of the liquor store sign earlier. Harvey's prolonged prayer at the altar of his curly-haired, good-natured boy from Jackson, Mississippi establishes Castro Street as the center of a national movement, but also points to Milk as an unapologetic exhibitionist—an in-your-face gay man who knows instinctively that discretion, in this case, has nothing to do with valor and who is willing to risk his life for the gay love he championed. This iconic moment, signaled by the abrupt cut and new camera angle from a bright sky, is accompanied by Danny Elfman's Carmina Burana-like soundtrack, a pulsating choir of sopranos, angelically serenading the couple as the camera zooms out on the kiss (see Figure 5.1). What gives this shot its power, aside from Elfman's choral approval of the liberated lovers, is the way the

Figure 5.1   Still from *Milk*

Source: © 2008 Focus Features. Courtesy of Universal Studios Licensing LLC zoom-out accompanies the soundtrack, the figures growing smaller as their image recedes in a subtle pulsing. Harris Savides's cinematography employs a "stop-action" movement that makes the camera subtly move to the beat of the angelic chorus as the kiss unfolds, Scott running his hands over Harvey's outstretched arms. The scene is both highly romantic and self-consciously formal, both real and expressionistic—passers-by walking down the sidewalk, unfazed by the two lovers, who diminish as the camera gives us a God's law view that is both adoring and strangely theatric, creating an *Angels-in-America* moment.

The Kiss scene captures the tonal ambiguity of Van Sant's film—its refusal to embrace the darkness of Milk's tragic narrative even as it inevitably rolls toward Harvey's martyrdom. Van Sant will later shoot the story of the shooting of Harvey in a mode that also recognizes the power of ideological framing and imbues the visual documents of this drama with an insouciant defiance that may for some downplay the gravity of Harvey's tragic death but for others does the important work of deftly shifting the focus from a Boalian poetics of oppression that inevitabilizes the eradication of the populist queer to a strange poetics of the queer oppressed—a parable of the power of performative culture.

Milk's Marriages

"As homosexuals, we can't depend on the heterosexual model," Harvey explained to Doug one night … "We should be developing our own life-style. There's no reason why you can't love more than one person at a time. You don't have to love them all the same. You love some less, love some more—and always be honest with everybody about where you're at. They in turn can do the same thing and it can open up a bigger sphere" (Shilts, *The Mayor of Castro Street*, 237–238)

The simultaneity of the release of *Milk* and the passage of Proposition 8 illustrates one of the central internal conflicts at work in critical queer studies—the debate over the priority and outcome of an LGBT political movement that has marriage equality as one of its primary goals while remaining dedicated to overcoming a heterocentrism that employs the same institution to underwrite gay discrimination. Harvey Milk's voracious sexual history, detailed in Shilts's *Mayor of Castro Street*, receives considerable taming in the feature film, even as Van Sant borrows from Shilts's biography to tell the story of the suicide of Jack Lira, Harvey's last full-time lover before the assassination.[20] Harvey had a penchant for thin men in their twenties and was in the process of romantically lavishing flowers and notes on lovers like Doug Franks and Billy Weigardt during the time surrounding his embarrassing relationship with Jack Lira, the troubled and alcoholic Fresno

---

20   Even Shilts' account of Harvey's sex life is not without its pejorative descriptors: "horny," "promiscuous," "randy."

kid (played by Diego Luna) who became Milk's dubious first lady. Before Jack Lira successfully hung himself, other lovers of Harvey—Craig Rodwell, Jack McKinley, and Joe Campbell—had also attempted suicide in New York City, a fact Harvey relates to Dan White in one of their discussions of the importance of gay politics during the film.

Black and Van Sant's adaptation departs markedly from the scripted narrative of Epstein's award-winning 1984 documentary (*The Times of Harvey Milk*)—not to narrate the supervisor's ribald sexuality but instead to depict the tragic suicide of Harvey's lover, Jack Lira, re-creating the hanging scene detailed in Shilts's biography, in which Lira pins on to a velvet curtain his suicide note: "You've always loved the circus Harvey. What do you think of my last act?"[21] The film establishes this scene with a high-angle shot of Harvey as he enters the dark foyer to his apartment and climbs its winding stairway toward the flat, notes from Jack pinned to the walls as Milk grows increasingly nervous, tripping over beer cans and reading messages like "It's all about you, honey." The previous scene in the film had taken place in City Hall, where Dan White told Harvey not to humiliate or demean him anymore. In the *mise-en-scène* of the suicide, the final circus note is pinned to a red curtain, held on by an election button. After Harvey pulls it back, the shot of the dangling Lira codes the famous ending of Wyler's *Children's Hour*, when Karen finds the swinging Martha (Shirley MacLaine). The camera cuts sharply to a crying Harvey comforted on the phone by the voice of his true love, Scott, the film then returning to the narrative "tape recording" frame in the same kitchen. "Jack was gone and there was no time to mourn," Harvey states, as the scene moves to the anti-Proposition 6 headquarters, the returns from the November election coming in.

The film's spliced-in news footage of Anita Bryant and others, who report widespread Christian support for the initiative, resonates eerily within the current context of the successful Proposition 8, attesting to the power of the Reagan revolution and the concomitant move in queer politics from 1960s liberation to 1990s post-gay conformity. In a dramatic redaction of Shilts's biography, the screenplay depicts Milk receiving a call during the middle of the election returns from the disabled Minnesotan Paul who tells his hero Harvey that he finally did board a bus for Los Angeles after the election victory, suddenly realizing he "didn't want to die anymore." The phone call from a disabled queer kid, which in Shilts's biography occurs late at night after Proposition 6 is defeated, could as easily have come—in another time and place—from the young Texas screenwriter, Dustin Black. Its placement after Lira's suicide and its specific mention of Paul's abandoned suicidal ideation gives Harvey the hope he needs to carry on, in spite of his strange premonitions days later in a box at the War Memorial Opera House as he watches Tosca commit suicide during the finale of Puccini's opera—a short time before his own death.

---

21   Shilts 233.

A production of *Tosca* with Pavarotti and Montserrat Caballe actually did take place in 1978, and Milk had multiple points of identification with the operatic plot: the martyred Cavaradossi—a painter of portraits—killed at the behest of the hypocritical and jealous Scarpia, causing the heroic Tosca to slay the antagonist Scarpia and jump to her death to avoid her imminent arrest. Van Sant's emphasis on Puccini's music and libretto—framing Harvey's shooting in a window that looks out on the opera house with its *Tosca* banners—foregrounds the heroine's suicide as eerily equivalent to the risk-taking Milk, whose rampant outness regularly brought written death threats. His almost willful martyrdom was Tosca's, and in many ways his active engagement with White invited the violent hetero-hate Harvey had witnessed all his life—in high school, in Central Park, in bar raids, in religious condemnation. This narrative conflation of operatic suicide and the dangers of populist queer politics—enhanced by references throughout the film to Harvey's insistence that he would not live past 50, supplies *Milk* with its sensibility of fated Aristotelian tragedy, even as Van Sant points to queer oppression as the source of both suicide and assassination—calling in Boalian fashion for Milk's legacy to enact change.

The shaping of biographic material in Van Sant's biopic together with recent media attention turned toward the prevalence of queer teen death point to the way suicide functions within the larger marriage debate as a dangerous byproduct of polarization between Milk's Marcusian vision of liberated eros and the Human Rights Campaign's promulgation of assimilatory marriage. Missing from the argument between the marriage promoters like Evan Wolfson and its "sex-positive" detractors like Michael Warner is a discussion of how suicide, the ultimate anti-social performance and one particularly rampant among gay teens and single men, functions as a citational act within queer culture—an engagement with the Real (in the Lacanian sense) that signals what Gambotta calls an absence of the Other.[22] Suicide is the irrevocable act of queer abjection par excellence; it represents a "haunting spectre of the subject's deconstitution," one which necessarily accompanies the struggle of LGBTIQ subjectivity to undo the history of erasure and a compulsory heterosexism that necessarily occludes queer subjectivity.[23] Though the causes of suicide are complex and varied—ranging from

---

22   Antonella Gambotto, *The Eclipse: A Memoir of Suicide* (Broken Ankle Books, 2004). The rash of gay suicides that received considerable publicity after Tyler Clementi jumped from the George Washington Bridge in September 2010 resonates with the prevalence of suicide in the Milk biography, not only among his intimates, but also among the men from small towns in America who regularly called him. Suicide is currently the tenth leading cause of death in the world, and in the west, suicide is most prevalent in the category of single middle-aged men. Though statistics vary, one out of three or four teenage suicide attempts involves an LGBTIQ-related individual. http://en.wikipedia.org/wiki/Suicide. See also, Karen Augé, "Young, Gay, and Bullied: Suicides Elsewhere Have Colorado Educators on Alert," *The Denver Post* (October 12, 2010): 1A-8A.

23   Butler 244.

genetics to substance abuse to discrimination—queer self-annihilation is arguably attributable to an oppression shaped not only by a history of discrimination in religious, employment, and educational venues, as David Segura testified in the *Perry* case, but also within the available social positions within queer culture itself.[24] In *Milk*, Jack's non-belonging emerges along ethnic, geographical, familial, and class lines as well as along the trajectory of his sexual orientation. His father beat him; he grew up in the conservative Central Valley with a migrant Mexican family; he hooked up with Harvey when he already was facing alcohol abuse and joblessness.[25]

Jack's suicide is dramatized as a "last act"—a performance of the tragic queer subject that takes place behind a curtain, sending Harvey the message that neither the sexual utopia of Castro Street in the 1970s nor the conferral of political status can fully uproot the deeply embedded paradigm of tragic anti-gay oppression that continues to thrive among social and cultural institutions, most recently through the likes of 50 Cent, who recently tweeted to his three million followers that he recommended suicide for any man who does not love women.[26] Critical queer studies requires scholars and activists alike to recognize the ways in which the binary of urban bathhouse and suburban wedlock perpetuates an endgame for many queer subjects, who recognize themselves in neither hegemony of marital bliss nor the dance floor of *Queer as Folk*. Van Sant's extensive filming of Lira's suicide takes place in close juxtaposition to his depiction of Harvey's assassination and as a result speaks directly to the way the tragic paradigm—permeating as it does the social and political fabric of queer and straight consciousness—perpetuates a deep-seated oppression that neither the happy hegemony of marriage nor the celebration of the gay ghetto has yet to uproot.

Though the events of the film takes place well before *Baehr v. Lewin* put marriage back on the lesbian and gay map in Hawaii during the 1990s, *Milk* does recast Harvey's biography in ways that transform this gay icon into a more monogamous subject. Dustin Black's screenplay does not dwell at any length on Milk's earlier sexual life; instead, the film recasts its hero as a politically driven organizer whose primary lover, Scott Smith, remains Harvey's "main squeeze"

---

24   *Perry* 101. "Religion is the chief obstacle for gay and lesbian political progress," testified Segura.

25   *Milk* has come under critical attack for its demonization of the Latino Lira as the self-loathing queer (no matter how closely the narrative follows Shilts's biography) and the idealization of Scott Smith as the loyal Milk supporter. The Lira portrayal bears a strange resemblance to the erasure of Philip Levine from *Boys Don't Cry*. See Katie Kane, "Glass of Hope: Drinking in the life and work of Harvey Milk," *The Missoula Independent* (February 12, 2009), http://missoulanews.bigskypress.com/missoula/glass-of-hope/Content?oid=1147982.

26   The text of 50 Cent's controversial comment is quoted in www.towleroad.com/2010/09/50-cent-tweet-encourages-gay-suicide.html; the rapper later explains its context in *The Advocate*, www.advocate.com/News/Daily_News/2010/09/30/50_Cent_Encourages_Gay_Suicide.

even after Harvey's endless campaigning leads Scott to move out. Yet from Shilts's *Mayor of Castro Street*, we know that the 17-year-old Glimpy Milch (Harvey's other name) found himself in a police paddy wagon in 1947, run out of Central Park along with a number of other gay men for indecent exposure—namely the removal of their shirts on a summer day (4). Besides cruising the Rambles, the big-eared Harvey, a clown in appearance and theatric in temperament, was also exploring gropes in standing room at the Met with "adolescent randiness" as he listened to his beloved Bidu Sayao (7).

Shilts's biography reminds us that the closeted Harvey of Long Island was a Goldwater Republican, one who emerged from the Navy with the reputation of a man's man, one who never even thought of himself as queer, one who led a double life that featured him fleeing from the police during bar raids. The wary Harvey took a series of lovers in Manhattan—Joe Campbell, Craig Rodwell, Jack McKinley. He traveled to San Francisco in 1969 with the *Hair* troop, having transformed himself dramatically into a longhaired and beaded hippie before he met, at the age of 41, Scott Smith, 20 years his junior. The film condenses these earlier parts of Milk's life, turning Scott into the catalyst for Milk's hippy-ization, when in fact Milk moved to San Francisco before he met Scott, and once they both set up shop together, neither of the two "put much faith in Harvey's once-dear devotion to fidelity. Promiscuity was practically an article of faith among the new gays of Castro Street," Shilts writes. "This proved particularly fortuitous for Harvey, whose sexual appetite never waned" (88). As the Castro evolved in the 1970s from queer Haight Ashbury into Village People clone-dom (140,000 strong), Harvey's persistence political ambition matched the ambit of his desire.

Given the widely surveillant self-regulation within neo-Puritan capitalism, a mainstream screening of the sexual openness of the Castro in the 1970s was probably, however, infeasible both economically and socially in the supposedly post-gay era of 2008. Not only have the voluntary Motion Picture Association of America (MPAA) ratings replaced the Hays Code as a way of effectively censoring explicit homosexual content at the cineplex; in the case of *Milk*, the rating system no doubt came to dictate the parameters of adaptation, in so far as a filmmaker like the increasingly famous Van Sant sought to produce and distribute a major motion picture. Though both are rated R, *Milk* is hardly *My Own Private Idaho,* even if Van Sant in the initial sex scene between Scott and Harvey uses some of the same pastiche and quick cuts of his earlier film about a male hooker. *Milk*'s sex takes place for the most part in the dark; there is little or no nudity in a film that steers clear of bathhouses and barebacking in favor of an occasional Cleve Jones blowjob or morning-after head-and-shoulders shot. The film moves in a primarily political realm in ways that capitulate to the voluntary sex code for purposes of appealing, presumably, to a wider hetero as well as homo-normative audience. As a result, the Harvey we witness in Van Sant's film is perforce a potentially marriageable subject—someone whose political ambition tragically lost him the love of his life (Scott) and led him to an ill-fated affair with the suicidal and alcoholic Lira. Our Harvey necessarily comes to us at the Opera House Plaza Multiplex in 2009 as a milquetoast by 1978 standards, a portrayal that belies the charged cruising that made the Castro's Elephant Walk a bar where just about everyone was on the make in 1978—including both me and Holy Harvey.

Yet even if the film bowdlerizes the sex-positive Milk, whose horniness was as legendary as his political perseverance, *Milk* nevertheless evokes, even in this toned-down biopic, a pre-AIDS era of free gay love in which "lovers were not meant to be chattels, locked into only one finite relationship."[27] That ethos stands in sharp contrast to the trajectory of the carefully orchestrated affidavits and testimonies of plaintiffs Kristin Perry and Sandra Steir (as well as Paul Katami and Jeffrey Zarrillo) in *Perry v. Schwarzenegger*, the successful post-*Strauss* federal court action against Proposition 8 filed by the lawyers in *Bush v. Gore* three days before the California Supreme Court upheld the amendment based on California law in the *Strauss* case. In contrast to the militant legacy propounded in *Milk*, the *Perry* plaintiffs describe themselves as long-term domestic partners raising children and seeking the imprimatur of wedlock. These conflicting accounts of gay and lesbian life underline the critical delineations of an ongoing debate over the wisdom of gay marriage, as articulated with particular perspicacity by gay activists like queer scholar Michael Warner and Human Rights Campaign lawyer Evan Wolfson.[28] While for some the release of *Milk* evidences how far the LGBT community has come from the early days of celebratory liberation to the current drive to gain access to the thousand rights and liabilities—in tax, tort, domestic relations, and estate law—that attach to a marriage license, for others the move from open sexual relations to the push for homo-assimilation represents a regression rather than a progression—a kind of betrayal of the Milk legacy rather than a citation of it as political if not social precedent.

In contrast to the flamboyant Milk, the plaintiffs in *Perry v. Schwarzenegger* (704 F. Supp. 2d 921 [N.D. Cal 2010]) turn out to be lesbian and gay everypersons— middle-class, hardworking couples interested in raising families and achieving the "special meaning" that attaches to the magic word "marriage," even if tantamount to the rights and liabilities provided by California's domestic partnership law.[29]

---

27   Shilts 238.

28   Michael Warner, "Beyond Gay Marriage," in *Left Legalism/Left Critique*, ed. Wendy Brown and Janet Halley (Durham, NC: Duke University Press, 2002), 259–289. See also Lisa Duggan, "Holy Matrimony!" *Nation* (March 15, 2004).

29   *Perry* at 12 ("special meaning"). The recent California legal history of the struggle for gay marriage begins with Proposition 22, a successful initiative in 2000 that amended California Family Code 308.5 to validate marriage only "between a man and a woman." After the Mayor of San Francisco, Gavin Newsom, ignored Proposition 22 and authorized city officials to issue marriage licenses in 2004, the Supreme Court of California (95 P.3rd 459 [Cal 2004]) stayed the Mayor's order, until the court's *In re Marriages* (189 P. 3rd 384 [Cal 2008]) held Proposition 22 unconstitutional. Approximately 18,000 same-sex couples married between the time of the court's decision, May 2008, and the passage of Proposition 8 in November 2008. Those marriages were held to be valid in *Strauss v. Horton* (207 P.3rd 48 [Cal 2009]), but Proposition 8, the initiative that amended the

Lead plaintiff Kris Perry was first contacted by Chad Griffin, a Los Angeles-based political organizer, who, along with his American Foundation for Equality, has led the charge for the federal lawsuit. After Griffin watched the November 2008 election returns with Mayor Gavin Newsom and Bruce Cohen, one of the producers of *Milk*, the disappointed group conceived of the lawsuit as a response to the agonizing passage of Proposition 8.[30] Forming a foundation to fund the legal challenge—on the board of which sits, ironically enough, Dustin Lance Black and Bruce Cohen—Griffin contacted the distinguished Theodore Olson, the attorney who successfully secured four more years of George Bush in *Bush v. Gore*, as well as David Boies, the attorney for Gore. After assembling these unlikely champions for queer rights, Griffin approached Kris Perry, an administrator of First 5, a California state agency that promotes health and education for young kids. Perry and her partner Sandra Steir, a tech support manager for Alameda County, live in Berkeley where they have raised four boys—ages 15 to 21. The other plaintiffs are a 30-something couple from Burbank: Paul Katami, a fitness expert and consultant, and Jeffrey Zarrillo, his partner of nine years. Because the hearing in *Perry* relied primarily on expert testimony from historians like Yale's George Chauncey (author of *Gay New York*) and gay psychologist Greg Herek, the sexual histories of these plaintiffs have not received the scrutiny that Harvey's has, but Judge Walker's decision nevertheless portrays them in large part as de facto heterosexuals, same-sex couples whose relationships are similarly situated to those of opposite-sex couples (*Perry* 130). The plaintiffs represent mainstream lesbians and gay men, people in committed relationships who, under the equal protection of the Fourteenth Amendment, desperately seek the security and privileges of the state-sanctioned sexuality that attaches to a marriage license.

Not incidentally, Vaughn Walker, the Chief Judge of California's Northern District Federal Court who handed down the *Perry* decision in favor of the plaintiffs, is himself a quiet queer, a Bush Sr. appointee to the federal bench whose position was initially opposed by Nancy Pelosi because the then practicing litigator had represented the United States Olympic Committee against the organizer of the Gay Olympics, later enforcing a lien on the latter's property for court costs while

---

California Constitution to limit marriage to opposite sex couples in November 2008, was upheld. Perry et al. then sued successfully in federal district court, Judge Walker holding Proposition 8 to be a violation of the equal protection and due process clauses of the United States Constitution. Walker's decision holding Proposition 8 unconstitutional was appealed to the Ninth Circuit where oral argument was simulcast on the net. On November 17, 2011, the Supreme Court of California ruled that the private backers of Proposition 8 had a right to defend the constitutional validity of the marriage ban in spite of the State of California's unwillingness to defend it. In February, 2012, the Ninth Circuit ruled Proposition 8 unconstitutional, but supporters of the ban are planning to appeal to the United States Supreme Court.

30   The story of *Perry* is detailed in Margaret Talbot, "A Risky Proposal," *The New Yorker* (January 18, 2010), www.newyorker.com/reporting/2010/01/18/100118fa_fact_talbot?currentPage=all.

he was dying of AIDS. Walker, known as a libertarian and follower of Richard Posner's theories of economic justice, finally gained his seat on the bench in 1989, and has since ruled (1) against an Oakland high school student who protested a teacher's assignment of pro-gay reading material and (2) in favor of a city's refusal to allow one of its employees to hand out anti-gay literature at work.[31] A Library of Congress website lists Walker as one of two federal judges in the country who is out of the closet, but sexual orientation has functioned largely as a nonissue during his years on the bench, at least until his 136-page decision ruled that there was no rational basis for denying same-sex couples marriage licenses. Affirmed in part on appeal, his thorough opinion reviews the history of queer discrimination and finds that there is no substantive difference between gay and straight couples, flying quite squarely in the face of Milk's anti-chattel legacy of opposition to finite relationships.[32]

Milk's social history, even if edited in Van Sant's film in order to fit within the parameters of a censorious Hollywood rating system, acts nonetheless as a dangerous form of authority, which marriage promoters must cover up even as they cite Harvey's political legacy—his passage, for example, of a gay rights ordinance while in office—as precedent for their campaign for marriage equality. Even though screenwriter Dustin Lance Black (who in his acceptance speech expressed his wish to marry one day) and producer Bruce Cohen were both part of this revisionary version of Milk's life and are both members of the foundation that supports the lawsuit, their cinematic reiteration in the Milk story does not entirely obscure the discontinuity of Harvey's domestic rowdiness. There is something of what José Muñoz calls "the antirelational turn in queer studies," as epitomized by Edelman's *No Future* and Bersani's earlier *Homos*, in the dangerous supplement of Harvey's biography—something of the un-interpellatable *jouissance* of sex for sex's sake that neither the producers of *Milk* can make over nor the legal reasoning of Judge Walker can fully rationalize in *Perry*'s extensive finding of facts that led to the overturning of Proposition 8. Van Sant foregrounds that celebratory gay legacy in part through his inclusion of documentary footage of the fabulous Castro way of life in the 1970s.

Yet equally present in the rhetoric of Milk's political ascent is Harvey's repeated canard, "You've gotta give them hope"—a motivational motto adopted as his credo, repeating it twice into his archival tape recorder at the close of the film. Though

---

31   See John C. Hopwood, "Is Vaughn Walker Gay? Federal Judge Who Struck Down Prop 8 is Homosexual," *AssociatedContent*, www.associatedcontent.com/article/5659714/ is_vaughn_walker_gay_federal_judge.html?cat=17associatedcontent 3.

32   On February 7, 2012, a three-judge panel of the Ninth Circuit upheld Walker's decision 2 to 1, but Judge Reinhardt limited his ruling to California, where Proposition 8 removed an *existing* right already granted to lesbian and gay citizens. Reinhardt thus avoided the large constitutional issue of the application of equal protection to *all* gay marriage. In what is now called *Perry v. Brown* (formally *Schwarzenegger*), proponents of Proposition 8 have requested an *en banc* hearing by 11 of the Ninth Circuit judges.

Muñoz in *Cruising Utopia* makes no mention of Milk's constant message of hope in relation to his own "hope" thesis about queer utopia as a localized and often aesthetic place of "forward dawning futurity," the Milk historical moment—with its collective excitement about LGBT power and exposure—arguably evidences a utopian era in the annals of gay culture. Milk, though anti-establishment, was hardly a nihilist or "romancer of the negative," as Muñoz characterizes Edelman's work on the way queer culture resists current narratives of family values; Harvey rather was a crusader for the potentiality of hope—even if his use of the term existed in a realm more openly politicized than the aesthetic modalities treated in *Cruising Utopia.*[33]

But what did Harvey hope for; what was the aim of his constant call? Was it the message a young Mormon Dustin Lance Black heard, as he related to the audience at the Academy Awards: "When I was thirteen ... I heard the story of Harvey Milk. And it gave me hope one day I could live my life openly as who I am and then maybe even I could even fall in love and one day get married."[34] Would Harvey, had he lived, championed the FreedomToMarry blog, or was his message of hope a response to teenagers in Minnesota and Altoona, Pennsylvania, who called Harvey in search of a way to avoid suicide? Would Milk—hope*ful* romantic that he was—have stuck to his open-relationship philosophy, or would he have supported—as the late Tom Stoddard did—the *right* to marry whether or not a queer individual chose to follow that path?[35] These questions—which are often couched in terms of resource allocation, civil rights priorities, and the benefits of ending discrimination through legal recourse—have particular bearing on the political and social future of queer culture. They also speak directly to the way the struggle for marriage equality and its resistors have taken center stage in the current queer drama in ways that sideline the work of a theater of the oppressed— the urgent need to dismantle an antagonistic heterocentrism that foments the narrative of the tragic and suicidal queer subject.

Protect Queers: Warner, Wolfson, Walker, and Forces of Wedlock

At first blush, the achievement of marriage equality for same-sex partners would seem not only to overcome deep inequities between gay and straight couples but also to send a message to queers across the country that "it gets better."[36] No

---

33   José Esteban Muñoz, *Cruising Utopia: The Then and There of Queer Futurity* (New York: New York University Press, 2009), 11.

34   Black's acceptance speech is quoted in http://movies.broadwayworld.com/article/ Dustin_Lance_Blacks_Oscar_Acceptance_Speech_for_Original_Screenplay_20090222.

35   See Aaron Goldstein, "Would Harvey Milk Have Opposed Gay Marriage?" *Canada Free Press* (February 17, 2009), www.canadafreepress.com/index.php/article/8571.

36   www.itgetsbetter.org/ is a Dan Savage inspired blog to let queer youth know that LGBTIQ life can improve. The IGB blog was started in fall 2010 to combat a rash of gay

doubt the horizon of possibility for lesbian and gay youth in Massachusetts, Iowa, and most recently the state of Washington expands with their knowledge that, as screenwriter Black stated, one day—after surviving the high-school assaults and epithets—they could "be who they are" and maybe even marry. Black's heartfelt sentiment recalls a genealogy of queer development that begins with coming out, leads to a fixed identity, and ends with love and marriage, yet tellingly this natural progression leaves out the possibility of love without marriage that Black's hero Harvey Milk envisioned, creating an impression that identity politics and marriage are the endgame for queers. Michael Warner and other scholars challenge assumptions underlying Black's well-known paradigm. "Squeezing gay couples into the legal sorting machine [of marriage] would only confirm the relevance of spousal status," Warner argues, "and would leave unmarried queers looking more deviant before a legal system that could claim broader legitimacy."[37]

For opponents of the legal push for marriage equality, it is ethically incumbent upon the queer subject to examine the way the conferral of this state license not only discriminates against those who are not coupled but more dangerously represents "a state-sanctioned program for normalizing gay sexuality," and thus delegitimizing the kind of sexual openness propounded by Harvey Milk (276). For Warner, the oft-cited "personal choice" argument that marriage equality would establish a *right* to participate in the "menu of privileges and prohibitions" tied to this state institution but not *mandate* that participation ignores the social consequences that would attach to all queers as a result of joining the jointure of marital privilege and championing the lockdown of wedlock. Even as it confers rights and obligations on the Kris Perries and Paul Katamis of the lesbian and gay world, the marriage initiative, from the perspective of its critics, "'makes bachelorhood equivalent to moral lassitude, where all sexual expression outside wedlock is morally tainted.'"[38] For Warner, "marriage, in short, would make for good gays: the kind who would not challenge the norms of straight culture, who would not flaunt sexuality, and who would not insist on living differently from ordinary folk" (277).

In effect, the freedom to marry would not only put the likes of Harvey Milk back in the closet but also feed the violent heterocentrism that cracks down on public displays of queer affection. Warner views marriage promoters like Rotello,

---

teen suicides.

37   Warner, "Beyond Gay Marriage" 282. See also *The Trouble with Normal: Sex, Politics, and the Ethics of Queer Life* (Boston: Harvard University Press, 2002).

38   Warner in "Beyond Gay Marriage" (276) quotes Fenton Johnson's review of William Eskridge's *The Case for Same-Sex Marriage: From Sexual Liberty to Civilized Commitment* (New York: Free Press, 1996). Johnson's "Wedded to an Illusion: Do Gays and Lesbian Really Want the Freedom to Marry?" appears in *Harper's* (November 1996): 4. In his *GayLaw: Challenging the Apartheid of the Closet* (Cambridge, MA: Harvard University Press, 2002), however, Eskridge discusses more open forms of domestic relations law, including the possibilities of polyamorous relations.

Eskridge, and Wolfson not as champions of equality but social engineers who view the marriage quest as a chance to put an end to the popper-snorting, White-Party libertinism of gay culture and instead foster long-term and stable coupling (276). Where does a queer kid from Warm Springs, Montana, find himself in this neo-Puritan discourse; what are his options and how are the parameters of his subjectivity—already condemned in churches, schools, and police departments—further circumscribed by a marriage movement that promotes a policing of his sexual expression? The conferral of marriage equality may give him the hope of possible connubial bliss in the future but that same conferral sends a message of further hopelessness to the solitary and single gay teenager on the lookout for unregulated same-sex connection.

For Human Rights Campaign lawyer Evan Wolfson, however, "marriage is first and foremost *about* a loving union between two people."[39] Radical academics that critique the freedom-to-marry movement as a sell-out, he argues, ignore both the power of love and the overwhelming will of a diverse LGBT populace that seeks to make a public statement about the validity of their unions (272). Moreover, Wolfson states, the marriage ship has sailed, and those who criticize the actions of legislatures and judges around the country are pissing into a prevailing wind (261). Needless to say, the dissenting opinions of Warner, Berlant, and Duggan do not for the most part figure into the deliberations of judges like Vaughn Walker and Margaret Marshall as they apply constitutional provisions to the denial of marriage licenses to same-sex couples, yet this legal anti-intellectualism, endemic to the pragmatic bent of the legal profession in general, does not diminish the value of Warner's discussion of the way "love" functions ideologically as a mystifier that covers over the material inequities which the state license perpetuates.[40] Marriage is a "public institution, not a private relation," Warner insists (274). "The ethical meaning of marrying cannot be simplified to a question of pure motives, conscious choice, or transcendent love. Its ramifications reach as far as the legal force and cultural normativity of the institution" (274). Romantic love, moreover, has its strongest cultural icons not in narratives of wedded couples but stories of passion outside of marriage—like *Anna Karenina* and more recently *Brokeback Mountain* or even *Boys Don't Cry*. The appeal to romantic love as an argument in favor of marriage overlooks the way this state license—obtained by couples for motives

---

39   Warner, "Beyond" (266) cites Evan Wolfson, "Crossing the Threshold: Equal Marriage Rights for Lesbians and Gay Men, and the Intra-Community Critique," *New York University Review of Law and Social Change* (1994) at 479.

40   Chief Justice Margaret Marshall's famous opinion in *Goodrich v. Dept. of Public Health* (798 N.E.2d 941 [Mass. 2003]) is available at http://scholar.google.com/scholar_ca se?case=16499869016395834644&q=goodrich+v.+department+of+public+health&hl=en &as_sdt=800000002&as_vis=1. The relatively ineffective status of Warner's arguments in the legal sphere, points to the way reasoned de-mystification of ideology, like Warner's, does not take into account, as Žižek has argued, how ideology functions irrationally, in spite of the exposure of its flaws.

that range from rights to immigrate to economic security to the legitimization of intimacy—continues to be a "profoundly antidemocratic" institution to the degree that it leaves out those who do not participate in the "long-term coupling" it supposedly fosters.

Warner's critique of the ideological smokescreen behind the isomorphic link of love and marriage has particular relevance for our understanding of the legacy of Harvey Milk and its revision in Van Sant's film. Although the Reverend Troy Perry, the founder of the gay positive Metropolitan Community Church, filed in 1970 an unsuccessful suit in Los Angeles Superior Court to allow him to perform a marriage ceremony for two lesbians, and Jack Baker eloquently brought his unsuccessful case for gay marriage before the courts of Minnesota in 1972, these cases were largely anomalous during the gay rights movement of the 1970s, which focused on employment discrimination, protection against police harassment, and combatting the efforts of Christian organizations to oppress queers. For Warner, the unpopularity of the marriage movement before 1990 reflected a queer commitment to "unprecedented kinds of commonality, intimacy, and public life" that resisted the regulation of sexuality by the state (264). If same-sex marriage was not on Harvey Milk's gaydar, his commitment to the power of love—no matter how obscurant its effects—was unwavering. Harvey *was* a hope*ful* romantic, but his passion for men saw the monogamous message of marriage as unsuitable to his form of intimacy, and his eventual dedication to populist principles as well as his fight against Proposition 6 not only made him deeply suspicious of matrimony as either a religious or secular institution but also turned the focus of his activism toward the promotion of an unrepressed and unregulated expression of same-sex love. The collapse of that expression into the privileged mode of marriage was probably unthinkable for a man whose private and public life struggled against the destructiveness of the closet, and thus the current crusade for marital rights would arguably have been understood as a move from one closet into another—producing a model of normalization that could limit as much as expand the horizon of the single, queer kid in Altoona, Pennsylvania.

The maverick legacy of Milk's biography in juxtaposition to the fast-moving marriage movement points to a deep division in the queer community between academics and legal activists, between constructivists and essentialists, between radical and reactionary forces among a population that is struggling, as Harvey stated in his address to the multitudes in the San Francisco Civic Center Plaza on June 25, 1978, to secure their inalienable right to freedom. Milk's inspirational recital of the Declaration of Independence in front of Gay Pride Paraders in spite of the death threats that the film dramatizes—establishes a common ground that both legal advocates ignore as they remain entrenched in the demands of our adversarial legal system and academics also stubbornly resist through the self-perpetuating certainty of their principles. That common ground—as symbolized by the public space of the plaza—derives its force from recognition of the shared source of oppression that exists in uncanny likeness between the forces of Anita Bryant's 1978 Moral Majority and the Protect Marriage campaign of 2010. Propositions 6

Figure 5.2   Still from *Milk* (City Hall dome)

Source: © 2008 Focus Features. Courtesy of Universal Studios Licensing LLC

and 8—in spite of their separation by 30 years of gay progress in film, television, statutes, schools, stamps, and holidays—are initiatives that have the same source— social and religious conservatives. Their opposition to Warner, Wolfson, and Walker does not discriminate, and Milk's blatant reference to them as impeders of freedom (through Sean Penn's unfortunately wooden hand motions in the film) encapsulates religious intolerance as a formidable force in the perpetuation of queer suicide, harassment, employment discrimination and institutional erasure. The achievement of marriage rights or civil unions or domestic partnership laws will not in and of itself defeat this tragic drama of oppression.

Before Milk gives his speech in the film, Savides's camera establishes the Civic Center Plaza as its location through a god's-eye shot of the open space from an oblique angle, with the dome of City Hall in the foreground—the dolly-in camera action taking place from an aerial position (Figure 5.2).. The high angle reminds us of a few of the salient tragic components in this historic moment, just months before Milk's assassination—a convergence of increasing lesbian and gay freedom, religious and political surveillance, and threats of violence in the face of public expression. Thirty years later an uncanny configuration of these same forces would find voice in the broadcast to an overflow crowd outside of City Hall during the proceedings of *Strauss v. Horton*, the initial legal challenge to the passage of the anti-gay constitutional amendment. When the federal case was filed in 2009, Judge Walker let the public hear *Perry v. Schwarzenegger* online, and a popular blog continues to provide updates on the appeal of his decision.[41] Needless to

---

41   http://prop8trialtracker.com.

say, Judge Vaughn Walker does not cite Michael Warner in his 136-page decision overturning Proposition 8, nor does he mention the legacy of Harvey Milk.

This subaltern magistrate Walker—whose queer quietism contrasts sharply with Milk's theatric sensationalism—builds his case for the constitutionality of same-sex marriage by reviewing the evolution of a civil institution that began as a contract which stripped women of their rights through coverture and maintained racial purity, but over time evolved into its current status as a state-sanctioned social tool for creating "stable households, which in turn form the basis of a stable, governable populace" (111).[42] Walker, who ruled that the due process clause of the United States Constitution is violated by the failure to extend the fundamental right of marriage to lesbians and gay men, established 80 Findings of Fact in his opinion, many of them based on the testimony of the plaintiffs' experts, including David Segura (a Stanford Political Science Professor), Gregory Herek (renowned Psychology Professor), Nancy Cott (American History Professor at Harvard), and George Chauncey (Yale historian). Those findings run the gamut from determinations that (1) gays and lesbians have experienced widespread and acute discrimination from both public and private authorities over the course of the twentieth century (96) to (2) marriage is "the happy ending to romance" or "destination of love" (80) to (3) "laws are perhaps the strongest of social structures that uphold and enforce stigma" (85), to perhaps most germanely, (4) "religion is the chief obstacle for gay and lesbian political progress" (101).

All of these findings lead to Walker's added conclusion of law that "same-sex couples are situated identically to opposite couples in terms of their ability to perform the rights and obligations of marriage under California law" (113), thus rendering the denial of their access to marriage licenses under Proposition 8 a violation of the equal protection clause of the Fourteenth Amendment. While Walker is careful to state that his findings do not require him to rule that lesbians and gays are a suspect class for purposes of heightened scrutiny under the equal protection clause, his findings certainly provide enough evidence for such a conclusion. What is remarkable about Walker's decision is the degree to which it documents the organized and diffuse opposition to the LGBTIQ community from the religious sector of society. David Segura's testimony points to what he calls an "unprecedented" coalition of religious groups, including the established Catholic and Mormon churches, in their opposition to gays and lesbian during the Protect Marriage campaign (59). Eighty-four percent of voters who regularly attend church voted in favor of Proposition 8 while 83 percent of those who do not attend voted against it, a statistic that crystallizes the common source of opprobrium that affects Warner and Wolfson alike.

Echoing Anita Bryant's Save Our Children campaign 30 years earlier, the continued belief that gay and lesbian relations are sinful has led, in the eyes of one expert, directly to violence against the queer minority (101). Hate crime statistics confirm a recent rise in crime against sexual minorities, which now consist of 17 to 20 percent of hate crime activity—a statistic made more alarming by the fact

---

42   *Perry* 111.

that 73 percent of this one-fifth are crimes that include a measurable degree of violence to the victim (97). The dissemination of this hate throughout society finds its evidentiary basis in Segura's so-called "warmness scores," which measure the public's comfort level with difference. Warmness scores for gays and lesbians fall consistently 20 points below other minorities (religious, racial, and ethnic groups), according to plaintiffs' experts (104). This information underscores the degree to which prejudice against queers continues to take the form of willful erasure as one of its principal tactics. In many ways, there is no greater suspect class than queers in America's social fabric, and the refusal to admit the prevalence of this animus is itself the most insidious form of that prejudice. By failing to rule that sexual minorities are a suspect class *tout court*, the thorough Walker decision evidences how deeply entrenched this animus is in the United States, even though his ground-breaking decision recognizes the denial of the right to marry as one of the offshoots.

At the close of *Perry*, Walker concludes, with tactical wisdom, that a holding that gays and lesbians are a historically suspect class is unnecessary because there is not even a rational basis for Proposition 8, no compelling government interest whatsoever for denying marriage to same-sex couples, who for all intents and purposes are no different from opposite-sex couples (117)—gender no longer playing a role in marriage law and procreation not being an obstacle to the license, since 18 percent percent of gay and lesbian couples now raise children (78). In Walker's opinion, the stigma that accompanies the separate track of alternative domestic partnership legislation affects not so much Warner's marginalized uncoupled but the population of lesbian and gay couples who are relegated to the discriminatory classification of second-class citizenship. At issue in the case is not the broader impact of marital rights on the rest of queer culture but more narrowly on the way heterosexual marriage excludes same-sex couples who understand themselves as the same as opposite-sex couples except for their sexual orientation. In order to establish this identical situatedness between the historically bifurcated homos and heteros, *Perry* must necessarily ignore both Harvey Milk and queer alternative culture today. His opinion thus dramatizes the deep necessity of conformity— the need for a subaltern *homo-hetero-ness* that can amplify the social contract to include lesbian and gay families.

In many ways Walker's conclusion belies the weight of the statistical evidence of the experts who testified during the hearing. As targets of discrimination from a religious right that has convinced the public that queers are affluent, self-absorbed disease mongers who recruit and molest children (*Perry* 98), the argument that gays and lesbians are similarly situated, nay, identical to opposite-sex couples seems disingenuous at best. What Walker must perforce cover over as he rules that gay couples are really straight couples in anatomical disguise includes not just a history of oppression that has defined queer subjectivity but also the culture of resistance to this oppression—the culture that Michael Warner champions even as he is ignored by the mainstream legal profession, a culture that includes the polyamorous principles of Harvey Milk, which Van Sant's retelling preserves even as its dissemination bowdlerizes the full sexual performance of Harvey's history.

To borrow Judith Butler's phrase, Walker's decision necessarily participates in a "collective amnesia" about queer history that Warner's argument resists.

Milk, for all its reduced 2-percent eroticism, still remains a strong cultural reminder of the ethical dilemma that the marital movement has created for gay and lesbian subjectivity. Even as most agree that Kris Perry and her partner deserve the right to participate in the 1,000 benefits and burdens that attach to the receipt of a secular marital license issued in City Hall as well as the right to recite what Austin calls the felicitous performative "I do," most would also agree that she has the right to call herself a lesbian, to enunciate the other performative that carries forward a history of oppression and resistance and has produced a LGBTIQ culture which includes queer kids who want "to be who they are" without becoming either tragic victims of violence or normalized spouses. Milk's political success and his messy romantic love life cannot be disowned by those in search of legal recognition without running the risk of serious complicity with the violent forces of oppression that still persist in our social fabric. The unmarried Harveys of the world are arguably in need of the same health, tax, and legal protections that are denied them because they refuse to enter into "stable" relationships, even though for some the recognition of gay marriage may function as an incremental step toward the legal recognition of other forms of intimacy like property-sharing households, which look toward continental models that extend benefits to other intimate configurations.[43] More dramatically, the gay marriage debate and the timing of its trials during the 40th anniversary of the death of the campaigner against Proposition 6 enhances the need to mobilize against the continued encroachment on the separation of church and state in our country, an encroachment that has found its rallying cry in the continued attempt to re-enact a theater of oppression against LGBT citizens across the country.

On November 14, 2010, *The Missoulian*, a newspaper in Montana, reported in its obituaries that a 38-year-old bank teller "had left us too early and will be dearly missed." Jason had "a magnetic personality and a wonderful sense of humor." He attended Valley Christian School and went to Seattle to study design. He "was liked by everyone" and could "make any bad situation more bearable with his witty one-liners." He enjoyed art, music, and his three cats, and he "should have been a comedian." Whether or not the deceased was in fact gay, this queer obituary—with its gay metonymies ("design," "comedian," "witty"), its unknown cause of death, its mention of a Christian background—typifies the kind of individual Harvey Milk attempted to reach out to in his plaza speeches, the kind of individual whose hopelessness comes from a place more fundamental than marital equality or the protection of sex-positive zones in Manhattan. *Milk* reminds us of the continued difficulty of queer survival in an era of post-gay urbanity and marriage assimilation. Van Sant's film interrupts the quest for rights and reminds us that many in the greater queer world are still fighting for their right to live, the right to challenge the tragic paradigms that haunt the cultural and legal narratives of queer subjectivity.

---

43   Warner 262.

Conclusion
Toward a Queer Political Aesthetic

Suddenly this Summer

On August 5, 2011, Patrick Murphy, co-creator of the popular television program *Glee*, admitted receiving death threats as a result of the queer content of his show, which dramatizes the travails of young singers in an American high school, often depicting gay and lesbian characters. "I think anytime you shine a spotlight on homosexuals or minorities and you try to say they are normal or worthy of acceptance," he stated in an interview after the announcement of 12 Emmy nominations, "people on the fringe will come after you."[1] Ironically, the proverbial lunatic "fringe" Murphy mentions has as its target the show's depiction of a queer marginalized "fringe" that seeks mainstream "normalcy," his remark resulting in a semantic confusion that exemplifies the changing face of America's social constituency and points to the way contemporary visual media acts as a powerful tool of cultural persuasion—one admittedly without the enforcement authority of the law, but one which functions through a similar process of widespread dissemination.

The potentially violent criticism *Glee* continues to receive from right-wing pundits and the Parents Television Council coincided in the summer of 2011 with two legal advances for gay rights that complicate any attempt to take an accurate reading of the current queer barometer. In June, 2011 the Human Rights Council of the United Nations passed by a narrow margin (23:19) a resolution expressing "grave concern" about worldwide abuses that occur as a result of sexual orientation or gender identity.[2] Though the resolution contained no enforcement mechanism and was opposed by Russia, Saudi Arabia, and Pakistan, among other nations, the Council established a reporting mechanism and set up a commission to hold hearings in the future. Consensual same-sex relations are illegal in 76 countries and discrimination against queer people is rampant in many others. The UN resolution passed just days before New York became the largest state in the union to legalize same-sex marriage, joining five other states who have bucked the trend of successful constitutional amendments banning such marriages in many other states.

These legal and cultural victories for same-sex rights, framed by powerful and dangerous dissent, attest to the queer arena as a central site of ideological struggle

---

1   "Emmys Q and A: Ryan Murphy about *Glee*'s 12 Emmy Nominations," www. deadline.com (August 5, 2011).

2   Frank Jordan, "U.N. Gay Rights Protection Resolution Passes, Hailed as Historic Moment," www.huffingtonpost.com (June 17, 2011).

between the left and right—in spite of the strong political differences within the LGBTIQ "community" itself. Because the recognition of lesbian and gay civil rights involves an expansion of the parameters of the social, legal, and even religious contract, queers have emerged as a point of condensation in the culture wars, a set of battles that often mask deeper issues about the role of government and the duty of a citizenry to recognize and support all elements of its populace. The chapters in this book understand the material concerns of this struggle as deeply embedded in the antagonism between competing discourses, what Foucault has called discrete bodies of knowledge that enable and constrain the social imagination, sometimes producing forms of social identity.[3] Through antagonism between discourses, Laclau and Mouffe contend, subjectivity is realized and radical democracy shaped.[4] Similarly, Stuart Hall has coined the term "articulation" to indicate "the complex set of historical practices by which we struggle to produce identity out of, on top of, complexity, difference, and contradiction."[5] Film, theater, fiction, and law represent on the one hand a set of discrete discourses that compete for a center stage in the shaping of legitimate forms of subjectivity, but as Foucault argued in his difficult *Archaeology of Knowledge*, the boundaries between these fields are often artificial constructs established to maintain a certain control over bodies of knowledge. My readings of the interface of legal discourse with the production and representation of artistic works endeavor to elucidate some of the connections between law and literature which these guarded domains have been reluctant to entertain.

The horizon of expectation associated with the genre of tragedy exists as a sub-discourse within the field of literature, one which, I have argued, has influenced law as well as drama and thus provides evidence of one important link between these fields. For Boal, the narrative structure of Aristotelian tragedy inevitably produces what he calls a "poetics of oppression"—a "catharsis of the revolutionary impulse" in which "dramatic action is substituted for real action."[6] The prevalence of this tragic paradigm of containment within legal, literary, and cinematic realms has extraordinary ramifications for the intersecting discourse of queer representation, which has a very long history of tragic scapegoating, as unfolded in the late Vito Russo's landmark

---

3   Alec McHoul and Wendy Grace, *A Foucault Primer: Discourse, Power and the Subject* (New York: New York University Press, 1993), 34, citing Michel Foucault, *The Archaeology of Knowledge,* trans. Alan Sheridan-Smith (New York: Pantheon, 1972).

4   Ernesto Laclau, "Power and Representation," *Politics, Theory, and Contemporary Culture,* ed. Mark Poster (New York: Columbia University Press, 1993), 291–292; see also Kevin DeLuca, "Articulation Theory: A Discursive Grounding for Theoretical Practice," *Philosophy and Rhetoric* 32:4 (199): 334–348. DeLuca writes, "A subject is constituted as the nodal point of a conglomeration of discourses—a position which leaves room for agency but not the free will of a preconstituted subject" (338).

5   Stuart Hall, "On Postmodernism and Articulation: An Interview with Stuart Hall," by Lawrence Grossberg, *Critical Dialogues in Cultural Studies"* ed. David Morley and Kuan-Hsing Chen (New York: Routledge, 1996), 131–150, at 135.

6   Augusto Boal, *Theatre of the Oppressed,* trans. Charles A. and Maria-Odilia Leal McBride (New York: Theatre Communications Group, 1985), 155.

Celluloid Closet (1981) and its subsequent film adaptation by Epstein and Friedman, a study that convincingly shows how the only-good-queer-is-a-dead-queer adage has largely controlled the history of LGBT cinema, with exceptions for comic relief and the silencing mandated by Hays Code censorship.[7] Through the queer likes of Tennessee Williams's *Suddenly Last Summer* or *Cat on a Hot Tin Roof*, Boal's 1974 reading of Aristotelian tragedy seems particularly apt, but his pre-post-structuralist theory of tragedy as a deeply conservative form of cultural containment also takes shape within a dramaturgic polemic, one which differentiates traditional tragedy from what he calls, relying in part on Brecht, a "poetics of the oppressed," in which spectators become actors and employ theater as a means of legislating social change.

Whether or not docudramas like *The Execution of Justice* or *The Laramie Project* produce social change through their subversive content or contain it through catharsis (as Boal maintains) is a question that is unanswerable definitively, even if reception theory were to allow us to gauge the causal relation between representation and behavior. Thus Boal's assumptions about the effect of Aristotelian tragedy derive their validity from an analysis of the structural elements of the genre itself, especially in so far as audience is represented within the play, exemplified for instance by the role of the townspeople in *The Project* as tragic chorus. But this inspirational Brazilian dramaturge also has recently come under criticism for overlooking the unpredictability of discourse in general. "There is an opaqueness, an essential impurity in the process of representation," Laclau has stated, "which is at the same time its condition of both possibility and impossibility"—an opaqueness that renders the effects of discourse as neither ultimately hegemonic nor subversive.[8] Even with this necessary corrective to Boal's un-nuanced theories, I have argued, the pervasiveness of the tragic paradigm within fiction, film, and law remains a pervasive and persistent scenario, one that moves from *Philadelphia* to *Milk*, from *Giovanni's Room* to *The Hours*. The controlling message of the tragic queer persists—in configurations as varied as Ford's *Single Man*, Sharia law, Republican Marlene Bachmann's church, and the homosexual panic defense—retaining its value as cultural and social capital in stubborn ways that demand continued examination of the terms of its viability.

These chapters have sought to explore how the tragic queer commodity retains its overdetermined force as both target and spark for a re-evaluation of the history of queer opprobrium, a history that continues to unfold in courtrooms and theaters. Through the process of interpreting these stories that portray the "law" of queer death, the visual power of cinema—its ability to *re-vise* legal process—has emerged as a compelling tool of this cultural "legislation," one that captures the imagination in all senses of that phrase, demonstrating how popular film functions as a compelling, if not compelled, message. This phenomenon makes the content

---

7   Vito Russo, *The Celluloid Closet: Homosexuality and the Movies*, revised ed (New York: Harper & Row, 1987). Arguably, the symbolic condensation that currently attaches to LGBTIQ rights carries on this scapegoat tradition, in so far as lesbians and gay have become the locus of all the sins of liberal society.

8   Laclau 291.

of these images even more charged, and challenges us as viewers to interrogate the so-called "take away" from these moving pictures that move us. To that end, the deadly way the queer is repeatedly represented on the screen must give us pause and compel us to interrogate the reasons for this unrelenting narrative.

Resisting the Fundamentalist Jihad

> They take [them] to be the cause of every disaster to the state, of every misfortune to the people. If the Tiber reaches the wall, if the Nile does not reach the fields, if the sky does not move or the earth does, if there is a famine, or if there is a plague, the cry is at once, "The Christians to the Lions." (From Tertullian, *Apologeticus*, XL.2, third century AD)

> Some are born gay, some achieve gayness, and some have gayness thrust upon them. (A transposition of Malvolio's "greatness" speech in Shakespeare's *Twelfth Night*)

The viability of the tragic paradigm in queer law and literature involves a social internalization of a history of opprobrium, a sedimentation of prejudice whose etiology springs from a complex matrix of historical, sociological, and psychological factors. This prejudice is also maintained by a deep complicity within the LGBT population that manifests in the availability and necessity of the closet as well as the social compulsion to assimilate or pass as straight— impulses found in characters as varied as Ennis del Mar and Brandon Teena. For Gordon Allport, prejudice gains its foothold through an epistemology that begins with the neutral mental processes of categorization, cognitive organization, and linguistic labeling, but in turn uses those mental operations to produce ideations or stereotypes that undermine careful modes of thinking by establishing shorthand methods of prejudgment.[9] How does this harmless mental process of ordering the data of consciousness relate to the violence of McKinney, Lotter, Dan White, and the alleged murderers of Jack Twist—acts of the so-called lunatic fringe? Patterns of discrimination, Allport's study maintains, exist in a continuum that ranges from verbal denunciation to avoidance and censorship, from reasoned bias to physical attack—moving in egregious cases to organized attempts at elimination, such as Exodus—the group that seeks to convert homosexuals from love of the same sex to the love of Jesus. Marcus Bachman, husband of one Republican candidate for president of the United States, not only has publically called gays "barbarians" who "need to be disciplined," but also continues to participate actively in an ex-gay ministry. The link between disciplining barbarians and assassination, between representation and conduct—between free speech and the imminent threat of assault—is regularly overlooked, even denied, by those in power who wish to

---

9　See chapter ten in Gordon W. Allport, *The Nature of Prejudice* (New York: Anchor, 1958), originally published in 1954.

police sexual minorities as a means of solidifying their own base. Ignored is Allport's now famous conclusion that violence "is always an outgrowth of milder states of mind. Although most barking ... does not lead to biting, yet there is never a bite without previous barking."[10] Discourse, Laclau and Mouffe remind us, cannot be divorced from material reality, in large part because all existence is mediated through representation.[11]

Discrimination, this book shows, takes many forms; it is often enshrined in common law, jury selection, and torts. Could it also contribute to the perpetuation of tragic paradigms in cultural representation? My thesis asks readers to consider that possibility, to entertain the notion that the repetition of the Mathew Shepard story works as much to maintain the image of the tragic and crucified queer as it does to foment a change in social attitudes—a set of ramifications that ultimately are not mutually exclusive even if opposed. After all, another of Allport's axioms maintains that those who are deeply prejudiced are inclined to deny that they are, a truism about the unconscious aspect of bias that Žižek has explored in *The Sublime Object of Ideology*, a study that illuminates the irrational side of racism.[12] Thus, films like *Boys Don't Cry* and *Milk*, though important cultural forays into under-represented forms of sexual identity, may perpetuate the very myths the filmmakers seek to undo. As windows on the world, these works may also instantiate other theories about the nature of prejudice: Adorno's view of authoritarianism as based on bias, for example, or social scientists' finding of projection, group favoritism, and competition for limited resources at work in prejudicial thinking.[13] Authoritarianism, for example, seems clearly visible in the religious dogma of the Baptist Fred Phelps, the projection at work in speculation about Dan White's sexuality, and the political economics that govern the impossibility of Jack's dream of a "cow and calf" operation with Ennis.

---

10   Allport 57. See also Alexander Tsesis, "Dignity and Speech: The Regulation of Hate Speech in a Democracy," 44 *Wake Forest Law Review* (2009): 497–532 ("Free speech is essential to collective decision making; however, when hate speech places reasonable people in fear for their well being or advocates discriminatory conduct, it eliminates ... collective autonomy," 532).

11   See Ernesto Laclau and Chantal Mouffe, "Post-Marxism Without Apologies," *New Left Review* 166 (1987): 79–106 and DeLuca 341.

12   Allport 334; Slavoj Žižek, *The Sublime Object of Ideology* (New York: Verso, 1989), 28–30 (on misrecognition).

13   Theodore Adorno on the proclivity of authoritarians to be prejudicial in S. Pious, "The Psychology of Prejudice," understandingprejudice.org (April 7, 2011): 3; Harry M. Sherif, O.J. White, W. Wood, and C. Sherif, *Ingroup Conflict and Cooperation* (Norman: University of Oklahoma Press, 1961) (on prejudice as a function of limited resource allocation); M.B. Brewer, "The Psychology of Prejudice: Ingroup Love or Outgroup Hate?" *Journal of Social Issues* 55 (1999): 429–444 (on prejudice as favoritism of one group rather than dislike of outsiders). Kirsten Anderson has written specifically on sexual orientation discrimination (*Benign Bigotry: The Psychology of Subtle Prejudice* [Cambridge: Cambridge University Press, 2010]).

Queers not only present a continual threat to a heterosexual inside that defines itself in relation to an ostracized outside; that inside has also historically dictated the nature of queer subjectivity itself. A critical queer consciousness must explore the possibility that debates about the genealogy of LGBT identity may participate in the very strategies of homophobia that are necessarily thrust upon the queer subject. "Since the 1970s," Jeffrey Escoffier writes,

> American political and cultural life has become polarized between secular liberalism ... and religious conservatism. The Religious Right is engaged in a campaign to achieve political and cultural hegemony in American life, and it has built this campaign on the revival of supposedly traditional "family values." Homosexuality is currently a major target in this hegemonic project.[14]

In reaction to this unrelenting fundamentalist *jihad*, the queer community has undergone its own internal struggles, arguably resorting to the essentialism of genetics to rationalize lesbian and gay identity, embracing family values like marriage and military participation in hopes of proving queer "value," and employing the rhetoric of privacy rights to maintain its privileged closet. These moves have engendered in turn a polemical response from queer constructivists who decry the "all but hetero" mentality of assimilationists and celebrate a culture of marginalization, whether utopic or anarchist. Lost in these internecine battles between conformists and separatists (Wolfson and Warner), idealists and nihilists (Muñoz and Edelman) is a realization of the radical contingency of queer subjectivity, framed as it is by the forces of homophobia, forces that have dictated legal and cultural production from the enactment of sexual deviancy codes to the production of *Boys in the Band* and *The Well of Loneliness*—from Brandon Teena's own homophobia to jury selection that excludes gays as inherently biased.[15] The tragic queer paradigm finds its foundation within this historic sedimentation of opprobrium and thus to a great degree partakes in the kind of citational epistemology that prejudice relies upon for its reproduction. A critical queer consciousness will recognize the way myriad forms of heteronormativity besiege and frame the debates over gay marriage and the roots of gay identity, realizing how LGBTIQ culture is sometimes divided and conquered as a

---

14   Jeffrey Escoffier, *American Homo: Community and Perversity* (Berkeley: University of California Press, 1998), 207.

15   David A.B. Murray, ed. *Homophobias: Lust and Loathing Across Time and Space* (Durham, NC: Duke University Press, 2009). In the Introduction to this collection, Murray writes that homophobia is a "deeply problematic" concept for a number of reasons. First, in many cases, "discrimination and/or violence against homosexuals is not due to an 'irrational' fear, nor can it be understood from a purely psychological framework." Homophobia is in fact a "socially produced form of discrimination located within relations of inequality." He continues: "discrimination against homosexual can be conveyed through a range of attitudes: form indifference to dismissal, 'scientific' logic, 'tolerance,' or even a carefully delimited embrace (as in 'love the sinner, not the sin')" 3.

result of a failure to acknowledge the workings of prejudice both within and without queer subjectivity.

For sexual minority cultures, a "poetics of the oppressed" may find a more apt assignation in what I want to coin as a "poetics of the unrepressed," a cultural attention not just to the happy endings of gay narratives like *Maurice* and romantic comedies like *Object of My Affection* but more pointedly to an intensified scrutiny of the continued workings of prejudice. An intensified investigation into the social factors that give rise to an Aaron McKinney or Dan White requires broader thinking about the current legitimacy of a political strategy Herbert Marcuse some time ago labeled "repressive tolerance," a doctrine that has recently manifested in the demand by some segments of the religious right that they receive legal protection for discrimination against sexual minorities under doctrines of free speech and religion.[16] A queer poetics must focus not only on the ways heteronormative institutions of law, business, and religion continue to sanction erasure of sexual difference but also on more recent attempts by backlash fundamentalists to claim legal protection for their intolerance under a rubric of free speech. If forced to give up their bigotry in order to do business in the public arena, religious groups claim they have become targets of reverse discrimination, even though they have not been historically criminalized, subject to electro-shock therapy, or the brunt of ridicule and violence in almost every high school in the nation—at least since the time of Tertullian. Their already empowered status is overlooked in favor of an ideology that masks a push to use anti-discrimination laws to protect discrimination itself. In a work like the now famous graphic novel *Fun Home*, for example, Alison Bechdel admirably portrays the effects of heteronormativity on a closeted father in small-town Pennsylvania, but an even more expansive antihomophobic poetics would examine the ways the legal legitimization of prejudice lays the groundwork for hate crimes.[17] Kaufman's *Laramie Project* no doubt broaches these issues with its various interviews; Proulx's story also intimates these links, but in what ways might a queer political aesthetics draw a sharper line between the Marcus Bachmanns of the social fabric and the death threats to Harvey Milk and the creators of *Glee* receive?

Marcuse published his "Repressive Tolerance" in 1965, and although its radical call for censorship of censors in a society that indoctrinates its constituents through media control and "heteronomany," as he calls it, includes admittedly a tinge of heavy-handed Leninism, his basic premise strikes at the heart of the current perversion of the principles of diversity as a means of safeguarding those who oppose the goals of equal protection. "When tolerance mainly serves the protection and preservation of a repressive society, when it serves to neutralize opposition and to render men immune against other and better forms of life," Marcuse writes, "then tolerance

---

16   Herbert Marcuse, "Repressive Tolerance," in, *A Critique of Pure Tolerance* (Boston: Beacon Press, 1969) 95-137.

17   Alison Bechdel, *Fun Home: A Family Tragicomedy* (New York: Houghton Mifflin, 2006).

has been perverted."[18] Marcuse's critique of pure tolerance stems from a Hegelian logic that realizes absolute freedom contains within it the possibility of its own negation (the freedom, for example, to restrict and even eliminate queer freedom); as a result, he concludes that "certain behavior cannot be tolerated without making tolerance an instrument for the continuation of servitude" (88). A new queer poetics, while not advocating for a censorship of queer censors, must dramatize the way statements by Supreme Court Justices like Antonin Scalia perpetuate a hetero-hegemony that endangers the very livelihood of the queer community. In his now notorious dissent in *Romer v. Evans*, the 1996 case that overruled a Colorado constitutional amendment that would have prevented the enactment of laws designed to prohibit discrimination against lesbians and gays, Scalia wrote:

> Of course it is our moral heritage that one should not hate any human being or class of human beings. But I had thought that one could consider certain conduct reprehensible—murder for example, or polygamy, or cruelty to animals—and could exhibit even "animus" toward such conduct. Surely that is the only sort of "animus" at issue here—moral disapproval of homosexual conduct.[19]

Under a discourse of morality, Scalia champions repressive tolerance—a righteous lack of hatred for homosexuals as long they do not do the deeds that define them, namely the same-sex acts that this Supreme Court justice links to homicide. Should a federal official who suggests that consensual sex is akin to murder (*homo-cide*) be allowed to make decisions that determine federal elections and the right to reproduction? A queer political aesthetic requires a focus on this new Orwellian chapter in our history, calling if not for censorship of Scalia at least for a dramatization of his ideological affiliation with the Dan Whites and Aaron McKinneys of the American social fabric. While to some extent the docudramas of Mann and Kaufman do explore the sources of censorious violence in the heterocentric West, these works also document the historical success of such volatile discourse and do not fully narrate the kind of poetics of the unrepressed which would champion queer subjectivity.

Obscene *Howl*

> Who let themselves be fucked in the ass by saintly motorcyclists, and screamed for joy
> Who blew and were blown by those human seraphim, the sailors, caresses of Atlantic and Caribbean love. (*Howl*, Part 1)[20]

---

18 Marcuse 111.

19 *Romer v. Evans* (1996) 116 S.Ct. 1620, at 1633; see Andre Koppelman, "*Romer v. Evans* and Invidious Intent," 6 *William and Mary Bill of Rights Journal* 89 (1997).

20 Allen Ginsberg, *Howl and Other Poems* (San Francisco: City Lights: 1956).

At the age of 29, Rob Epstein won an Academy Award for *The Times of Harvey Milk* (1984). He subsequently directed or produced *Common Threads: Stories from the Quilt* (1989), *The Celluloid Closet* (1993), *Paragraph 175* (2000), and most recently *Howl* (2010 with Jeffrey Friedman), a dramatization of the events surrounding Allen Ginsberg's composition and publication of his ground-breaking poem in 1956. Epstein and Friedman's experimental film, created in celebration of the 50th anniversary of Ginsberg's poem, dramatizes the famous obscenity trial in San Francisco criminal court, the conservative Judge Clayton Horn presiding. The film not only adds to the archive of contemporary queer legal cinema; it also situates itself outside the familiar world of adaptation and biopics through establishing literature itself as filmic subject. On trial in *Howl* is the validity of artistic production, and Epstein and Freidman's film introduces a new layer to this field by artistically depicting the trial of an artistic work, thus complicating further the segues *Critical Queer Studies* is mapping.

Howl, which received mixed reviews, presents a nonlinear pastiche of interwoven segments: an interview framework in which Allen Ginsberg sitting in his apartment answers questions about his poem and life, flashback black-and-white scenes from Ginsberg's college and traveling days with Cassidy and Kerouac (including his landmark reading of *Howl* at Six Gallery in San Francisco in 1955), animated scenes based on illustrations Ginsberg worked on during his life, and finally a depiction of the courtroom obscenity prosecution that drew national attention to the nascent poets of the San Francisco Renaissance. While recommending the film as a whole, A.O. Scott identified the animation sections as a disastrous if ambitious misstep, while Mick La Salle of the *San Francisco Chronicle* expressed surprise that the makers of *The Times of Harvey Milk* would put together such an uneven narrative.[21] James Franco in the title role of Allen has generally received praise for his capture of the cadence of the young Ginsberg's reading style, but his image as Gucci model and *Spiderman* star, for some critics, make him an unlikely choice to enact the unglamorous Ginsberg, replete with a fake beard, even though Franco does have a Jewish mother and an MFA from Columbia in creative writing. *Howl*'s poignant depiction of Ginsberg's "irrepressible need to shock," Colin Carman writes, stems in large part from the poet's willingness to come out of the closet with a studied bang, as Franco's performance captures with an effective confessional sincerity.[22]

The more subdued critic Stanley Fish, in the *New York Times*' Opinionater, calls *Howl* the first film about literary criticism, reviewing how the author's interview provides biographical criticism, complemented by the *explication de texte* undertaken in the screenplay by lawyers, professorial expert witnesses, and

---

21   A.O. Scott, "Leaping Off the Page: A Beatnik's Poetic Rant," *The New York Times* (September 23, 2010); Mick LaSalle, "Poet and Patience on Trial in *Howl*," *San Francisco Chronicle* (September 4, 2010): E1.

22   Colin Carman, "A Movie Based on a Poem," *Gay and Lesbian Review Worldwide* 18:2 (March–April 2011) in http://www.glreview.com/article.php?articleid=316.

animators.[23] Fish's observations underline the connections between processes of legal proof and literary interpretation: both involve a hermeneutics of assessing narratives or representational evidence; both undertake a process of judgment. Even if that determination of worth—in a post-Matthew Arnold twenty-first century—involves not so much a critical rating as the application of theory to text, the process still shares its methodology with the way statutes are applied to statements of facts in courts of law. The obscenity trial, depicted in the film, melds these two practices of interpretation when literature professors take the stand as experts on the "redeeming value" of Ginsberg's epic poem.

Howl, in spite of its shortcomings, serves, I think, a broader purpose than illustrating the connections between law and literature. By portraying the successful defense against criminal obscenity charges for a poem that celebrates queer sex, Epstein and Friedman's "lit flick" arguably renders a poetics of the unrepressed, paving the way for a new queer political aesthetic.[24] Produced by *Milk*'s Gus Van Sant and starring the actor who played Harvey's lover Scott in that film, Franco's Ginsberg captures the genuine self-discovery and frankness of the self-effacing young poet in the process of finding his voice in the poem. Toward the end of the film, Ginsberg tells his interviewer that he deliberately wrote "joy" instead of "pain" at the end of his ass-fucking line (quoted above) in order to unseat the expectations of his readers.[25] The insouciant writer, however, understands his project as something he would not want his father to read, but one that nonetheless comes from his gut. The screenplay, drawn entirely from archival language as the opening credits insist, includes a statement by Ginsberg that *Howl* is not primarily a promotion of homosexuality but of "frankness." The poet follows this comment with another about how his homosexuality "broke the ice" and became a "catalyst for self examination" in his composition process. *Howl* covers a lot of sexual ground, but its punch comes largely from the poem's willingness to celebrate same-sex attachments, and Epstein and Freidman's screenplay emphasizes the gay coming-of-age aspect of this narrative about a young mensch from Patterson, New Jersey.

In March of 1957, customs officials confiscated 520 copies of *Howl and Other Poems* as they arrived in San Francisco from the London printer. One of the City Lights publishers, Shigeyoshi Murao, was arrested, and he and Lawrence Ferlinghetti were subsequently prosecuted for criminal obscenity, generally defined as the distribution of materials that appeal primarily to a prurient interest, have a tendency to incite lustful thoughts, and have no redeeming social or literary value. The film does not depict Murao's arrest, but instead cuts from the first animation sequence to a shot of the trial scene, Clayton Horn presiding. The courtroom sequences, shot with an almost sepia filter in the wood-paneled San

---

23   Stanley Fish, "Literary Criticism Comes to the Movies," Opinionater, *The New York Times* (October 4, 2010).

24   "Lit flick" is Carman's term.

25   Stanley Fish calls this part of the interview "a reader response" moment, when the author deliberately disrupts the semantic expectation of his reader (see note 23 above).

Francisco setting, retain some of the surreal quality of the previous animated sequences, which cut unexpectedly to the trial section of the film's larger montage as the screenplay develops. This surrealism resides not in the realistic footage of the courtroom scenes, which begins with a bird's-eye view through a chandelier, but in the almost *Law and Order* sensibility of the trial's historical re-enactment—as if the filmmakers were turning fact into fiction, turning this documentary into a prime-time serial. The trial is peopled with familiar character actors: John Hamm from *Mad Men* is Jake Erlich, the famous defense attorney upon whom the Perry Mason character was based; Mary Louise Parker of *Weeds* appears as a white-gloved Dominican College teacher who assures us that she did not "dwell long" on the crude text of Ginsberg's poem. Jeff Daniels plays the conservative University of San Francisco English professor with particular brilliance, arguing that the poem has no redeemable form, theme, or "opportunity." Epstein and Friedman transform the closely watched 1957 trial into an HBO movie, rendering the courtroom drama as the almost incredulous stuff of a *Perry Mason* episode, making casting choices that remove the audience from documentary sensibility and thrust them into the familiar realm to television drama.

The directors commented on the insidious banality of the trial transcript in an interview with Kirsten McCracken, pointing out how the prosecution, which ironically catapulted the poem into immediate fame, seemed predictably based on "fear and scapegoatism," what the filmmakers called "an eternal dialectic" now at work in the gay marriage debates.[26] Their understanding of the potentially tragic dimension of the trial ("scapegoatism") is balanced by a portrayal that highlights the inability and "ridiculousness" of legal discourse's attempt to cope with the determination of the value of artistic representation, in spite of a statute that promised fines and imprisonment for Ferlinghetti should the judge determine that *Howl* appealed to prurience, instilled lustful thoughts, and had no redeeming social value. Importantly, in the film's presentation of the trial, the prosecutor avoids repeating Ginsberg's famous "fucked in the ass" line and skips to the next, asking experts what "blew and were blown by human seraphim" means. Although the expert suggests that the line may refer to being blown by the wind, the prosecutor's final translation of the line into oral copulation produces an almost smirking reaction from the courtroom audience, film viewers no doubt struck by the petty and almost ludicrous nature of the expert testimony. Had the prosecutor read the line about "anal intercourse," however, it would be hard to believe that the judge and audience would not have found Ginsberg's language ob-scene or in the etymological sense, "hard to look at."

At some more fundamental level, *Howl is* a deeply obscene work in so far as it brings "alcohol and cock and balls" into poetic discourse and claims joyful gay sex as aesthetically acceptable and pleasing. The poem's redeeming value lies in its *challenge* and shock to those who refuse to recognize that gay anal intercourse

---

26 Kirsten McCracken, "Film and Literature: *Howl*," www.tribecafilm.com (September 20, 2010).

can be joyful, those who cannot countenance the publication of a poem about the return of the unrepressed, seeking instead to police and eliminate the content of Ginsberg's queer story. When defense attorney Jake Ehrlich in his closing argument calls for light to be shed through honesty, he reminds the judge that there is much in the world that is "visible but unseen." Ginsberg's epic poem does the aesthetic work of making "seen" the obscene, in even making a scene out of the obscene—of forcing society to hold the mirror up to queer desire and relinquish their stubborn insistence on the occlusion of those acts which gave Ginsberg his understanding of his difference—the basic reality of his joy in loving other men. Unlike Oscar Wilde, Ginsberg himself is not specifically charged with any crime in this case, but metonymically, his queer work is under scrutiny as purely prurient, lust-based, and valueless—all descriptors that have attached and continue to be applied to the LGBTIQ subject. The obscenity statute, at some level, stands in metonymically for the censorship of queer desire, in this case a desire expressed in the work product of the gay poet. The *Howl* criminal trial seeks not just to punish the publisher of the poem, but to ban its content as anti-social, irredeemable, and outside the parameters of civil community.

Judge Horn's holding that *Howl*, though vulgar in many places, is not without some redeeming artistic value serves as both a critique of the First Amendment's repressive tolerance and a triumph of the elusive power of aesthetics in the legal arena. Horn refuses to allow the government to enact its censorious law, commenting that those who see evil in literature often reveal the evil in themselves, concluding that *Howl* speaks to a different audience than the average man, but one that cannot be erased. In fact, the state's attention on the queer material in Ginsberg's poem—seeking to know the truth about its sexual content—acted ironically as an erotic exercise itself, creating, in Foucauldian fashion, a spiral of power and pleasure in the courtroom as experts tried to parse the meaning of "angel-headed hipsters" and the caresses of sailors.[27] The trial, in other words, backfired, spotlighting material that the prosecutor sought to occlude, shining light on the allegedly obscene content of Ginsberg's epic.

As Mark Shorer, one of the literary experts in the trial opined to the prosecutor, "you can't turn poetry into prose; that's what makes it poetry." The legal attempt to reduce artistic expression to statutory pornography—to fit representation into the prosaic formula of valueless prurience—has of course vexed the courts for decades, most famously with Supreme Court Justice Potter Stewart's exasperated statement that he knew pornography when he saw it, but the law's frustration with its incapacity to define and police literary representation in many ways mirrors the myriad critiques of literature's inexact portrayal of legal procedure, in spite of both disciplines' common mode of interpretation. The value of the epic *Howl*, the judge determines, depends on the epistemological standpoint of its reader,

---

27 For the relationship between power and pleasure, see Michel Foucault, *The History of Sexuality: Volume 1: An Introduction*, trans. Robert Hurley (New York: Vintage, 1980), 45.

and the court was unwilling to gainsay the existence of those readers, no matter how un-average they might be. The *Howl* trial dramatizes the uncanny ability of aesthetic discourse to elude the grasp of censorious law and in this case employ legal process to challenge intolerance and champion breaking the boundaries of heteronormative values. In the *Howl* trial, the law's attempt to censor Ginsberg's poem served finally to champion literary representation by staging, as Stanley Fish notes, a drama of critical interpretation.

The real uncertainty of whether or not a poem like *Howl* could find a publisher today in our neo-Victorian era no doubt calls for a degree of speculation, but that open question speaks to the need not only to document, film, and narrate stories of queer censorship but also to represent through myriad forms of social discourse a poetics of the unrepressed—on local and national levels. Dan Savage's YouTube project *It Gets Better*, created in response to the rash of gay teen suicides in 2010, presents a case in point, even if the IGB collection of interviews has been criticized as a kind of whitewash, not only because of the largely white and gay participation but also because the majority of the testimonials fail to document the ways life often does *not* get better for queers of color and global queers.[28] IGB and its critics, including the blog *Make it Better*, have nevertheless spawned an interactive queer debate that allows LGBTIQ people to tell their stories, even if many of them are not the hopeful Horatio-Alger narratives that the upwardly mobile urban gay class would like to promote. IGB stands as an important online development for the lesbian and gay movement in so far as this website engages the visual and narrative in ways that harness the power of story and image to counter anti-queer messages within religion, law, and even some cinema—messages that perpetuate narratives of the queer as damned, deviant, and doomed. A future queer political aesthetic must work both to expose the myriad machinations of bias still at work in society and at the same time to tell stories of poets like Allen Ginsberg, who at the end of the film, in his inimitable and charming way, confesses to his interviewer:

> Homosexuality is a condition. Because it alienated me or set me apart from the beginning, it served as a catalyst for self-examination or a catalyst for a detailed realization of my environment and the reasons why every one else is different— and why I am different.

---

28   www.itgetsbetter.org; for criticism, see Jasbir Puar, "In the Wake of *It Gets Better*," *Guardian* (November 16, 2010). See also www.makeitbetter.org.

Bibliography

50cent. *Twitter.com*. September 29, 2010. http://twitter.com/#!/50cent/status/25954812348. (accessed March 16, 2012).

"50 Cent: Tweet Wasn't Antigay." *Advocate.com*. September 30, 2010. www.advocate.com/News/Daily_News/2010/09/30/50_Cent_Encourages_Gay_Suicide/. (accessed March 16, 2012).

"A Compilation of Critiques on Hate Crime Legislation." *Blackandpink.org*. N.d. www.blackandpink.org/revolt/a-compilation-of-critiques-on-hate-crimes-legislation. (accessed March 16, 2012).

Adorno, Theodore. In S. Pious, "The Psychology of Prejudice," April 7, 2011. www.understandingprejudice. org. (accessed March 12, 2012).

Agamben, Giorgio. *Homo Sacer: Sovereign Power and Bare Live*. Trans. Daniel Heller-Roazen. Stanford: Stanford University Press, 1998.

Alexander, Gregory S. "Talking About Difference: Meanings and Metaphors of Individuality." 11 *Cardozo Law Review* 1355–1375 (1990).

Allport, Gordon W. *The Nature of Prejudice*. New York: Anchor, 1958.

Anderson, Kirsten. *Benign Bigotry: The Psychology of Subtle Prejudice*. Cambridge: Cambridge University Press, 2010.

Aristodemou, Maria. *Law and Literature: Journeys from Her to Eternity*. Oxford: Oxford University Press, 2000.

Armstrong, Elizabeth A. *Forging Gay Identities: Organizing Sexuality in San Francisco, 1950–1994*. Chicago: University of Chicago Press, 2002.

Armstrong, Elizabeth A., and Suzanna M. Crage. "Movements and Memory: The Making of the Stonewall Myth." *American Sociological Review* 17 (October 2006): 724–751.

Augé, Karen. "Young, Gay, and Bullied: Suicides Elsewhere Have Colorado Educators on Alert." *The Denver Post*. October 12, 2010, sec. 1A–8A.

Bagnall, Robert G., Patrick C. Gallagher, and Joni L. Goldstein. "Burdens on Gay Litigants and Bias in the Court System: Homosexual Panic, Child Custody, and Anonymous Parties." 19 *Harvard Civil Rights-Civil Liberties Law Review* 497–515 (1984).

Baldwin, James. *The Evidence of Things Not Seen*. New York: Henry Holt, 1995.

Baron, Jane B. "Law's Guilt about Literature." *Studies in Law, Politics, and Society* 36 (2005): 17–30.

Bechdel, Alison. *Fun Home: A Family Tragicomedy*. New York: Houghton Mifflin, 2006.

Bell, David, and Gill Valentine, eds. *Mapping Desire*. New York: Routledge, 1995.

Benshoff, Harry M. "*Milk* and Gay Political History." *Jump Cut: A Review of Contemporary Media.* www.ejumpcut.org/archive/jc51.2009/Milk/index.html (accessed July 12, 2011).

Binder, Guyora. "Aesthetic Judgment and Legal Justification." *Studies in Law, Politics, and Society: A Special Issue: Law and Literature Reconsidered* 43 (2008): 79–113.

Binder, Guyora, and Richard Weisberg. *Literary Criticisms of the Law.* Princeton: Princeton University Press, 2000.

Birch, Elizabeth, and Paul Weyrich. "Symposium—Debate for Specific Hate Crime Legislation Protecting Homosexuals." *Insight on the News.* July 24, 2000. http://findarticles.com/p/articles/mi_m1571/is_27_16/ai_63692894/?tag=mantle_skin;content (accessed July 12, 2011).

Black, David A. *Law in Film: Resonance and Representation.* Champaign Urbana: Illinois University Press, 1999.

Black, Dustin Lance. "Dusting Lance Black's Acceptance Speech For Original Screenplay." *Movies.Broadwayworld.com.* February 22, 2009. http://movies.broadwayworld.com/article/Dustin_Lance_Blacks_Oscar_Acceptance_Speech_for_Original_Screenplay_20090222. (accessed March 16, 2012).

Boag, Peter. *Same-Sex Affairs: Constructing and Controlling Homosexuality in the Pacific Northwest.* Berkeley: University of California Press, 2003.

Boal, Augusto. *Theatre of the Oppressed.* Trans. Charles A. and Maria-Odilia Leal McBride. New York: Theatre Communications Group, 1985.

Bornstein, Kate. *Gender Outlaw: On Men, Women and the Rest of Us.* New York: Vintage, 1995.

Boyd, Blanche McCrary. "Who Killed Susan Smith?" *Oxford American* (August/September 1996): 36–42.

Brewer, M.B. "The Psychology of Prejudice: Ingroup Love or Outgroup Hate?" *Journal of Social Issues* 55 (1999): 429–444.

Bridgewater, Pamela D., and Brenda V. Smith. "Introduction to Symposia: Homophobia in the Halls of Justice: Sexual Orientation Bias and its Implications within the Legal System." 11 *American University Journal of Gender, Social Policy, and the Law* 1–128 (2002).

Brody, Jennifer Devere. "Boyz Do Cry: Screening History's White Lies." *Screen* 43:1 (spring 2002): 91–96.

Bronski, Michael. "A Troubling Vision of Matthew Shepard." *Boston Phoenix.* November 26-December 2, 2004.. www.bostonphoenix.com/boston/news_features/this_just_in/documents/04285820.asp.(accessed July 15. 2005).

Brooks, Peter, and Paul Gerwitz, eds. *Law's Stories: Narrative and Rhetoric in the Law.* New Haven: Yale University Press, 1996.

Brown, Wendy. *States of Injury.* Princeton: Princeton University Press, 1995.

Brown, Wendy. "Suffering the Paradoxes of Rights." In *Left Legalism/Left Critique*, Wendy Brown and Janet Halley, eds., 432. Durham, NC: Duke University Press, 2002.

Bull, Chris. "Anatomy of a Gay Murder." *Alicia Patterson Reporter* 20:1 (2001). http://aliciapatterson.org/stories/anatomy-gay-murder (accessed July 12, 2011).

Bull, Chris. "When Hate Isn't Hate." *Planet Out*. November 24, 2004. www.planetout.com.

Butler, Judith. *Bodies That Matter: On the Discursive Limits of Sex*. New York: Routledge, 1993.

Butler, Judith. "Deconstruction and the Possibility of Justice: Comments on Bernasconi, Cornell, Miller, Weber." 11 *Cardozo Law Review* 1715 (1990).

Butler, Judith. *Gender Trouble: Feminism and the Subversion of Identity*. New York: Routledge, 1990.

Butler, Judith. *Psychic Life of Power: Theories of Subjection*. Stanford: Stanford University Press, 1997.

Califia, Pat. "San Francisco: Revisiting the City of Desire." In *Queers in Space*: *Communities, Public Spaces, Sites of Resistance*, Gordon Brent Ingram, Anne-Marie Bouthillette, and Yolanda Retter, eds., 177–196. San Francisco: Bay Press, 1997.

Canady, Margot. *The Straight State: Sexuality and Citizenship in Twentieth Century America*. Princeton: Princeton University Press, 2010.

Carman, Colin. "American Eden: Nature, Homophobic Violence, and the Social Imaginary." In *The Brokeback Book: From Story to Cultural Phenomenon*, William R. Handley, ed., 123–136. Omaha: University of Nebraska Press, 2011.

Carman, Colin. "A Movie Based on a Poem." *Gay and Lesbian Review Worldwide* 18:2 (March–April 2011). In http://www.glreview.com/article.php?articleid=316 (accessed March 16, 2012).

Carman, Diane. Editorial. *Denver Post*. October 10, 1998. http://www.democraticunderground.com/discuss/duboard.php?az=view_all&address=389x336565. (accessed March 16, 2012.)

Carter, David. *Stonewall—The Riots that Sparked the Gay Revolution*. New York: St. Martin's Griffin, 2010.

Charles, Casey. "Panic in *The Project*: Critical Queer Studies and the Matthew Shepard Murder." *Law and Literature* 18:2 (summer 2006): 225–252.

Chase, Anthony. *Movies on Trial: The Legal System of the Silver Screen*. New York: New Press, 2002.

Chen, Christina Pei Lin. "Provocation's Privileged Desire: The Provocation Doctrine, 'Homosexual Panic,' and the Non-violent Unwanted Sexual Advance Defense." 10 *Cornell Journal of Law and Public Policy* 195–235 (2000).

Churchill, David S. "The Queer Histories of a Crime: Representations and Narratives of Leopold and Loeb. *Journal of the History of Sexuality*. 18:2 (2009): 287–324.

Claycomb, Ryan M. "(Ch)oral History: Documentary Theatre, the Communal Subject and Progressive Politics." *Journal of Dramatic Theory and Criticism* 17 (spring 2003): 95–119.

Comstock, Gary David. "Dismantling the Homosexual Panic Defense." 81 *Law and Sexuality: Review of Lesbian and Gay Legal Issues* 81–102 (1992).

Comstock, Gary David. *Violence Against Lesbians and Gay Men.* New York: Columbia University Press, 1991.

Cooper, Brenda. "*Boys Don't Cry* and Female Masculinity: Reclaiming a Life and Dismantling the Politics of Normative Heterosexuality." *Critical Studies in Media Communication* 19:1 (March 2002): 44–63.

Cornell, Drucilla. *Transformations: Recollective Imagination and Sexual Difference.* New York: Routledge, 1993.

Cvetkovich, Ann. *An Archive of Feelings: Trauma, Sexuality, and Lesbian Public Cultures.* Durham, NC: Duke University Press, 2003.

Davies, Jon. "Alberta, Authenticity, and Queer Erasure." In *The Brokeback Book: From Story to Cultural Phenomenon*, William R. Handley, ed., 249–266. Omaha: University of Nebraska Press, 2011.

Dawson, Gary Fisher. *Documentary Theatre in the United States: An Historical Survey and Analysis of Its Content, Form, and Stagecraft.* Westport: Greenwood, 1999.

Delgado, Richard. "Storytelling for Oppositionists and Others: A Plea for Narrative." 87 *Michigan Law Review* 2411–2441 (1989).

DeLuca, Kevin. "Articulation Theory: A Discursive Grounding for Theoretical Practice." *Philosophy and Rhetoric* 32 (1999): 334–348.

D'Emilio, John. *Making Trouble: Essays on Gay History, Politics, and the University.* New York: Routledge, 1992.

Derrida, Jacques. "Force of Law: The 'Mystical Foundation of Authority.'" In *Deconstruction and the Possibility of Justice*, David G. Carlson, Drucilla Cornell, and Michel Rosenfeld, eds., 13. New York: Routledge, 1992.

Derrida, Jacques. "The Law of Genre." Trans. Avital Ronell. *Critical Inquiry* 7:1 (autumn 1980): 55–81.

Derrida, Jacques. *Of Grammatology.* Trans. Gayatri Chakravorty Spivak. Baltimore: Johns Hopkins University Press, 1974.

Dimock, Wai Chee. *Residues of Justice: Literature, Law, Philosophy.* Berkeley: University of California Press, 1996.

Dolan, Kieran. *A Critical Introduction to Law and Literature.* Cambridge: Cambridge University Press, 2009.

Draz, Christian. "Lost in Adaptation." *The Gay and Lesbian Review Worldwide* 13:3 (May–June 2006): 12.

Dreger, Alice D. *Hermaphrodites and the Medical Invention of Sex.* Cambridge, MA: Harvard University Press, 1998.

Dressler, Joshua. "When 'Heterosexual' Men Kill 'Homosexual' Men: Reflections on Provocation Law, Sexual Advances, and the 'Reasonable Man' Standard." 85 *Journal of Criminal Law and Criminology* 726–763 (1995).

Dreyfuss, Robert. "The Holy War on Gays." *Rolling Stone.* 18 March 1999, 38–41.

Duggan, Lisa. "Holy Matrimony!" *The Nation.* March 15, 2004. In http://www.thenation.com/article/holy-matrimony. (accessed March 16, 2012).

Duggan, Lisa. *The Twilight of Equality: Neoliberalism, Cultural Politics and the Attack on Democracy.* Boston: Beacon, 2004.

Dunne, John Gregory. "The Humboldt Murders." *New Yorker*. January 13, 1997, 45–62.

Dwyer, Paul. "*Theoria Negativa:* Making Sense of Boal's Reading of Aristotle." *Modern Drama* 48:4 (winter 2005): 635–658.

Ebert, Roger. "Brokeback Mountain." *Chicago Sun-Times*. December 16 2005. http://rogerebert.suntimes.com/apps/pbcs.dll/article?AID=/20051215/REVIEWS/51019006. (accessed March 16, 2012).

Edelman, Lee. *No Future: Queer Theory and the Death Drive*. Durham, NC: Duke University Press, 2004.

Eden, Kathy. *Poetic and Legal Fiction in the Aristotelian Tradition*. Princeton: Princeton University Press, 1986.

Egelko, Bob. "Vaughn Walker, Retired Judge, Reflects on Prop. 8." *SFGate.com*. April 7, 2011. www.sfgate.com/cgi-bin/article.cgi?f=/c/a/2011/04/06/MN661IRCO5.DTL. (accessed March 16, 2012).

"Emmys Q and A: Ryan Murphy about *Glee*'s 12 Emmy Nominations." August 5, 2011. www.deadline.com. (accessed March 16, 2012).

Eribon, Didier. *Insult and the Making of the Gay Self*. Trans. Michael Lucey. Durham, NC: Duke University Press, 2004.

Escoffier, Jeffrey. *American Homo: Community and Perversity*. Berkeley: University of California Press, 1998.

Eskridge, William N. *The Case for Same-Sex Marriage: From Sexual Liberty to Civilized Commitment*. New York: Free Press, 1995.

Eskridge, William N. *GayLaw: Challenging the Apartheid of the Closet*. Cambridge, MA: Harvard University Press, 1999.

Eugenides, Jeffrey. *Middlesex*. New York: Farrar, Straus, and Giroux, 2002.

Faderman, Lillian. *Scotch Verdict: Miss Pirie and Miss Woods v. Dame Cumming Gordon*. New York: Columbia University Press, 1994.

Felman, Shoshana. *The Juridical Unconscious: Trials and Traumas in the Twentieth Century*. Cambridge, MA: Harvard University Press, 2002.

Ferguson, Robert A. *Law and Letters in American Culture*. Cambridge, MA: Harvard University Press, 1984.

Fetner, Tina. *How the Religious Right Shaped Lesbian and Gay Activism*. Minneapolis: University of Minnesota Press, 2008.

Fish, Stanley. "Literary Criticism Comes to the Movies." *The New York Times*. Opinionater. October 4, 2010. In http://opinionator.blogs.nytimes.com/2010/10/04/literary-criticism-comes-to-the-movies/ (accessed March 6, 2012).

FitzGerald, Frances. *Cities on a Hill: A Journey through Contemporary American Cultures*. New York: Simon & Schuster, 1981.

Foucault, Michel. *The Archaeology of Knowledge and the Discourse on Language*. Trans. A.M. Sheridan Smith. New York: Pantheon, 1972.

Foucault, Michel. *The Foucault Reader*. Paul Rabinow, ed. New York: Pantheon Books, 1984.

Foucault, Michel. *The History of Sexuality: Volume 1: An Introduction*. Trans. Robert Hurley. New York: Random House, 1978..

Foucault, Michel. *Power/Knowledge: Selected Interviews and Other Writings: 1972–77.* Trans. Colin Gordon et al. (New York, Pantheon, 1980).

Freeman, Chris. "'Jack I Swear:' Some Promises to Gay Culture from Mainstream Hollywood." In *The Brokeback Book: From Story to Cultural Phenomenon,* William R. Handley, ed., 105. Omaha: University of Nebraska Press, 2011.

Freeman, Michael, and Andrew D.E. Lewis, eds. *Law and Literature.* Oxford: Oxford University Press, 1999.

Gamboa, Antonio R. Letter to the Editor. *The Gay and Lesbian Review Worldwide.* 13:5 (September–October 2006): 7.

Gambotto, Antonella. *The Eclipse: A Memoir of Suicide.* Broken Ankle Books, 2004.

Geertz, Clifford. *Local Knowledge: Further Essays in Interpretive Anthropology.* New York: Basic Books, 1983.

Ginsberg, Allen. *Howl and Other Poems.* San Francisco: City Lights, 1956.

Gleiberman, Owen. "The Searchers." *Entertainment Weekly.* December 9, 2005, 59–60.

Glendon, Mary Ann. *Rights Talk: The Impoverishment of Political Discourse.* New York: The Free Press, 1991.

Goldstein, Aaron. "Would Harvey Milk Have Opposed Gay Marriage?" *CanadaFreePress.com.* February 17, 2009. www.canadafreepress.com/index. php/article/8571. (accessed March 16, 2012).

Goldstein, Richard. "The Matthew Shepard Icon." *The Village Voice.* March 13– 19, 2002, 52.

Goodrich, Peter. *Legal Discourse: Studies in Linguistics, Rhetoric and Legal Analysis.* New York: St. Martin's, 1987.

Gorton, Michael. "The Hate Crime." *The Gay and Lesbian Review Worldwide.* 13:3 (May–June 2006): 13.

Greenfield, Steve, Guy Osborn, and Peter Robson. *Film and Law: The Cinema of Justice.* Portland: Hart, 2010.

Gutíerrez-Jones, Carl. *Critical Race Narratives*: *A Study of Race, Rhetoric, and Injury.* New York: New York University Press, 2001.

Halberstam, Judith. *In A Queer Time and Place: Transgender Bodies, Subcultural Lives.* New York: New York University Press, 2005.

Halberstam, Judith. "Not So Lonesome Cowboys: The Queer Western." In *The Brokeback Book: From Story to Cultural Phenomenon,* William R. Handley, ed., 190–204. Omaha: University of Nebraska Press, 2011.

Hale, Jacob. "Consuming the Living, Dis(Re)Membering the Dead in the Butch/ FTM Borderlands." *GLQ* 4:2 (1998): 311–348.

Hall, Donald E. *Queer Theories.* New York: Palgrave, 2003.

Hall, Stuart. "On Postmodernism and Articulation: An Interview with Stuart Hall." By Lawrence Grossberg. In *Critical Dialogues in Cultural Studies,* David Morley and Kuan-Hsing Chen, eds. New York: Routledge, 1996.

Halley, Janet, and Andrew Parker. "Introduction to a Special Issue: After Sex: On Writing since Queer Theory." *The South Atlantic Quarterly* 106:3 (summer 2007): 422.

Halliwell, Stephen. *The Poetics of Aristotle: Translation and Commentary.* Chapel Hill: University of North Carolina Press, 1987.

Handley, William R., ed. *The Brokeback Book: From Story to Cultural Phenomenon.* Omaha: University of Nebraska Press, 2011.

Hanson, Ellis, ed. *Out Takes.* Durham, NC: Duke University Press, 1999.

Hardison Jr., O.B. *Aristotle's Poetics: A Translation and Commentary for Students of Literature.* Trans. Leon Golden. Gainsville: University of Florida Press, 1981.

Harrison, Eric. "A Filmmaker Fictionalizes to Get at Difficult Truths." *Los Angeles Times.* February 6, 2000. http://articles.latimes.com/2000/feb/07/entertainment/ca-61809. (accessed March 16, 2012).

Hawker, Philippa. "Seeing Doubles." *TheAge.com.au.* March 1, 2002. www.theage.com.au/articles/2002/03/01/1014704987942.html. (accessed March 15, 2012).

Heald, Paul J. "The Death of Law and Literature: An Optimistic Eulogy." *The Comparatist* 33 (May 2009): 20–26.

Heilbrun, Carolyn, and Judith Resnik. "Convergences: Law, Literature and Feminism." 99 *Yale Law Journal* 1912–1956 (1990).

Heinzelman, Susan. *Riding the Black Ram: Law, Literature, and Gender.* Stanford: Stanford Law Books, 2010.

Herek, Gregory M. "The Social Context of Hate Crimes: Notes on Cultural Heterosexuality." 89–101. In *Hate Crimes: Confronting Violence Against Lesbians and Gay Men*, Gregory M. Herek and Kevin T. Berrill, eds. Newbury Park: Sage 1992.

Herring, Scott. *Another Country: Queer Anti-Urbanism.* New York: New York University Press, 2010.

Hinckle, Warren. *GaySlayer!* Virginia City: Silver Dollar Books, 1985.

Holleran, Andrew. "'If They Know Us…'." *The Gay and Lesbian Review Worldwide* (April–May 2009), www.glreview.com/article.php?articleid=148. (accessed March 16, 2012).

Holleran, Andrew. "The Magic Mountain." 13:2 *The Gay and Lesbian Review Worldwide* (March–April 2006): 13.

Hopwood, John C. "Is Vaughn Walker Gay? Federal Judge Who Struck Down Prop 8 is Homosexual." *AssociatedContent.com.* www.associatedcontent.com/article/5659714/is_vaughn_walker_gay_federal_judge.html?cat=17associatedcontent%203. (accessed March 16, 2012).

Hunt, Alex. "West of the Closet, Fear on the Range." In *The Brokeback Book: From Story to Cultural Phenomenon*, William R. Handley, ed., 146. Omaha: University of Nebraska Press, 2011.

Huston, Johnny Ray. "*Milk* (Gus Van Sant, US)." *Cinema Scope.* www.cinema-scope.com/cs37/cur_huston_milk.html. (accessed March 16, 2012).

I Promise You This: Collected Poems in Memory of Harvey Milk. In the Gay and Lesbian Archive, San Francisco Public Library (1979).

Ingebretsen, Edward. *At Stake: Monsters and the Rhetoric of Fear in Public Culture.* Chicago: University of Chicago Press, 2001.

Ireland, Doug. "'20/20' and Matthew Shepard." *Direland.* December 6, 2004. http://direland.typepad.com/direland/2004/11/index.html. (accessed July 15, 2005).

Jacobs, James B., and Kimberly Potter. *Hate Crime: Criminal Law and Identity Politics.* New York: Oxford University Press, 2001.

Johnson, Barbara. "Translator's Introduction." In Jacques Derrida. *Dissemination.* Chicago: University of Chicago Press, 1981, vii–xix.

Johnson, E. Patrick, and Mae G. Henderson, eds. *Black Queer Studies: A Critical Anthology.* Durham, NC: Duke University Press 2005.

Johnson, Fenton. "Wedded to an Illusion: Do Gays and Lesbian Really Want the Freedom to Marry?" *Harper's.* November 1996, 4.

Jones, Aphrodite. *All She Wanted: A True Story of Sexual Deception and Murder in America's Heartland.* New York: Pocket Books, 1996.

Jordan, Frank. "U.N. Gay Rights Protection Resolution Passes, Hailed as Historic Moment." June 17, 2011. www.huffingtonpost.com. (accessed March 16, 2012).

Kamir, Orit. *Framed: Women in Law and Film.* Durham, NC: Duke University Press, 2006.

Kane, Katie. "Glass of Hope: Drinking in the life and work of Harvey Milk." *The Missoula Independent.* February 12 2009. http://missoulanews.bigskypress.com/missoula/glass-of-hope/Content?oid=1147982. (accessed March 16, 2012).

Kaufman, Moisés. *Gross Indecency: The Three Trials of Oscar Wilde.* New York: Vintage, 1998.

Kaufman, Moisés, and the Members of Tectonic Theater Project. *The Laramie Project.* New York: Dramatists Play Service, 2001.

Knopp, Lawrence. "Sexuality and Urban Space: Gay Male Identity Politics in the United States, the United Kingdom, and Australia." In *Cities of Difference*, Ruth Fincher and Jane M. Jacobs, eds., 164–168. New York: Guilford, 1998.

Kohn, Sally. "Greasing the Wheel: How the Criminal Justice System Hurts Gay, Lesbian, Bisexual and Transgendered People and Why Hate Crime Laws Won't Save Them." 27 *New York University Review of Law and Social Change* 257 (2001–2002).

Konigsberg, Eric. "Death of a Deceiver." *Playboy.* January 1995. http://course1.winona.edu/pjohnson/h140/boysstory.htm. (accessed March 16, 2012).

Koppelman, Andrew. *The Gay Rights Question in Contemporary American Law.* Chicago: University of Chicago Press, 2002.

Koppelman, Andrew. "*Romer v. Evans* and Invidious Intent." *William and Mary Bill of Rights Journal* 6 (1997): 89.

Kushner, Tony. "The Art of the Difficult." *Civilization*. August–September 1997, 62–67.

Lacan, Jacques. "The Mirror Stage." *Ecrits: A Selection*. Trans. Alan Sheridan. New York: Norton, 1977.

Laclau, Ernesto. "Power and Representation." In *Politics, Theory, and Contemporary Culture*, Mark Poster, ed., 291–292. New York: Columbia University Press, 1993.

Laclau, Ernesto, and Chantal Mouffe, "Post-Marxism Without Apologies." *New Left Review* 166 (1987): 79–106.

LaSalle, Mick. "Poet and Patience on Trial in *Howl*." *San Francisco Chronicle*. September 4, 2010, E1.

Leavitt, David. "Men in Love: Is *Brokeback Mountain* a Gay Film?" In *The Brokeback Book: From Story to Cultural Phenomenon*, William R. Handley, ed., 30. Omaha: University of Nebraska Press, 2011.

Leigh, Danny. "Boy Wonder." *Sight and Sound* 10:3 (March 2000): 18–20.

Leonard, Jerry, ed. *Legal Studies as Cultural Studies: A Reader in (Post)Modern Critical Theory*. Albany: SUNY Press, 1995.

Levi, Ross D. *The Celluloid Courtroom: A History of Legal Cinema*. Westport: Praeger, 2005.

Loffreda, Beth. *Losing Matt Shepard: Life and Politics in the Aftermath of Anti-Gay Murder*. New York: Columbia University Press, 2000.

Make it Better. www.makeitbetter.org. (March 16, 2012).

Manalansan IV, Martin F., and Arnaldo Cruz-Malavé. *Queer Globalizations: Citizenship and the Afterlife of Colonialism*. New York: New York University Press, 2002.

Mann, Emily. *The Execution of Justice*. In *Testimonies: Four Plays*. New York: Theatre Communications Group, 1997.

Marcuse, Herbert. "Repressive Tolerance." In.*A Critique of Pure Tolerance*. Boston: Beacon Press, 1969. 95–137.

Mason, Gail. *The Spectacle of Violence: Homophobia, Gender, and Knowledge*. New York: Routledge, 2002.

Matsuda, Mari J. "Crime and Affirmative Action." *Georgetown Journal of Gender, Race and Justice* 1 (1998): 309.

Matsuda, Mari J. *Where is Your Body? And Other Essays on Race, Gender and the Law*. Boston: Beacon, 1996.

McCracken, Kristen. "Film and Literature: *Howl*." September 20, 2010. www.tribecafilm.com. (accessed March 16, 2012).

McHoul, Alec, and Wendy Grace. *A Foucault Primer: Discourse, Power, and the Subject*. New York: New York University Press, 1993.

McMillen, Liz. "The Importance of Storytelling: A New Emphasis by Law Scholars." *Chronicle of Higher Education*. 26 July 1996, A10.

Mendelsohn, Daniel. "No Ordinary Love Story (*Brokeback Mountain*)." *Gay and Lesbian Review Worldwide* 13:3 (May–June 2006): 10.

Metz, Christian, *The Imaginary Signifier: Psychoanalysis and the Cinema.* Trans. Celia Britton et al. Bloomington: Indiana University Press, 1986.

Metz, Christian. "The Imaginary Signifier." *Screen* 16:2 (1976): 14–76.

Miller, D.A. "Brokering *Brokeback*: Jokes, Backlashes, and Other Anxieties." *Film Quarterly* (spring 2007): 50–60.

Miller, J. Hillis. "Laying down the Law in Literature: The Example of Kleist." 11 *Cardozo Law Review* 1491–1514 (1990).

Minkowitz, Donna. "Love Hurts." *Village Voice.* April 19, 1994, 24–30.

Mison, Robert. "Homophobia in Manslaughter: The Homosexual Advance as Insufficient Provocation." 80 *California Law Review* 133–178 (1992).

Mogul, Joey L., Andrea J. Ritchie, and Kay Whitlock. *Queer (In)Justice: The Criminalization of LGBT People in the United States (Queer Acts/Queer Ideas).* Boston: Beacon Press, 2011.

Moran, Leslie J., Emma Sandon, Elena Lozidou, and Ian Christie, eds. *The Law's Moving Image.* London: Glass House, 2004.

Morrison, James. "Back to the Ranch Ag'in: *Brokeback Mountain* and Gay Civil Rights." In *The Brokeback Book: From Story to Cultural Phenomenon*, William R. Handley, ed., 81–100. Omaha: University of Nebraska Press, 2011.

Mortimer-Sandilands, Catriona, and Bruce Erickson, eds. *Queer Ecologies: Sex, Nature, Politics, Desire.* Bloomington: Indiana University Press, 2010.

Muñoz, José Esteban. *Cruising Utopia: The Then and There of Queer Futurity.* New York: New York University Press, 2009.

Murphy, Sara. "The Law, the Norm, and the Novel." In *Studies in Law, Politics, and Society: A Special Issue: Law and Literature Reconsidered*, Austin Sarat, ed., 53–77. Bingley, UK: JAI, 2008.

Murray, David A., ed. *Homophobias: Lust and Loathing across Time and Space.* Durham, NC: Duke University Press, 2009.

"New Details Emerge in the Matthew Shepard Murder," *20/20.* ABC. November 26, 2004. The Transcription Company, Burbank, CA. www.transcripts.tv/2020. cfm. (accessed July 15, 2005).

Nussbaum, Martha. *Poetic Justice: The Literary Imagination and Public Life.* Boston: Beacon, 1995.

Olsen, Mark. "He Loves Being Bad--And He's Good At It: Interview with Peter Sarsgaard." N.d. www.angelfire.com/film/petersarsgaard/interview.html. (accessed March 16, 2012).

Ossana, Diana. "Climbing Brokeback Mountain." In Annie Proulx, Larry McMurty, and Diana Ossana. *Brokeback Mountain: Story to Screenplay*, 147. New York: Scribner, 2005.

Oswin, Nancy. "Critical Geographies and the Uses of Sexuality: Deconstructing Queer Space." *Progress in Human Geography* 32:1 (2008): 89–103.

Patterson, Eric. *On Brokeback Mountain: Meditations about Masculinity, Fear, and Love in the Story and the Film.* Lanham: Lexington Books, 2008.

Peters, Julie Stone. "Law, Literature, and the Vanishing Real: On the Future of an Interdisciplinary Illusion." *PMLA* 120:2 (March 2005): 442–453.

Peterson, David. "'Everything built on that:' Queering Western Space in Proulx's 'Brokeback Mountain.'" In *Queering Paradigms*, Scherer Burkhard, ed., 281–298. Oxford: Peter Lang, 2009.

Pidduck, Julianne. "Risk and Queer Spectatorship." *Screen* 42:1 (spring 2001): 97–102.

Polletta, Francesca. "The Structural Context of Novel Rights Claims: Southern Civil Rights Organizing, 1961-1966. *Law and Society*. 34 (2000): 367–398.

Posner, Richard. *Law and Literature*. Cambridge, MA: Harvard University Press, 2009.

Prosser, Jay. *Second Skins: The Body Narratives of Transsexuality*. New York: Columbia University Press, 1999.

Proulx, Annie. "Blood on the Red Carpet." *Guardian*. March 11, 2006. In http://www.guardian.co.uk/books/2006/mar/11/awardsandprizes.oscars2006. (accessed March 16, 2012).

Proulx, Annie. "Brokeback Mountain." In *Brokeback Mountain: Story to Screenplay*. New York: Scribner, 2005. 1–28.

Proulx, Annie. *Close Range: Wyoming Stories*. New York: Scribner, 2000.

Proulx, Annie. "Getting Movied." In *Brokeback Mountain: Story to Screenplay*. New York: Scribner, 2005. 129–138.

Puar, Jasbir. "In the Wake of It Gets Better." *Guardian*. November 16, 2010. www.guardian.co.uk/commentisfree/cifamerica/2010/nov/16/wake-it-gets-better-campaign. (accessed March 16, 2012).

Puar, Jasbir. *Terrorist Assemblages: Homonationalism in Queer Times*. Durham, NC: Duke University Press, 2007.

Rao, Radhika. "Editor's Review of *The Aesthetic of the Oppressed* by Augusto Boal, translated by Adrian Jackson and *The Theatre of Urban Youth and Schooling in Dangerous Times* by Kathleen Gallagher." *Harvard Education Review* (fall 2008). In http://www.hepg.org/her/abstract/660. (accessed March 16, 2012).

Rapold, Nicholas. "Come with Us." *Sight and Sound* 19:2 (February 2009): 28–30.

Reichman, Ravit. *The Affective Life of Law: Legal Modernism and the Literary Imagination*. Stanford: Stanford Law Books, 2009.

Rhode, Deborah. *Justice and Gender*. Cambridge, MA: Harvard University Press, 1989.

Rich, Ruby B. "Ghosts of a Vanished World." *Guardian*. January 16, 2009. www.guardian.co.uk/film/2009/jan/16/harvey-milk-gus-van-sant. (accessed March 16, 2012).

Robson, Ruthann. *Gay Men, Lesbians, and the Law*. New York: Chelsea House, 1997.

Ronner, Amy D. *Homophobia and the Law*. Washington, DC: APA, 2005.

Rosenblum, Darren. "Queer Intersectionality and the Failure of Recent Lesbian and Gay 'Victories'." 4 *Law and Sexuality* 83 (1994).

Rudnicki, Stephen. *Wilde*. Los Angeles: Dove, 1998.

Russo, Vito. *The Celluloid Closet*. New York: Harper & Row, 1987.

Salter, Kenneth W. *The Trial of Dan White.* El Cerrito: A Market and Systems Interface Publications Book, 1991.

Sandel, Michael. *Liberalism and the Limit of Justice.* Cambridge: Cambridge University Press, 1982.

Sarat, Austin and Jonathan Simon, eds. *Cultural Analysis, Cultural Studies, and the Law: Moving Beyond Legal Realism.* Durham, NC: Duke University Press, 2003.

Sarat, Austin, Laurence Douglas, and Martha Umphrey, eds. *Law on the Screen.* Stanford: Stanford University Press, 2005.

Savage, Michael, creator. *It Gets Better.* www.itgetsbetter.org. (accessed March 16, 2012).

Schneck, Richard. "The Laws of Fiction: Legal Rhetoric and Literary Evidence." *European Journal of English Studies* 11:1 (April 2007): 47–63.

Scott, A.O. "Freedom Fighter in Life Becomes Potent Symbol in Death." *The New York Times.* November 26, 2008. http://movies.nytimes.com/2008/11/26/movies/26milk.html.

Scott, A.O. "Leaping Off the Page: A Beatnik's Poetic Rant." *The New York Times.* September 23, 2010. (accessed March 16, 2012).

Sedgwick, Eve Kosofsky. *Epistemology of the Closet.* Berkeley: University of California Press, 1990.

Shafer, Scott. "When a Gay Judge Rules on Gay Rights." *NPR.org.* June 13, 2011. www.npr.org/2011/06/13/137109321/when-a-gay-judge-rules-on-gay-rights. (March 16, 2012).

Shelley, P.B. "A Defence of Poesy." In http://www.fordham.edu/halsall/mod/shelley-poetry.asp. (accessed March 16, 2012).

Sherif, Harry M., O.J. White, W. Wood, and C. Sherif. *Ingroup Conflict and Cooperation.* Norman: University of Oklahoma Press, 1961.

Sherrill, Kenneth. "The Political Power of Lesbians, Gays and Bisexuals." *Political Science* 29:3 (1996): 469–470.

Shewey, Don. "Town in the Mirror." *American Theatre* 17:5 (2000): 14–15.

Shilts, Randy. *The Mayor of Castro Street: The Life and Times of Harvey Milk.* New York: St. Martin's, 1982.

Siegel, Carol. "Curing Boys Don't Cry," *Genders* 37 (2003): 1–25.

Sloop, John M. "Disciplining the Transgendered: Brandon Teena, Public Representation, and Normativity." *Western Journal of Communication* 64:2 (spring 2000): 165–189.

Slotkin, Richard. *Gunfighter Nation: Myth of the Frontier in Twentieth-Century America.* Norman: University of Oklahoma Press, 1998.

Smith, Dinita. *The Illusionist.* New York: Scribner 1997.

Stacey, Jim, ed. *Reading Brokeback Mountain: Essays on the Story and the Film.* Jefferson: McFarland, 2007.

Stein, Arlene. *Shameless: Sexual Dissidence in American Culture.* New York: New York University Press, 2006.

St. Joan, Jacqueline, and Annette Bennington McElhiney, eds. *Beyond Portia: Women, Law, and Literature in the United States*. Boston: Northeastern University Press, 1997.

Stryker, Susan, and Jim Van Buskirk. *Gay by the Bay: A History of Queer Culture in the San Francisco Bay Area*. San Francisco: Chronicle Books, 1996.

Suffredini, Kara S. "Pride and Prejudice: The Homosexual Panic Defense." 279 *Boston College Third World Law Journal* 279–282 (2001).

Sullivan, Andrew. "Us and Them." *The New Republic*. (April 2, 2001) 8.

Sullivan, Andrew. "What's So Bad About Hate?" *New York Times Magazine*. September 26, 1999. In http://www.nytimes.com/1999/09/26/magazine/what-s-so-bad-about-hate.html?pagewanted=all&src=pm. (accessed March 16, 2012).

Szasz, Thomas. "'J'Accuse': Psychiatry and the Diminished American Capacity for Justice." In the Mike Weiss Papers, San Francisco Public Library Archives (1979).

Talbot, Margaret. "A Risky Proposal." *The New Yorker*. January 18, 2010. www.newyorker.com/reporting/2010/01/18/100118fa_fact_talbot?currentPage=all. (accessed March 16, 2012).

Tavers, Robert. *Anatomy of a Murder*. New York: St. Martin's, 1957.

Thernstrom, Melanie. "The Crucifixion of Matthew Shepard." *Vanity Fair*. March 1999, 209–275.

Thomas, Kendall. "Beyond the Privacy Principle." 92 *Columbia Law Review* 1431–1514 (1992).

Tigner, Amy. "*The Laramie Project*: Western Pastoral." *Modern Drama* 45:1 (spring 2002): 144.

Tomain, Joseph P. *Creon's Ghost: Law, Justice, and the Humanities*. Oxford: Oxford University Press, 2009.

Travers, Robert. *Anatomy of a Murder*. New York: St. Martin's, 1957.

Tsesis, Alexander. "Dignity and Speech: The Regulation of Hate Speech in a Democracy." *Wake Forest Law Review* 44 (2009): 497–532.

Turan, Kenneth. "Breaking No Ground: Why *Crash* Won, Why *Brokeback* Lost, and How the Academy Chose to Play It Safe." In *The Brokeback Book: From Story to Cultural Phenomenon,* William R. Handley, ed., 101–103. Omaha: University of Nebraska Press, 2011.

Turner, Victor. *From Ritual to Theatre: The Human Seriousness of Play.* New York: Performing Arts Journal Publications, 1982.

Wallace, Stewart, and Michael Korie. *Harvey Milk: Opera in Three Acts.* In the Gay and Lesbian Archive, San Francisco Public Library (1994) (opera).

Warner, Michael. "Beyond Gay Marriage." *Left Legalism/Left Critique*. Wendy Brown and Janet Halley, eds., 259–289. Durham, NC: Duke University Press, 2002.

Warner, Michael. "Homo-Narcissism; or, Heterosexuality." *Engendering Men*. Joseph A. Boone and Michael Cadden, eds. 191–206. London: Routledge, 1990.

Warner, Michael. *The Trouble with Normal: Sex, Politics, and the Ethics of Queer Life*. Boston: Harvard University Press, 2002.

Warren, Patricia Nell. "Real Cowboys, Real Rodeos." *The Gay and Lesbian Review Worldwide* 13:4 (July–August 2006): 19.

Weisberg, Richard. *Poethics and Other Strategies of Law and Literature*. New York: Columbia University Press, 1992.

Weiss, Mike. "Dan White's Last Confession." *San Francisco Magazine*. October 1998, 32–33.

Weiss, Mike. *Double Play: The City Hall Killings*. Menlo Park: Addison Wesley, 1984.

West, Robin. *Narrative, Authority, and the Law*. Ann Arbor: University of Michigan Press, 1994.

White, James Boyd. *The Legal Imagination*. New York: Little, Brown, 1973..

White, Patricia. "Girls Still Cry." *Screen* 42:3 (2001): 122–128.

Wickberg, Daniel. "Homophobia: On the Cultural History of an Idea." *Critical Inquiry* (Autumn 2000): 42–57.

Williams, Patricia. *Alchemy of Race and Rights: Diary of a Law Professor*. Cambridge, MA: Harvard University Press, 1992.

Winterson, Jeanette. *Written on the Body*. New York: Vintage, 1992.

Wolfson, Evan. "Crossing the Threshold: Equal Marriage Rights for Lesbians and Gay Men, and the Intra-Community Critique." 21 *New York University Review of Law and Social Change* (1994): 567

Woolner, Ann. "Suicide After Sex Video Leaves Shared Guilt Behind." *Bloomberg.com*. September 30, 2010. www.bloomberg.com/news/2010-10-01/suicide-after-sex-video-leaves-shared-guilt-behind-ann-woolner.html. (accessed March 16, 2012).

Wypijewski, Joann. "A Boy's Life: For Matthew Shepard's Killers, What Does It Take to Pass as a Man?" *Harper's*. September 1999, 61–74.

Wypijewski, Joann. "Hate Crime Laws' Won't Cure Homophobia." *Counterpunch*. November 27/28, 2004. www.counterpunch.org/jw11272004.html. (accessed March 16, 2012).

Yabroff, Jennie. "Trans America: Documentary Filmmakers Susan Muska and Gréta Oláfsdottir Talk About the Story Behind *The Brandon Teena Story*." *Salon.com*. February 25, 1999. www.salon.com/entertainment/movies/int/1999/02/25int.html. (accessed March 16, 2012).

Young, Iris Marion. *Justice and the Politics of Difference*. Princeton: Princeton University Press, 1990.

Žižek, Slavoj. *The Sublime Object of Ideology*. New York: Verso, 1989.

Filmography

Amores Perros. Dir. Alejandro Iñárritu. Filmax: 2000.

Anatomy of a Murder. Dir. Otto Preminger. Columbia Pictures: 1959.

A Single Man. Dir. Tom Ford. Artina Film: 2009.

Boys Don't Cry. Dir. Kimberly Peirce. Fox Searchlight Pictures: 1999.

Boys in the Band. William Friedkin. Cinema Center Films: 1970.

Brandon Teena Story. Dirs. Susan Muska and Greta Olatsdottir. Zeitgeist Films, 1998.

Brokeback Mountain. Dir. Ang Lee. Paramount Pictures: 2005.

Cat on a Hot Tin Roof. Richard Brooks. MGM: 1958.

The Celluloid Closet. Dir. Rob Epstein and Jeffrey Friedman. Sony Pictures: 1995.

The Children's Hour. Dir. William Wyler. United Artists: 1961.

Desert Hearts. Dir. Donna Deitch. Samuel Goldwyn Company: 1985.

Fire. Dir. Deepa Mehta. Trial by Fire Films: 1997.

The Hours. Dir. Stephen Daldry. Paramount: 2003.

Howl. Dir. Robert Epstein and Jeffrey Friedman. Werc Werk Works: 2010.

Laramie Inside Out. Dir. Bev Seckinger. New Day Films: 2004.

Maurice. Dir. James Ivory. Cinecom: 1987.

Milk. Dir. Gus Van Sant. Focus Features: 2008.

My Own Private Idaho. Dir. Gus Van Sant. New Line Cinema: 1991.

Object of My Affection. Nicholas Hytner. Twentieth-Century Fox. 1998.

Philadelphia. Jonathan Demme. TriStar Pictures. 1993.

Oscar Wilde. Dir. Gregory Ratoff. Vantage Film: 1960.

Suddenly Last Summer. Dir. Joseph L. Mankiewicz. Columbia Pictures: 1959.

These Three. Dir. William Wyler. Samuel Goldwyn Co.: 1936.

The Times of Harvey Milk. Dir. Robert Epstein. Cinecom International: 1986.

The Trials of Oscar Wilde. Dir. Ken Hughes. Viceroy Films: 1960.

W. Dir. Oliver Stone. Lions Gate: 2008.

Wilde. Dir. Brian Gilbert. Sony Pictures: 1998.

Index